W9-AEL-855

The Jews of Odessa

THE JEWS OF ODESSA

❖

A Cultural History, 1794-1881

Steven J. Zipperstein

Stanford University Press, Stanford, California
1985

STANFORD UNIVERSITY PRESS
Stanford, California

Printed in the United States of America

CIP data appear at the end of the book

FOR SALLY

Acknowledgments

I began my research on Odessa Jewry under the shrewd and exacting guidance of Hans Rogger, of the University of California at Los Angeles, who co-supervised the dissertation on which this study is based. His example as both scholar and teacher has most influenced my academic work. The guidance of Amos Funkenstein set high standards for my research, and I appreciate his many stimulating suggestions. The advice and friendship of Jonathan Frankel, Igor Kotler, Eli Lederhendler, and Robert M. Seltzer were of great help at several crucial periods. Chimen Abramsky's close reading of the manuscript and his many other kindnesses cannot be adequately acknowledged or repaid. Others who helped in various ways include Abraham Ascher, Arnold Band, Lucjan Dobroszycki, Todd Endelman, David Feldman, Arthur Hertzberg, Giora Hon, George Jewsbury, Richard Judd, Tony Judt, George Mandel, Ron May, Alexander Orbach, Moshe Pearlmann, Eli Sha'altiel, Chone Shmeruk, and J. S. G. Simmons. I owe a great deal to two distinguished scholars now deceased, Zosa Szajkowski and Isaiah Trunk. Mitchell Cohen read and reread this manuscript more times than he would probably care to remember, and his judgments were consistently sound. I am much in his debt.

I am grateful to the libraries, archives, and individuals that helped provide the materials for this study: Dina Abramowicz of the YIVO Institute for Jewish Research; Mordecai Nadav of the

Jewish National and University Library of Jerusalem; Michael Heymann of the Central Zionist Archives; the late Hillel Kempinsky of the Bund Archives of the Jewish Labor Movement; Philip Miller of the Klau Library, Hebrew Union College–Jewish Institute of Religion, New York; the librarians of the Upper, Slavonic, and Oriental Reading Rooms of the Bodleian Library; and the staffs of the Slavic Division of the University of Helsinki; the Slavonic and Jewish Divisions of the New York Public Library; the Klau Library, Hebrew Union College–Jewish Institute of Religion, Cincinnati; the British Library; the Public Record Office; and the Kressel Library and Archive of the Oxford Centre for Postgraduate Hebrew Studies.

It is a pleasure to acknowledge the institutions that supported this study financially: the National Foundation for Jewish Culture; the Memorial Foundation for Jewish Culture; the Max Weinreich Center for Advanced Jewish Studies; the Regents of the University of California, who awarded me their generous Chancellor's Intern Fellowship; and the Sir Simon Marks Fund of the Jewish Federation Council of Greater Los Angeles. I owe an immense debt to the President, David Patterson, and the Governors and Fellows of the Oxford Centre for Postgraduate Hebrew Studies for appointing me the first incumbent of the Frank Green Fellowship in Modern European Jewish History. I benefited, moreover, from the opportunity of spending two years in residence at the Centre's Yarnton Manor, which provided me with an atmosphere of rare beauty and intellectual stimulation. I owe thanks to the Warden and Fellows of St. Antony's for inviting me into their college as a Senior Associate Member in 1982. And I thank the President and Fellows of Wolfson for appointing me to my present Research Fellowship.

I am grateful for permission to use (in revised form) material from my articles published elsewhere: "Jewish Enlightenment in Odessa: Cultural Characteristics, 1794–1871," *Jewish Social Studies*, vol. 44, no. 1 (Winter 1982): 19–36; "Russian Maskilim and the City," *The Legacy of Jewish Migration: 1881 and Its Impact*, ed. David Berger, Brooklyn College Studies on Society in Change, no. 24 (Highland Lakes, New Jersey: Atlantic Research and Publications, 1983), pp. 31–45; and "Haskalah, Cultural Change, and

Nineteenth-Century Russian Jewry: A Reassessment," *Journal of Jewish Studies*, vol. 34, no. 2 (Autumn 1983): 191–207.

I would like to thank J. G. Bell and Karen Brown Davison of Stanford University Press for their interest in this work. The dicta of my copy editor, Mark Graham, on the virtues of brevity and clarity are much appreciated, and my manuscript has benefited from being placed in his able hands.

On a more personal level, my parents provided me with many of the skills and commitments that made this work seem meaningful, even in times of apparent drudgery. It was, above all, the example of my father, a maskil of the most unusual sort, that set me on this course. Finally, my thanks go to my wife, Sally Goodis, who, by reminding me of things other than Russian Jewish history, has enhanced my life more than she can possibly imagine. I dedicate this book to her.

S.J.Z.

Contents

A Note on Transliteration and Dates

In transliterating Hebrew, Russian, and Ukrainian, I have followed the Library of Congress rules except that I have eliminated most diacritical marks and have presented well-known names (e.g., those of the Tsars) in their most familiar form. For Hebrew words I have not used diacritical marks to distinguish between letters *het* and *hei*, and I have rendered the letter *tsadi* into the English *ts*. The Yiddish transliteration is based on the system devised by the YIVO Institute for Jewish Research, though I follow some of the modifications suggested by the *Encyclopedia Judaica*. Personal names appear in different versions, depending on the geographical or cultural context in which the individual was most active.

Dates follow the Julian or Old Style calendar, which in the nineteenth century was twelve days behind the Gregorian.

The Jews of Odessa

Livonia
Riga
Petchora
Wenden
Ostrow
Pskov
Kholm
Valdai or Valdai
Borovitchi
Krasnoi Kolm
Volotchok
Ostachkov
Torjok
Tver
Kaschin
Koliazan
Rjev
Klin
Moscow
1812
Mojaisk
Serpoukhov
Kaluga
Riazan
Toula
Bielev
Bogorodi
Mittau
Bauske
Frederickstadt
Jacobstadt
Lutzen
Dunabourg
Nevel
Toropetz
Polotsk
Braslav
Memel
Kowno
Wilna
Troki
Vitebsk
Smolensk
Lepel
Orsa
Minsk
Borisov
Grodno
Bialystok
Slonim
Novogrodek
Mohilew
Mstislav
Roslavl
Bobroujsk
Propoisk
Briansk
Bolkhov
Orel
Ephremov
Slousk
Pinsk
Brzesc Litevski
Homel
Staradoub
Novosil
Telez
Kromy
Sevsk
Novgorod Seversk
Kursk
Michailovka
Dolgoe
Tschernigov
Vladimir
Loutsk
Dubno
Ostrog
Zitomir
Kiev
Oster
Niegin
Glinsk
Lebedino
Belgorod
Ohoiane
Oskol
Brody
Lemburg
Berdichev
Constantinov
Bogouslaf
Poltava
1709
Charkov
Khorole
Kremen
Zolotonocha
Zvenigorod
Kamieniec
Braslav
Ouman
Elizabethgrad
Czernowitz
Mohilov
Olgopol
Olviopol
Jekaterinoslav
Bakmout
Pavlograd
Novomoskovsk
Alexandrovsk
Nikopol
Jassy
Kichinev
Bender
Grigoriopol
Voznesensk
Akerman
Odessa
1854
Nicolaiev
Cherson
Berislav
Perekop
Gulf of Perekop
Gulf of Odessa
Kinburn
Taganrog
Mamoupol
Berdiansk
Genitchi
Sea of Azov
Kertch
Kaffa
Taman
Anapa
Ismail
Mouths of the Danube
Tarkan
Eupatoria
Sevastopol
Simferopol
Baktchiserai
C. Chersonese
1855
Balaklava
Yalta
Bukarest
Silistra
Rustchuk
Shumla
Bazardjik
Varna
Mangalia
Burgas T. & Gulf
BLACK SEA
Bosphorus
Constantinople
Scutari
Sea of Marmora
Ineboli
C. Indjeh
Sinope or Sinoub
1853
Bafra
Bartan
Eregri
Trebizond
Gagra
Weljaminovsk

Introduction

Nineteenth-century Russian Jews saw the city of Odessa as many things. In Yiddish folklore it came to be associated with a life of comfort and pleasure-seeking ("lebn vi Got in Odes," "to live like God in Odessa"), with indifference to religion ("Zibn mayl arum Odes brent der gihenum," "Seven miles around Odessa burn the fires of hell"), with the criminal underworld ("Got zol ophitn fun . . . Odeser hultayles," "God protect us from . . . Odessa rakes"), and even with glamorous women (called "Odesere levones," "Odessa moons"). The city, according to admirers and detractors alike, was different from all others, and though Vilna, it was said, could be best likened to Minsk, Mogilev to Vitebsk, and Ekaterinoslav to Elizavetgrad, no other city in Russia resembled Odessa. If Odessa could be compared at all, it was only to the port cities of America, and then only to those on the frontier, like Chicago or San Francisco, where a mixture of enterprise, license, and violence combined to create environments free from the restraints of the past.

Despite Jews' fascination with and attachment to Odessa, the city's Jewish community has never been studied in and of itself. The careers of several of Odessa's most prominent Jewish intellectuals of the last quarter of the nineteenth century have been examined, and its innovative Jewish press has been discussed, but a study of the development of the city as a whole—whether social, economic, political, or cultural—has never been attempted.[1]

Detail of an antique map, showing the Pale of Settlement and some adjacent provinces. From George W. Colton, *Colton's Atlas of the World*, vol. 2 (New York, 1856).

The lack of such research reflects the evolution of Russian Jewish historiography. Before the rise of the Jewish nationalist movement in the 1880's and 1890's, Russian Jewish intellectuals showed little interest in Jewish history. The few who did, like Vilna's Samuel Joseph Fin, concurred with the German Jewish *Wissenschaft des Judentums* (Science of Judaism), which held that the proper focus of Jewish history after the fall of the Judean state and the destruction of the Second Temple was the intellectual sphere, and that Jews otherwise entered history only as the passive objects of a ruler's benevolence or wrath. Consequently, the few histories of Russian or Polish Jewish communities written before the 1890's concentrated on local rabbinic scholarship or on disabilities and restrictions. Odessa, the site of neither intensive traditional Jewish learning nor singular mistreatment at the hands of authorities or local townspeople, did not lend itself to such investigation.

In the highly productive three decades before the 1917 revolution, Russian Jewish historiography was dominated by Iulii Gessen and Simon Dubnow, both ardent liberals and Jewish nationalists, who believed the liberation of Russian Jewry from the tyranny of Tsarism to be the precondition for meaningful internal Jewish reform. The history of the Russian government's attitude toward the Jews was, they felt, a far more pressing concern than internal Jewish history. Their works, still standard treatments, clearly reflect these preferences. The social, economic, and cultural history of Russian Jewry briefly became the focus of considerable attention in the Soviet Union during the mid- and late twenties, but after the tightening of Stalin's hold in 1929, research on Jewish topics all but ceased and archives closed. Until recently, research on Imperial Russian Jewish history remained at a virtual standstill.

Odessa in particular may have been neglected because the fast pace of life in this new Black Sea port (founded in 1794) and the alleged preoccupation of its residents, Jewish and non-Jewish alike, with moneymaking and the pleasures of the moment made it a place where the past was considered irrelevant or was overshadowed by the demands of the present. Simon Dubnow, who lived in Odessa between 1890 and 1903, referred to it in his autobiography as the "least historical of all cities." Odessa contrasted markedly in this respect with Vilna, Grodno, Kiev, and Brest-Litovsk—the subjects of the first communal histories—where, as the Zionist publicist Shmarya Levin observed, "the dust of generations lay . . . like an invisible shadow." A city of stature in the communal hierarchy of Ashkenazic Jewry had traditionally been distinguished by learning and piety, central to the intellectual sphere on which Jewish history often focused. Neither modern nor traditional Jews wanted to celebrate (or study) a setting in which both seemed of tertiary importance.

Thus Odessa occupies an ambiguous place in the history of the cultural transformation of Russian Jewry. Though several of the most successful modern Jewish institutions in the Pale of Settlement were in Odessa, and though it attracted many of Russia's most distinguished Jewish intellectuals (among them Hayim Nahman Bialik, Saul Tchernikhovsky, Ahad Ha'am, and Simon Dubnow), the city was seen as curiously inhospitable to Jewish cultural concerns. Odessa's achievements, it was suggested, were the work of outsiders new to the city and thus little affected by it. Its rise as a center of Yiddish publishing in the 1860's, for instance, was attributed to its backward character: Yiddish literature took root there, it was said, because Odessa's Jews didn't know Hebrew well enough. The success of its modern Jewish school—the first in the Pale to survive more than a few months—was generally credited to the efforts of newcomers from Galicia, who were said to have imposed the school on an indifferent, even hostile Jewish community.

Implicit in this perception of Odessa as inhospitable cultural soil is the assumption that the modern transformation of Russian Jewry, and of European Jewry as a whole, is synonymous either with civic emancipation or with the comprehensive revolution in self-awareness that accompanied the *Haskalah*, the Jewish Enlightenment. Those who place their emphasis on self-awareness see Jewish modernization as the result of a self-conscious, systematic reassessment; in the absence of factors conducive to this process, they contend, traditional patterns persisted. (Their thesis is indeed more applicable to the Jews of Imperial Russia, who achieved emancipation only in 1917.) Stimulated by the work of Azriel Shohat and Jacob Katz, however, within the last decade Jewish historians have become increasingly conscious of the social as well as the intellectual component of modernization.[2] The Jewish social historian Todd Endelman, for example, points out that Haskalah was less typical of the experience of European Jews than was an alteration of practices and customs in imitation of non-Jewish manners. In the modern age, Endelman relates, Jews began "to expand the parameters of their social and cultural world to include much that was not Jewish. Jewishness became only a part of their sense of self. . . . In a world that was becoming increasingly despiritualized and compartmentalized, Judaism ceased to be a civilization, a culture, a social order, and became instead a religion in the contemporary sense of the term."[3]

The recent emphasis on acculturation in addition to Haskalah, and on changes in behavior and attitude as well as ideology, invites a fresh appraisal of Odessa Jewry's cultural history. Studies of the Russian Haskalah, having focused on the most prominent intellectual figures and the most fertile centers of Haskalah scholarship and literary creativity, have not taken into account the whole range of factors that influenced the transformation of Russian Jewry in the nineteenth century, and thus they leave the student of the period with a fairly constricted perspective. An examination of cultural change in Odessa serves to highlight the inadequacies of such an approach. Rather than measure Odessa Jewry against centers of classical Haskalah, one must analyze its cultural history on its own terms and within the context of the development of the city as a whole.

The cultural transformation examined in this study is the breakdown of rabbinic Judaism and its replacement by more secular and rational ways of interpreting the world among many Odessa Jews—a "change of heart," to paraphrase Auden, that involved an attitudinal as well as an ideological transformation. My primary concerns will be the acculturation of the local Jewish community (or at least substantial segments of it) as reflected in the genesis and development of its schools, newspapers, and other institutions, as well as the impact of this acculturation on the local Jewish intelligentsia. I use the term "acculturation" to describe the process of cultural change in which contact between two or more culturally distinct groups results in one taking over elements of the other's culture. Such an emphasis on acculturation is particularly appropriate, since in Odessa, far more than elsewhere in the Pale, the local gentile mercantile elite and others presented a westernized model suitable for Jewish emulation. In most areas, until late in the century Jews saw even wealthy Russian merchants as obscurantists bound by a primitive and inferior set of traditions. In Odessa, however, traditional Jewish claims of moral and cultural superiority were less binding.

Yet acculturation, as the term will be used in this study, was prompted not exclusively or even primarily by a belief in another culture's superiority; instead, it resulted from a recognition of the usefulness of the other culture's skills (linguistic, technical, or otherwise), quite independent of larger cultural benefits. The economic and social opportunities available to Jews in Odessa motivated many to adapt to gentile society in ways that would have been unthinkable, or at least unlikely, elsewhere in the Pale. Utility, not ideology, was the primary motivation. Yet local concerns were reflected in the ideological preoccupations of Odessa's Jewish intelligentsia, and the openness of local Jews often made them receptive to the intelligentsia's ideas and innovations.

The process of Jewish cultural change was by no means linear; indeed, the movement most often associated with it, the Haskalah, promoted "modern" as well as "traditional" strategies. Moreover, the various classes and subgroups in local society responded differently, at times radically so. I use terms such as "modernization," "secularization," and "acculturation," then, not to suggest uniformity of influence or response, but only for want of more precise substitutes. Indeed, I use "modern" primarily to characterize the perceptions of certain nineteenth-century East European Jews who believed that society operated according to a set of fundamental and uniform rules. The history and cultural development of Odessa's Jews confirmed, it seemed to the modernizers, these presuppositions. In this study I examine both how their understanding of "modernity" came to be formed and how it was eventually challenged, particularly in the 1870's.

This book is not a comprehensive study of Odessa Jewry's cultural life. The literary history of the city has already been ably charted by several students of Hebrew and Yiddish literature; beyond this, my choice of themes was determined in part by the availability of source material, a particular problem in view of the restrictions placed on research on Jews in the Soviet Union.

Hence, the existence of primary material on the city's Jewish schools is reflected in Chapters 2 and 6; similarly, I have drawn on a rich body of periodical literature on synagogal and rabbinic matters in Chapters 2 and 3. Underlying this study are several interrelated questions: What impact did social and economic factors have on Odessa Jewry's cultural development? What influence did these factors have on the attitudes and interests of the city's Jewish intelligentsia, in particular? How did institutions established by maskilim ("enlightened Jews") and designed along "modern" lines influence the self-perceptions of local Jews?

I devote much attention to the city's influential Jewish intelligentsia, especially after their rise to prominence in the 1860's. In particular, I examine their response to local conditions and the ways in which the community's institutions absorbed the intellectual currents they generated. (My emphasis, in this respect, is the social background of intellectual production.) In Chapter 4, for instance, I examine how Osip Rabinovich integrated the abstract commitments of a Jewish "russifier" into his life as a Jew in Odessa; in Chapters 4 and 6 I discuss the work of Joachim Tarnopol and Moses Leib Lilienblum in order to show how particularly pressing local concerns (such as fear of Jewish assimilation) shaped their thinking.

My concern, then, will be the interrelationship between culture and society. My examination will be limited largely but not entirely to the community's articulate Jews, inevitably in the minority. My focus on communal institutions and my reliance on the Russian-Jewish press (in Hebrew, Yiddish, and Russian)—a press published by self-consciously modern figures—necessarily slight less articulate, perhaps poorer and more traditional Jews. Social historians have recently found, however, that the poor, especially in areas undergoing rapid industrialization or urbanization, were often more ready than the middle class to turn their backs on religious ritual. In any event, as we shall see, the more acculturated among the city's Jews frequently established precedents that were imitated, however grudgingly, by other segments of the community. Further documentary clarification must await the opening of Soviet archives.

This study begins with the city's establishment and closes in 1881. I end on the eve of the pogroms that erupted in the aftermath of Alexander II's assassination, and I do not treat the intense Jewish cultural and political activity that centered in Odessa in the subsequent decade. I felt that a treatment of the later period—when many of the ideological presuppositions of the previous century were discarded by intellectuals in favor of "postliberal" alternatives—was beyond the scope of the present study. The later period has been studied (though from the restricted perspective of the city's nascent Zionist organization), but historians have almost entirely neglected the years covered by this book. Moreover, patterns set during the earlier period continued to inform the community's cultural development into the second decade of the twentieth century.

ONE

Historical Background

Tradition and Change in the Pale of Settlement

The social and cultural transformation of European Jewry in the modern age constituted one of the most profound upheavals in Jewish history. Earlier Jews were a social unit possessing distinct religious practices and institutions, performing specific economic functions outside the hitherto dominant corporations and guilds, and sharing a collective awareness of exile and an expectation of redemption, but increasingly large segments of the Jewish community ceased to define themselves primarily in these terms. Jews moved in significant numbers from the economic periphery into (or at least near) the center of commercial and financial activity. They came to justify normative decisions by explicitly using the ideas and beliefs of the larger society, and they increasingly viewed emancipation as an unquestionable (if still frequently inaccessible) right. They were bound more closely to the various countries in which they lived, or so many of Jewry's leading spokesmen now claimed, than to the people of Israel as a whole.[1]

Before the 1917 revolution, Russian Jewry appears at first glance to have remained largely outside this process. In marked contrast to the middle-class character of Central European Jewry by the late nineteenth century, the vast majority of Russian Jews continued to be concentrated in typically Jewish occupations like the clothing and needlework trades, with many in petty commerce. Russian Jews were confined largely to the Pale of Settlement and the Polish region and bound by a host of other restrictions, which were periodically augmented by expulsions from previously accessible urban and rural settings, by a *numerus clausus* for secondary and university students, and by pogroms, which, many believed, testified to the continuance of a primitive Judeophobia among not only the masses but also St. Petersburg officials. Talmudic academies of great distinction (such as Mir, Slobodka, and Telz) flourished in Lithuania, in contrast to their precipitous decline in the West; the hasidic courts of Lubavich, Stolin, Talnoye, and Gora remained the unchallenged centers of Jewish cultural life for many Jews in Belorussia, the Ukraine, and Poland. Even those Jews unmoved by the mysteries and regimen of traditional Judaism, be it hasidic or rabbinic, continued to communicate in a Jewish language largely incomprehensible to non-Jews.

This portrait, however, fails to take into account new tendencies inimical to traditional Jewish patterns. The westernization of the Russian autocracy in the eighteenth century—part of an effort to strengthen Russia's military capability and improve the efficiency of its government—introduced new ideas and encouraged new trends, both of which would eventually challenge the stability of the regime. New economic pressures and opportunities linked Russia more closely with the international community and encouraged landowners to produce a surplus for market, to abandon unprofitable lands for industrial investment, and to reevaluate the advantage of enserfed labor. Moreover, Jewish particularism, permitted and even encouraged in Poland-Lithuania, was, in the aftermath of the Polish partitions, increasingly seen as antithetical to the presumably homogeneous character of the "regulated state" envisaged by Tsars since Peter I. Jewish autonomy was increasingly restricted, and Jewish cultural distinctiveness was discouraged, most visibly by the network of government-sponsored Jewish schools established under Nicholas I. Jewish economic life was progressively threatened by the regime, resulting in repeated expulsions from villages and in occupational prohibitions. To be sure, in their treatment of Jews the authorities vacillated between policies aimed purportedly at Jewish integration and efforts that singled Jews out for special disabilities. These shifting policies (coupled with the transformation of European Jewry in the same period) resulted in a markedly uneven course of cultural development.

The forcible breakdown of traditional Jewish patterns has received great and perhaps undue prominence in the secondary literature on Russian Jewish history, a reflection of the impact of Western historiographical models on the self-understanding of Russian Jewry. Traditional institutions retained a far larger following in the region than did more modern ones; even Eastern European Jewish political movements remained relatively peripheral—except during rather brief, highly charged periods—until the 1917 revolution.[2] Nonetheless, the cultural insularity of the community was breached in this period, and the character of traditional Jewish society was transformed.

In Jewish historiography the term Haskalah, or "Enlightenment," has come to be most closely associated with modernizing trends in Eastern Europe.[3] The Haskalah movement, stimulated by the German Jewish philosopher Moses Mendelssohn (1729–86), was characterized by the belief that the fundamental features of Judaism were entirely reconcilable with the modern world and that Jewish life could be judged by outside standards; it was also marked by a hunger for ideas and a readiness to sacrifice for their sake. It assumed somewhat different forms in the various regions of Eastern Europe, but it was consistently pedagogic in character and optimistic in tone. It stressed the centrality of those aspects of Jewish life that non-Jews presumably considered positive: the purity of biblical Hebrew, the stability of Jewish family life, Jews' financial aptitude, their agricultural past, and Judaism's philosophical legacy. The followers of the Haskalah, called *maskilim*, did not simply mimic the larger society; they subscribed, at least in part, to its values. The Haskalah denounced aspects of contemporary Jewish life at variance with the beliefs of the larger society (and presumably with the true character of Judaism as well), such as mystical speculation, disdain for secular study, and ignorance of the vernacular.

The Haskalah's social program was vague. The maskilim encouraged the integration of Jews into the middle class, even in Eastern Europe, where this group was small and where the population consisted largely of peasants. Yet they also hoped to promote Jewish participation in agriculture; the Haskalah's leading Russian spokesman, Isaac Baer Levinsohn, suggested that at least one-third of Russia's Jews should be farmers. Integration into the larger cultural world was stressed, even though the maskilim themselves (insulated intellectuals, for the most part) denounced assimilation no less vehemently than did their traditionalist opponents. The exemplary Haskalah center was Vilna, with its distinguished circles of scholars, poets, and essayists knowledgeable in both Jewish and secular sciences, its Jewish residents better acquainted with Hebrew than were Jews elsewhere, and its stress on the cerebral rather than the emotive side of Judaism. The Haskalah's link with the rabbinic past was more apparent there, especially in view of the movement's rather spurious claim to be the legitimate heir to the legacy of the brilliant eighteenth-century talmudist Elijah the Gaon of Vilna. In contrast to the exponents of the German Jewish Enlightenment in the decades after Mendelssohn's death, Russian maskilim hoped to see Jewry rendered acceptable to its neighbors without relinquishing its distinctive social or religious character. In their view Judaism was to be purified but not entirely stripped of its idiosyncratic tendencies. By the middle of the nineteenth century, nearly every sizable Jewish community in the Pale and in Poland possessed at least a handful of maskilim, called "Berlinchiks" by critics who accused them of aping the latest Prussian fashions. They differed from more traditional Jews in dress (German-style coats rather than kaftans), in language (German and sometimes Polish or Russian, rather than Yiddish), at times in the degree of their compliance with ritual law, and, most of all, in their commitment to an intellectual movement that sought to redefine the nature of Jewish identity.

In the absence of emancipation (civic or political) or of increased contact between Jewish and non-Jewish intellectuals, the Haskalah offered a haven for Jews caught between an inaccessible larger cultural world and an unacceptable Jewish one. The assumption, however, that Haskalah is synonymous with the "modernization" of Russian Jewry emphasizes the history of ideas and pays little attention to the social components of the transformation. Literary historians of the Haskalah, among them Moshe Kleinman, Hayim Nahman Shapira, and Dan Miron, have been sensitive to the interrelationship between the social and the literary dimensions of the Haskalah, but they have concentrated on literary questions rather than on the broader process of Jewish cultural change in the Russian Empire.[4]

The Haskalah, with its emphasis on the reconciliation of old and new forms, made more headway in Russia than in the West, where it was supplanted by less moderate ideological and social responses to modernity. In Russia, the virtual nonexistence of a bourgeoisie espousing a secular *Weltanschauung* that might be emulated by Jews, the absence (except for brief periods) of the prospect of emancipation, and the weakness of Russia's primary and secondary school system, coupled with the lack of practical incentives for pursuing a secular education, all reinforced traditional standards, with the result that Haskalah was seen as the primary agent of Jewish adaptation to modernity. But Haskalah was, in fact, only one of several influences on Jewish cultural change in the region. One must also consider the impact that various social factors—such as regional variations within the Pale (in the literacy of Jews, for instance), urbanization, wars, occupational patterns, and the railway—had on the dissemination of ideas, the substitution of "modern" for traditional attitudes, and the disintegration of previously obdurate taboos.

The Pale of Settlement was by no means a homogeneous geographical, ethnic, or cultural unit, and the sharp differences within it were reflected in Jewry's far from unified cultural development. The area, in fact, consisted of at least three fairly distinct regions: Lithuania-Belorussia (the provinces of Grodno, Minsk, Vilna, Vitebsk, Kovno, Mogilev); the Ukraine (Volhynia, Podolia, Kiev, Chernigov, Poltava); and New Russia (Kherson, Ekaterinoslav, Taurida, and eventually Bessarabia). Much of the Pale, as it was finally constituted in 1835, comprised the area absorbed by Russia during the Polish partitions, though the provinces of Central Poland themselves—Kalisz, Suwalki, Plock, Lomza, Warsaw, Piotrikow, Kielce, Radom, Lublin, and Siedlce—remained officially outside of it, though effectively within it. New Russia and Bessarabia had been under Turkish hegemony until the late eighteenth and early nineteenth centuries, respectively. The sparsely populated provinces of Chernigov and Poltava were opened to Jewish colonization, despite their inclusion in Russia since the seventeenth century.[5] In each of these regions, different historical backgrounds and ethnic compositions, the size of the Jewish communities relative to the larger population, the degree to which Jews were concentrated in urban or rural settings, the ethnic and cultural character of these settings, and, eventually, the level of industrialization all had an effect on the acculturation of the Jewish community.

Curiously, however, Russian Jewish history has played down regional differences. This in part reflects the impact of Simon Dubnow, who saw Jewry (as did the seminal German Jewish historian Heinrich Graetz) as *ein lebendiger Volkstamm*, one tribe whose members, though scattered, were nonetheless unified by a common spiritual consciousness and shared aspirations. This tendency to play down regionalism was, of course, consistent with the general inclination of Russian historiography to accentuate uniformity over diversity, in line with the relatively unified climatic and geographical character of Russia, the largely homogeneous ethnic composition of the central region of the empire, and the autocratic, highly centralized nature of its government.[6]

Yet the differences within the Pale were significant, and these influenced the Jewish community's uneven cultural transformation. Perhaps the most fundamental variation was demographic concentration. In 1897 Jews amounted to 11.6 percent of the population of the Pale. In areas with only a few Jews, however, they were more susceptible to the influence of the larger society. In 1852, for instance, only 5 percent of the population of the province of Kherson, 1 percent of Ekaterinoslav, and 0.2 percent of Taurida were Jewish. By 1897 Jews constituted just 4.8 percent of the population of Ekaterinoslav, 4 percent of Poltava, and 5 percent of Chernigov.[7] Because on the whole Russian Jews were more concentrated than Jews in the West, integration was generally less attractive and the resistance of traditionalists more effective. However, if one evaluates Jewish demographic density province by province, a somewhat different picture emerges. In the provinces with the fewest Jews, Jewish acculturation often proceeded more quickly.

By contrast to the West, in Russia acculturation seldom resulted from a sense of cultural inferiority, at least not until late in the century. Rather, the mere recognition of the usefulness of learning Russian was more likely to be felt and acted upon by Jews living in areas where relatively few other Jews resided. This was reflected in Jewish literacy rates: in 1897, for example, 24.6 percent of all Jews were literate in Russian, as compared with 21.1 percent of non-Jews. But in areas where Jewish density was relatively low, as in the province of Chernigov, Russian literacy reached 70.2 percent for males between the ages of 20 and 29, as compared with 53.1 percent in Grodno and 59.3 percent in Mogilev.[8]

Regional variations in urbanization also affected acculturation. Few Russian Jews lived in large cities in the first half of the nineteenth century. The largest cities in Imperial Russia—the capitals, St. Petersburg and Moscow—were outside the Pale of Settlement and off limits to all but a few Jews. Residence in Kiev and in Polish Warsaw was also restricted; in Kiev, it was at times completely prohibited. At the beginning of the century, only 10 to 15 percent of Russia's Jews lived in cities with total populations of ten thousand or more.[9] Russia in this period, observes a student of Russian urbanization, "was essentially a country of small provincial centers completely dominated by two capitals."[10]

As the century wore on, the level of Jewish urbanization continued to fall well below that of Western and Central Europe, where 95 percent of Denmark's Jews and 85 percent of Prussia's lived in cities by the 1890's. However, when regional differences are taken into account, one finds that Jewish concentration in the cities of New Russia and central Poland nearly matched that of Western Europe. In the provinces of Kherson and Ekaterinoslav, 85 to 90 percent of all Jews lived in cities by 1897. In four of the five largest cities of Poland, including Lublin and Zamosc, the majority of the inhabitants in 1827 were Jewish. By 1897 fully one fifth, or 219,141, of Poland's Jews lived in Warsaw, as compared with 40,062 fifty years earlier.[11] As a result of such urbanization (and despite Poland's large concentration of hasidim, who as a group were particularly hostile to modern society), there was significant acculturation and even assimilation. Admittedly, some Russian "cities" were little more than hamlets, designated as urban centers by the regime for administrative purposes. Few offered the variety characteristic of nineteenth-century European city life. Yet even Kremenchug or Uman had distinctly urban features.

Nineteenth-century Eastern European Jews associated heterodox behavior with city life. Nearly all of Galicia's maskilim lived in three cities: Brody, Tarnopol, and Lemberg. Few of Odessa's middle-class Jews in the 1850's still wore entirely traditional Jewish clothing (or so it was claimed); it is estimated that by the 1840's some 2,500 Jewish men in Warsaw dressed in "German-style" clothes.[12] Relatively small cities could achieve a high standing in the cultural world of Eastern Europe's modernized Jews: Shklov's importance between the first and third partitions of Poland (greater even than Vilna's) resulted from its location on the new boundary between Russia and Poland, which enabled it to play a major part in the trade between St. Petersburg and the West. Zagare, because of its closeness to Courland, came to play a similarly vital commercial and cultural role.[13]

Location along a convenient transportation route—river routes before the 1860's and 1870's, and later, railways—significantly affected the degree to which a particular setting was influenced by modern currents, either economic or cultural. In the earlier period, most of the leading commercial centers of the Pale and Poland were located on or near rivers, by which merchants shipped grain, lumber, and other products to foreign and domestic markets. Pinsk's commercial importance, for instance, depended on the Pripet, Kamenetz-Podolsk's on the Dniestr, and Mogilev's on the Dniepr. Russia's first railway system, built in four major spurts of activity in 1868–71, 1877–79, 1885–87, and 1890–1900, opened up other, hitherto isolated environments to the larger world.[14]

By the late 1880's, Minsk, Warsaw, Siedlce, Kovno, Brest-Litovsk, Kiev, Grodno, Bialystok, Kovel, Rovno, Proskurov, Mogilev (Podolsk), Kishinev, Bender, Odessa, and Fastov, all cities with sizable Jewish communities, were joined by rail. Many smaller places were linked as well. Hebrew and Yiddish literature offers vivid vignettes of the railway's coming. As Israel Weisbrem wrote in his novel *Bein ha-zemanim* (Between the Times):

> The place in which our story took place . . . was a small town in Lithuania. Its residents were, then as always, pious and unblemished before God, as is true of Jews in all the small towns of Lithuania. But from the day the railway was laid down through this town, the spirit of Haskalah began to infect its youth. . . . The flutelike sounds of those chariots of fire were like manifestos for a nation walking until then in darkness, prompting it to come out and be enlightened, so that the glory of the Haskalah might shine upon it. . . . From the day the railway tracks were laid through this

town, its residents . . . began to wander throughout the entire world and to travel to faraway cities, whose ways and customs and characteristics they learned and brought back with them. Little by little, these new values came to be nurtured here as much as in the large cities.[15]

Sacrosanct customs were challenged as previously remote places were transformed into busy points of transit. Large cities were suddenly no longer inaccessible. The simultaneous decline of traditional Jewish occupations, as well as a general movement from trade and personal services to craft and industrial employment, also contributed to the disintegration of previously stable social and communal patterns.

Several factors led to a heightened interest in the events of the larger world. Of special importance was the impact of war. However, war by no means inevitably had this effect; the Napoleonic wars, for instance, made little impression (on the values, at least) of the cloistered Lithuanian Jews, with whom the French came into direct contact. The long-standing Jewish inclination to favor the present authorities, a visceral distrust of revolutionary sentiment by the conservative Jewish masses, and the pro-Russian exhortations of the Belorussian hasidic leader Shneur Zalman of Liady rendered the Russian Jewish community largely indifferent to the French and relatively unmoved by the conflict's broad political and cultural implications.[16] By contrast, the war conducted in the remote Crimea four decades later apparently evoked considerable interest. Jewish children as well as adults, wrote Lev Levanda in his unfinished novel *Pokhod v Kolkhidu*, found news of the war intoxicating. "I followed the exploits of the Crimean War in a completely different way from that in which I had followed previous events; they were absolutely singular," says the child who acts as the story's narrator. Some Jews in the novel's hamlet would travel to the provincial capital for the sole purpose of "smelling out" what was happening at the front. Since newspapers were all but unobtainable, rumors flourished. News of the whole of Europe uniting against Russia—with the exception of "our father-in-law in Prussia," as the narrator calls Friedrich Wilhelm IV—filled Jews with concern and hunger for additional information. "The interest of [our] Jews was strained to an intolerable degree."[17]

The deaths of approximately five hundred Jewish soldiers at

Sevastopol no doubt heightened this concern,[18] but if Levanda is to be believed, it originated in events that had little direct bearing on Jews. Indeed, the newspaper *Korot ha-ittim* was founded in Romania in 1855 in response to this new curiosity about what was happening outside the immediate orbit of the Jewish community.[19] A character of Reuven Braudes's 1888 novel *Shete ha-ketsavot* (The Two Extremes) speaks of news of "great and mighty events, . . . of the affairs of war, of heroes, the crash of horses, the roar of cannons, and the sound of bows."[20] Such news could open up the wider world for a Jewish provincial and make Jewish affairs seem lackluster by comparison.

Certain occupational groups especially inclined toward the larger world: physicians, notaries, and merchants, particularly merchants involved in commercial dealings with Western and Central Europe. A recognition of the value of familiarity with languages other than Yiddish, and perhaps a chance encounter with Reform Jewish practices at the Leipzig fair (where services accompanied by organ music had been held since 1820) may have served to open such merchants to modernizing influences.[21] In Warsaw several of the richest merchants assimilated; in Pinsk the wealthiest commercial family, the Lurias, were among the first to speak Russian at home, though they maintained close ties with Orthodox Judaism; in Odessa assimilation proceeded along lines more radical than in Pinsk but less pronounced than in Warsaw. Jewish clerks and accountants employed by commercial firms—and by the municipal government, which by the 1850's employed many Jews in Pinsk—were also particularly susceptible to the attractions of the modern world.[22]

Perhaps the most striking example of the relationship between occupation and acculturation was the *otkupshchiki*, the holders of government concessions for distilling and selling liquor. In the 1840's the Russian government introduced public leases, which were purchased by Russian Jewry's wealthiest financiers, Guenzburg and Warshawsky. These were in turn subleased to Jewish tax farmers, distillers, and tavern keepers; subsequently a class of affluent Jewish tax farmers emerged who functioned as financial agents of the treasury, with many Jewish subagents, who also served as officials of a sort. Otkupshchiki were often the community's richest men, economically independent of the Jewish community and at the same time enjoying a close economic association and occasional social contacts with non-Jewish officials and merchants—contacts that frequently led to a degree of acculturation and weakened their attachments to the Jewish community. By 1851, 476 Jewish otkupshchiki were members of the first Russian merchant guild. Even relatively unsuccessful otkupshchiki, according to the Jewish writer Aharon Paperna, earned between 400 and 500 rubles annually, as compared with a Jewish tutor or clerk, who might earn 150 to 200 rubles.[23]

Regarded by contemporaries, traditionalists and maskilim alike, as haughty and ignorant of Jewish culture, the otkupshchiki—numbering in the tens of thousands or more by the 1880's—were among the least traditionally Jewish groups in Russia. In his novel *Be-emek ha-bakhah*, Sh. Y. Abramovitsch tells of an otkupshchik who, after spending an evening playing cards with non-Jews, sits down to a meal of meat cooked in milk and then to sausages and cheese.[24] In the 1850's otkupshchiki formed an association whose membership was restricted to those literate in Russian.[25] A well-known Yiddish folk song claimed that they "shave their little beards / And ride on ponies. / They parade in the streets / And gorge themselves without ritually washing their hands."[26] Reuven Kulisher remarked in 1879 that the most apt symbol for the Russian Haskalah would be a picture of a Jew on a liquor barrel with a sausage in his hands.[27] Though meant to be sadly ironic, this was, despite its apparent incongruity, hardly as farfetched a symbol for modernization as Kulisher may have believed.

Other factors contributed to the community's cultural transformation, including the 1874 military reform, which required universal military service but also drastically reduced the length of service required of those who held higher educational degrees. Jewish parents, previously reluctant to send their children to Russian schools, now increasingly relented. The number of Jewish students in gymnasiums more than doubled between 1870 and 1879 (from 2,045 to 4,913) and rose nearly eightfold between 1865 and 1887 (from 990 to 7,657). Jewish university enrollment rose thirteen times (from 129 to 1,739).[28] The establishment of a series of new Lithuanian *yeshivot* in the last decades of the nineteenth century (the formidable Volozhin *yeshiva* closed in 1893, but its place was filled by the *yeshivot* of Mir, Vilna, Slobodka, and Telz, the latter two founded in the 1870's and 1880's) testified to a recognition by Eastern European traditionalists that only a concerted effort could check the tendency of Jewish youth to prefer gymnasiums over talmudic study houses.[29]

By the 1880's a russified Jewish leadership (whether liberal, Zionist, or socialist) had emerged and spoke for broad segments of the Jewish population. The pogroms of 1881–83 were followed by a redefinition of the meaning of Jewish politics, which now essentially ceased to encourage adaptation to the larger environment in order to achieve emancipation, and stressed instead the creation of a new world, either in Eastern Europe or elsewhere. Moreover, the pogroms quickened the migratory process that had begun in the late 1860's and that by 1914 saw nearly one-half of Eastern European Jewry migrating within the region or beyond it.[30] The flow of some Jewish youth into the revolutionary and Zionist movements created close ties, familial and otherwise, between sections of the Jewish masses generally unsympathetic to radical ideals and new political movements. By the first decade of the twentieth century, the heroism of Jewish radicals (especially the Bundists), their organization of Jewish self-defense, their participation in philanthropic activities throughout the Pale, even their conspiratorial form of internal organization, conferred on them an almost legendary aura. Mass migration, radically new political formulations, and chronic underemployment all challenged the foundations of traditional Jewish society before the 1917 revolution. The ability of the various forms of traditional Judaism to maintain themselves, to the extent to which they did, in the face of these pressures attested to their durability and resilience. However, once the Pale of Settlement was effectively abolished in 1915, when Jews were expelled from the battle zone to the Russian interior, traditional Judaism's defenses proved unequal to the task.

Perhaps nowhere in the Pale was acculturation more pervasive than in Odessa. The character of this Jewish community's cultural life may be traced to Odessa's newness, its multinational character, and, in particular, its remarkable commercial growth. ("The commercial history of Odessa," wrote A. A. Skal'kovskii, "*is* the history of Odessa.")[31] Though commercial enterprise was generally distrusted by the Russian authorities and consequently restrained, since Odessa's establishment its merchants had been decidedly less restricted because the city's potential value as a center of Russian grain export outweighed traditional misgivings. The close and continuous commercial relations that Odessa enjoyed with Western and Central Europe, Asia, and the United States facilitated contact with the larger world to a much greater extent than was typical for Russian Jews. Many Odessa Jews studied foreign languages, because knowledge of Italian, French, or German was deemed essential for participation in local economic life. Encouraged by the commercial opportunities open to Jews, many otherwise self-conscious traditionalists, unlike Orthodox Jews elsewhere in Russia, had their children study secular subjects to prepare for potentially lucrative commercial careers. For significant numbers of Jews, what occurred in Odessa—a community considered by many Russian Jews to be the Pale's most modern—was not, for the most part, the intellectually rigorous transformation that characterized the Haskalah. Rather, Odessa Jews began to participate more fully in various ways in the larger society, since in this setting the economic, social, and cultural benefits from such participation were more apparent.

The City of Odessa

Beginning in the seventeenth century, the Muscovite state viewed the acquisition of the northern littoral of the Black Sea, then under the control of the Ottoman Empire, as a major objective of its foreign policy. In this area, which had been lost by Kievan Rus' to foreign invaders in the eleventh century, three of Russia's major rivers, the Dniepr, Bug, and Dniestr, flowed into the Black Sea. Attempts to regain the territory in the late seventeenth and early eighteenth centuries ended in disaster. Then in 1739 the Treaty of Belgrade, following a successful campaign, ceded to Russia the territory between the Donets and Bug rivers, which was later incorporated into the province of Ekaterinoslav, as well as the right to maintain a civilian settlement in Azov, but the possession of the territory was of little value since the seacoast remained in Turkish hands.

The conquest of the region was completed in the reign of Catherine II. Russia had emerged from the Seven Years' War (1756–63) with a strengthened and expanded army, and its forces routed the Turks in 1769 in Jassy (Moldavia), and defeated them the following year in a naval battle in the Bay of Chesme. With the Treaty of Kuchuk Kainarji in 1774, Russia gained a small area of Black Sea coastline between the mouths of the Dniepr and Bug rivers as well as additional territory along the Sea of Azov. The treaty also guaranteed Russian vessels the right of free commercial navigation in Turkish waters. Within two decades, following the Second Turkish War (1787–92) and the Treaty of Jassy (1792), Russia secured the remaining Black Sea coastline between the Kuban and Dniestr rivers, and its 1783 annexation of the Crimea was confirmed. In 1789, in the midst of one of the campaigns in the second war, Russia captured a Tatar fortress on the Black Sea, twenty miles north of the mouth of the Dniestr. Called Yeni-Dunai (New World), it was located beside the town of Khazhibei, which six years later would be renamed Odessa.[32]

The territory was first named New Russia in 1764 (Novorusskaia guberniia; Novorossiiskaia guberniia after 1796) and divided in 1802 into the guberniias (provinces) of Nikolaev (called Kherson from 1803), Ekaterinoslav, and Taurida. Enlarged in 1828 by the addition of Bessarabia, New Russia was made up mostly of steppe, a treeless expanse covered by coarse and abundant herbaceous vegetation—flat, monotonous land that, despite a generally extreme climate and poor rainfall, had some of the richest soil in the world. The area had been inhabited by Cossacks and Tatars for centuries, and indeed the Zaporozhskaia Sech', an autonomous settlement of Cossacks located along the Dniepr river in the area acquired by Russia with the Treaty of Belgrade, maintained its independence until 1775, when it was dissolved by the Russian authorities. The government was acutely aware that this barely tamed, sparsely populated (52,000 people lived in the newly conquered southern steppe in 1768), and potentially rich agricultural territory was in need of intensive settlement.[33]

In order to encourage immigration, the Russian state used the same inducement that had drawn enserfed Polish and Ukrainian peasants, Circassian slaves, and others to the steppe for centuries—the lure of freedom. Runaway serfs from the interior, who otherwise would have continued their flight across the border, were persuaded to settle in the area, since the state assured them that their personal freedom would be protected. All non-noble settlers, as stipulated by a ukase of December 12, 1796, were to remain in the locale and the occupation in which they were registered in 1795; attempts by owners to reclaim runaway peasants were thereby obstructed and southern landlords were assured of a labor force. Peasants from central Russia were resettled by their landlords in the south and promised terms similar to those of leaseholders. In 1801, 93.7 percent of the peasants in New Russia were juridically free, and by the 1840's, of the total 3,127,000 inhabitants of New Russia only 658,000 were bonded serfs. Large numbers of runaway peasants were attracted to the region, and as a character in G. P. Danilevskii's 1860 novel, *Beglye v Novorossii* (Fugitives in New Russia), declares, "It is here that Russia's serfs have found a refuge. Here is their Kentucky and Massachusetts. If there had not been fugitives, there would have been nothing either in the Don, or the Black Sea region, or in the good and fertile lands beyond the Rapids."[34]

Catherine II offered sizable grants of land to leading government officials, naval commanders responsible for the conquest of the area, several Greeks who had served Russia during the Turkish wars, and a large number of Russian merchants. In the absence of an established agrarian system based on serfdom, the landowners were freer to respond to the demands of the market—especially the grain market—which became increasingly important in the first decades of the nineteenth century, when England began to look to foreign markets to supplement its domestic grain needs. A more commercially minded nobility thereby emerged in the southern provinces. Between 1815 and 1820, in Odessa, Kherson, and Kerch, several landowners formed exporting companies of their own, dealing not only in the sale of grains but also in meat, tallow, hides, flax, butter, and wax. Until the 1830's most New Russia landowners avoided the use of middlemen, negotiating directly with exporters at the port cities. In an effort to expedite the transportation of produce to harbor, a local landowner built the first waterway connecting the Dniestr river to Odessa.[35]

Foreigners were actively sought out as settlers and offered generous inducements, in contrast to the traditional distrust of non-Russians prevalent elsewhere in the empire. The first settlement of foreigners in the region was the military-agricultural colony

New Serbia, composed of Austrian Serbs and established in 1752 between the Dniepr and Sinitsa rivers in what was later the province of Kherson. Religious minorities (such as German Mennonites), refugees from the French Revolution, Greeks, and Bulgarians established agricultural colonies as well, and by 1839 as many as 40,591 foreign colonists lived in the province of Kherson alone. By the early 1840's colonists were responsible for a total of roughly 24 percent of Russia's exported grain.[36]

Foreigners were also attracted to the new cities—Elizavetgrad (originally St. Elizabeth), Kremenchug, Rostov-on-Don, Kherson, and Nikolaev—located along, or not far from, the Black Sea and Sea of Azov. The cities were established to serve primarily military functions as part of the new Dniepr defense line, but their commercial potential was soon apparent, and commercial settlers, initially mostly Old Believers and Greeks, were drawn to them. The cities soon gained the attention of the St. Petersburg authorities, aware that the southern ports were the natural outlet for the rich agricultural belt stretching for an area of 200,000 square miles from Penza to Kiev, and in 1782 the government decided to establish a commercial port, though it was uncertain whether to choose Kherson or Nikolaev. After the Second Turkish War it considered two new sites—Ochakov and Khazhibei—and selected the latter in 1794.[37]

Located on the west coast of the Black Sea, on a bluff about two hundred feet above sea level, Khazhibei possessed a deep natural port and nearly year-round accessibility, and was free of the silting and swamps that made Nikolaev and Kherson unhealthy and uncomfortable.[38] The construction of port facilities was soon begun, and measures were taken to attract settlers, in particular commercially experienced Greeks. Khazhibei's conqueror, Admiral Osip Mikhailovich DeRibas, served as its first administrator (the first of several foreign-born officials), and Khazhibei was renamed Odessa in 1795. The very choice of Odessa's name—recalling the ancient Greek colony of Odessos, which was thought to have been located nearby—may have been motivated by this wish to settle Greeks. The government allocated 15,000 *desiatinas* of land for a Greek settlement just outside the city's limits and granted 10,000 rubles for the construction of houses and other buildings in the compound. It offered generous inducements to other settlers as well, freeing them from all taxes and state services for ten years and exempting them from military service and the quartering of troops. The government offered loans for building houses and churches. It also guaranteed freedom of religion.[39]

The city experienced a period of uneven growth in its first decade. The funds allocated for the building of port facilities were largely misspent and few buildings were constructed. In 1800 only 86 ships docked in Odessa, and 64 left with freight. Many of Odessa's residents were seasonal laborers. In 1799, 3,182 of the city's 4,573 inhabitants were men, as were the vast majority of the city's 8,000–9,000 residents four years later. Its merchants generally saw Odessa as but one of several southern ports through which they exported produce to Turkey. Armand Emanuel, Duc de Richelieu, a French émigré in Russian service, who arrived in Odessa as *gradonachal'nik* (prefect) in 1803, thought that the city looked like "nothing more than a village."[40]

During the decade of Richelieu's administration Odessa was transformed into a city of international repute, Richelieu himself observing that though he entered a city of sand he left it one of stone.[41] Selected in 1805 to serve simultaneously as governor-general of Ekaterinoslav, Kherson, and Taurida, he applied himself to his tasks with great energy, honesty, and shrewdness. He immediately proceeded to standardize the requisitions at the port (2.5 kopecks on each *chetvert* of grain exported from the city, increased to 5 kopecks in 1813) and applied the funds collected to the building of port facilities. Allocations and loans from St. Petersburg were now treated with greater care and responsibility. Committed to free trade, Richelieu lobbied for a one-fourth reduction on all duties collected in the ports of the Black and Azov seas, and presented the case personally before Alexander I, whom he persuaded. Furthermore, he permitted the storage of imports in Odessa free of charge for a period of up to one and a half years.[42]

The building of port facilities, the stabilization of procedures at the port, and the reduction of duties helped create closer ties between Odessa and the Near East, Italy, and Marseilles. By 1808, consuls from France, Austria, Spain, and Naples were established in the city. Trade with France and Spain alone amounted to 10 million rubles in the period between 1813 and 1815. In 1816 an Odessa merchant, the wealthy French émigré Charles Sicard, opened the Black Sea Company, with its central office in Paris and branches in Marseilles, Constantinople, and Odessa. The number of merchants in the city's first merchant guild rose from 32 in 1808 to 53 in 1812. Under Richelieu's administration a discount bank, exchange, insurance company, customs district, quarantine facility, and commercial court were established.[43]

The city, wrote the aristocratic visitor F. F. Vigel' in the 1820's, had become a bourgeois republic, unbearably resolute, earnest, and self-absorbed.[44] Merchants were its paradigmatic figures, and, observed Skal'kovskii, they would often skip meals, avoid friends, disregard the feelings of their families, dine in the meanest taverns, and spend evenings in the Casino, where business was conducted, in order that correspondence not be delayed or a shipment of grain missed. Moneymaking became a consuming, all-important preoccupation, and every merchant, speculator, exporter, and entrepreneur, however small, felt that his fortune could be made at any moment.[45]

Already Odessa was beginning to be seen as a cultural center as well. The poet K. N. Batiushkov, who visited Odessa in 1818, declared that the city offered all that a cultured man would ever need, and the local opera, he felt, compared with Moscow's.[46] A public library and an antiquarian museum were established within a decade of the poet's visit. The editor of the first volume of the *Odesskii almanakh* (1831) opened his essay on contemporary Odessa life with the rhetorical question, "Is Odessa an agreeable place in which to live?" and responded with a vigorous affirmation of the city's merits:

> Here can be found everything that an active, educated man might ever need. If you want to make use of your time and capital in Odessa, you have a wide range of possible enterprises. If you love to read, you can satisfy your passion for books and journals in the Odessa library and local bookstores. Would you like to enjoy a few hours of leisure? You may turn for pleasure to the winter ball, in the summer to the promenade by the sea, and, of course, to the Italian Opera House.[47]

Richelieu's policies were largely responsible for promoting this image and encouraging conspicuous cultural activity. Visitors to

Odessa frequently criticized these policies (as have nineteenth- and twentieth-century historians) as strangely out of touch with the still-primitive character of the city. It was noted that almost immediately after Richelieu arrived in Odessa in 1803, and when a sufficient number of local artisans could not be found to build even the chairs for his residence (the chairs had to be transported from Kherson), he launched plans for the construction of an opera house and a series of majestic buildings in the city's center. Reluctant to impute extravagance to the much-lauded Richelieu, several Odessa historians credited these decisions to his overwhelming love for culture, a love so strong, they suggested, that it may have overwhelmed his sense of priority.[48] The Soviet historian Elena Druzhinina, however, has persuasively argued that Richelieu's insistence that cultural institutions be built immediately was consistent with a comprehensive plan aimed at transforming not only the city itself but, perhaps even more significant, the way it was perceived by foreign exporters and Russian merchants. Richelieu understood, she suggests, that the construction of port facilities alone would not alter the perception of Odessa as a remote port of little consequence, and that in order to call attention to it in the international community, a well-appointed city with notable cultural landmarks would have to be built quickly and dramatically.[49] The shrewd gamble paid off generously. By the 1820's Odessa was already a popular vacation spot for the Polish nobility, and its elegant shops, Italian opera, and strikingly beautiful promenade dazzled visitors. It was now sometimes referred to as a "Russian Florence" and "St. Petersburg in miniature."[50]

Richelieu, who returned to France in 1814 to become foreign minister and then chairman of the Council of Ministers in the Restoration government of Louis XVIII, was the first of several New Russia administrators who shared a positive orientation toward commercial enterprise, foreign investment, and free trade. His immediate successor, the French count Alexandre de Langeron, followed Richelieu's lead in most matters of policy. Count Mikhail Vorontsov (governor-general from 1822 to 1855)—whose father had been the Russian ambassador to Britain from 1784 to 1800, and who had spent many years abroad—was also an enthusiastic supporter of free trade (and a shrewd businessman himself), and he believed emphatically that freedom was as essential to healthy commercial life as were capital turnover and moderate governmental protection.[51]

The city now grew rapidly. By 1813 its population was 25,000–30,000, and the value of its exports rose from 1,787,000 rubles in 1802 to nearly 9 million, out of a total of 45 million for the New Russia region as a whole.[52] Sixty-five commercial houses were now located in the city, over half of all those in the Black Sea area. These enormous strides were due, in part, to the farsighted policies of Richelieu, but developments in the international arena, especially the Napoleonic wars and the Continental Blockade (1807–12), contributed significantly as well by setting the basis for the growth of the Russian grain trade, in which Odessa came to play a pivotal role.

Odessa became in this period the foremost port of entry for Asian goods bound for European markets. These were transported across Persia by land to Turkey, shipped to Odessa, and then sent by river or road through Brody and Leipzig to the northwest, and in particular to England. The Napoleonic wars also depleted Western grain reserves and disrupted agricultural production, forcing European buyers to begin to turn elsewhere to satisfy their countries' domestic needs. These needs remained when peace was reestablished, since England was compelled by accelerated industrialization to turn to foreign producers to supplement its domestic production. Russia emerged as Europe's chief granary, and Odessa eventually overtook St. Petersburg as Russia's major grain-exporting port.[53]

Odessa's growth was further enhanced by free-port status—a privilege championed by Richelieu—which was conferred upon the city in 1817 and not revoked until 1859. It was thereby transformed into the foremost warehouse of goods transported from the Near East and the Caucasus to Poland and Austria, securing for itself an important role in the import of luxury items, a less volatile and unpredictable business than grain trade. The first provincial branch of the commercial bank established in the capitals in 1818 opened in Odessa the same year, with initial assets of 3 million rubles. The bank served the activities of merchants throughout the southern area, and merchants as far away as Moscow used its services.[54] Duty-free luxury goods flooded the local market—subject to taxes only if transported outside the city limits—and Odessa residents grew accustomed to foreign wines, liqueurs, perfumes, and spices.[55] Laborers came to the city in large numbers (especially during the summer and fall seasons), attracted by the high wages paid for work at the port. Between 1815 and 1820, wagoners could earn five to six rubles merely for transporting a load of goods from harbor to warehouse—more than four times the normal wages for a day's labor.[56]

As a result of its commercial importance, Odessa became a major administrative center, though the city of Kherson was the capital of Kherson province, in which Odessa was located. The governor-general of New Russia resided in Odessa; the offices of the school district, post and telegraph, New Russia statistical committee, and medical administration were located here. It was also the home of the best schools in the region: a commercial gymnasium was started in 1804, and an institute for the children of the nobility soon afterward. The Richelieu Lyceum was opened in 1817, and transformed into the New Russia University in 1865. Three classical gymnasiums were located in the city, as well as a Russian Orthodox seminary, a school of fine arts, a conservatory, and many private schools, including special primary schools for Catholics, Armenians, Germans, and Jews.[57]

Widely traveled foreign visitors were impressed by Odessa's Continental appearance. "Europe was once more before our eyes," exclaimed a French visitor in 1838, upon his first glimpse of Odessa from aboard a ship bound from Constantinople, "and the aspect of the straight lines of the streets, the wide-fronted houses and the sober aspect of the buildings awoke many dear recollections in our minds. . . . [It was] a European town, . . . full of affluence, movement, and gaiety."[58] Odessa's streets, paved with broad limestone slabs, reminded another visitor of Naples, and its promenade recalled that of Genoa. The city's population continued to grow rapidly, to 41,700 in 1841 and 73,686 ten years later.[59]

Odessa's continental flavor was all the more pronounced since a large portion of its population was born abroad, coming from Greece, Italy, Germany, France, and even from Sweden, Denmark, the United States, Turkey, Egypt, and Persia. In the city's first few decades foreigners constituted the overwhelming majority of the population (in 1819 only about one-fourth of Odessa's population was Russian and the Ukrainian population was still small). Even in 1851 more than 10,000 of the city's 90,000 residents were registered as foreigners; many other residents had been born abroad but had acquired Russian citizenship. (Government policy encouraged naturalization by such measures as prohibiting foreign firms from buying wholesale grain for export.)[60] Though the numerical supremacy of foreigners declined significantly in the second half of the century, their wealth, prominence, and concentration in the city's center lent credence to the claim that Odessa was less Russian than European. "In Odessa," wrote August von Haxthausen after his visit in 1843, "is found the most motley mixture of nationalities I have ever seen." He was particularly struck by the way different nationalities tended to dominate particular occupations: Greeks, Italians, and Germans were concentrated in wholesale trade; the French sold wine and other retail goods; the Jews were bankers, agents, and brokers; the Karaites traded in tobacco and oriental goods.[61] The daily listing of current exchange rates was posted in Greek; local society spoke French; and the street signs were in Italian and Russian. Theater performances, according to another German visitor to Odessa in 1844, were presented in the same theater in five different languages.[62]

The grain market continued to dominate local commerce, with the value of grain exports rising from 6,962,000 rubles in 1823 to over 33 million rubles forty years later, and the amount of grain trade tripling between 1839 and 1853 to 3,818,000 chetverts. This progress was by no means uninterrupted, and poor grain harvests led to a sharp contraction in exports in 1820, 1822–24, and again in 1827–29. After the Treaty of Adrianople, which guaranteed the passage of Russian merchant ships through the Straits, Odessa's standing was secure, and the city now experienced two decades of steady, even dramatic growth. Indeed, by 1847 Odessa exported more grain than any other port in Europe, and 37 percent of all of Russia's grain was now exported through it. The value of Odessa's total exports rose from 10,289,000 rubles in 1842 to 51,372,000 in 1872, and more than tripled again within the next nine years to 160,202,000 rubles.[63] Odessa's central streets were now lined with numerous and fine shops—a reflection of the city's role in the import of luxury items—of which several rivaled the best specialty shops in the capitals. "Throughout the whole city," wrote the German geographer Johan Georg Kohl in 1844, "up to its remotest extremities runs a garland of shops and booths which present a curious assemblage of all that is found in the many lands whose fragments are here reflected as if in a broken mirror."[64] The number of stores and stalls in the city increased from 490 in 1827 to 743 in 1837 and 1,214 twenty years later.[65]

Among the most distinct indications of the city's commercial character were the thousands of ox-drawn wagons that filled Odessa's streets between May and September, carrying the grain from hinterland to harbor. Though a recommendation for the construction of a railway system to connect Odessa with the interior was presented to St. Petersburg in 1842, for three more decades much of the grain from the *chernozem* (the Black Earth belt of the Ukraine) was transported to the port by oxen, every wagon hauling about eight sacks of wheat (up to two bushels). Wheat was also brought to the port on barges along river routes. An American visitor to Odessa in 1854 left a particularly vivid account of wagons converging on the city: "As we approached Odessa everything betokened that we were coming into the neighborhood of a great city. We dashed past long caravans of ox-wagons, laden with the wheat of the Ukraine and the tallow of the steppes; with charcoal from the forests of Kishneff a hundred miles away; with dried-reeds and rushes which are used for fuel . . . ; with watermelons from the sandy plains in fabulous quantities."[66] In the 1850's, during the spring and summer months, about one hundred wagons arrived in the city daily.

These wagons laden with grain streaming toward Odessa's port indicated both the city's commercial vibrancy and the anachronistic state of the New Russian transportation system. The chernozem of Podolia, the source of much of the grain exported from Odessa, was located about two hundred miles away, and it took up to fifteen days to transport a wagon to the port. This arduous and inconvenient system, made all the more difficult in the late summer by seasonal heavy rains, added considerably to the cost of the grain and contributed to Odessa's relative eclipse in the face of North American competition in the period following the Crimean War.[67]

The problem of unsatisfactory transportation was only one of several serious and persistent concerns that New Russia officials failed to address satisfactorily until the mid-1860's: Odessa's streets were almost impassable when it rained, built as they were out of soft limestone, which turned easily into mud. During the dry summer months the air was filled with blinding particles of dust, also resulting from the erosion of the soft building material.* Furthermore, supplies of water were inadequate, and private entrepreneurs, who charged exorbitant prices for it, controlled most of the wells in the city. In view of the shortage of drinking water and the large numbers of ships anchoring in Odessa's harbor, sanitation was poor and difficult to control, and plagues periodically erupted despite strict quarantine procedures at the port. In 1812 and 1813, during Richelieu's tenure, intermittent plague claimed close to three thousand of Odessa's twelve thousand residents. Plagues erupted again in 1829 and 1837, and cholera in 1830, 1848–49, 1855, 1865–66, and 1872.[68]

Though the city's charms were often blithely overrated, immigrants continued to pour into Odessa in large numbers, and its population soared from 86,729 in 1849 to 193,500 in 1873, tripling in size between 1860 and 1892 to 404,000.[69] The second largest group of immigrants, surpassed in numbers only by Russians, were the Jews. As of 1892, out of the total population of 404,000, 198,233 were Russians, 124,511 Jews, 37,925 Ukrainians, 17,395 Poles, and 25,751 foreigners.[70] Only 38.5 percent of Odessa's Jews, according to the same survey, had been born in the city.[71] Drawn to Odessa, and to the southern provinces in general, in large numbers, the Jewish population of New Russia increased 333 percent between 1844 and 1880, and the percentage of Jews in the overall population rose in the same period from 2 to 5.6 percent.[72] Jewish immigrants looked upon Odessa, with its wide streets and limestone buildings, as a world apart from the ancient

*One of the best descriptions of the condition of Odessa's streets is in Shirley Brooks, *The Russians of the South* (London, 1854), p. 22: "The dust lies like a universal shroud of some two or three inches thick. The slightest breeze flings it over the town in clouds, the lightest footstep sends it flying high in dense heaps. When, therefore, I tell you that hundreds of the carriages of the places, driven at high speed . . . are perpetually racing about, and that the sea breezes are as perpetually rushing through the streets, the statement that Odessa lives in a cloud is no figure of speech."

settlements to which they were accustomed, and Odessa came to represent to Jews elsewhere, particularly in Lithuania, the option of a fresh start, offering a change in climate, economic possibilities, and perimeters of acceptable religious behavior. As the Zionist publicist Shmarya Levin observed when confronted with the "youth, freshness, and gaiety" of New Russia in 1898:

> I had been accustomed for a long time to Lithuania, an ancient land, with ancient cities and villages; the dust of generations lay upon it, and the worry of old age was like a visible shadow—it was a land that looked backwards. . . . That northern country was one in which beginnings were no longer made; men could only continue what the anonymous and forgotten past had begun. In every respect this rich, young southern country was the antithesis of the northern country of my birth. . . . Here, where the generations had not preempted everything, man could still write his name into something.[73]

Origins of the Jewish Community

The few studies of Odessa Jewry written while the records of the Jewish community were still accessible invariably commented on the lack of source material for the first few decades. This period, researchers observed, was "shrouded in mystery," in part because Odessa's *Kehillah* (the committee administering Jewish communal affairs; pl. *Kehillot*) functioned until the 1820's in an informal, haphazard fashion.[74] Such organizational laxity was not uncommon in frontier communities, where it frequently took several years for institutions to be consolidated and communal records carefully maintained. What made Odessa seem, in retrospect, unique was the importance the city would rapidly achieve in the second quarter of the nineteenth century. The paucity of material on the earlier period helped to reinforce the illusion that the history of Odessa Jewry truly began only with the immigration of enlightened Galician Jews to the city in the 1820's, an assumption these self-confident, often wealthy settlers themselves helped to foster.[75] Nevertheless, an examination of the relevant non-Jewish materials, a rereading of the Jewish ones, and a willingness to view the Jewish community within the larger social context all suggest that the early period cannot be so easily dismissed, and that the city's first two decades strongly influenced the future development of the community.

The geographical remoteness of the formerly Turkish areas surrounding the Black Sea, together with sober economic calculation by the St. Petersburg authorities, helped establish the region as a relatively hospitable setting for prospective Jewish immigration. Permission for Jewish settlement in the area was a distinct exception to the principle defining the Pale of Settlement, namely, that Jewish residents be restricted to areas annexed from Poland that already contained many Jews. Few Jews lived in the southern steppes, but as of 1769 the Russian government nevertheless permitted Jewish prisoners taken captive during the war with Turkey to settle there. In decided contrast to the 1791 reaffirmation of Jewish exclusion from cities in the interior of Russia, in New Russia the right of residence was officially extended to all Jews.[76]

Reasons for Jewish exclusion from the interior included the fear of Jewish economic competition, alarm over alleged Jewish commercial exploitation of the peasantry, and religious obscurantism. The merchant estate, burdened by tax obligations and forced to compete with the privileged gentry, and at times even with the peasantry, in commercial and manufacturing activities, insisted on the exclusion of Jewish businessmen from the interior—a prohibition consistent with anti-Jewish sentiments shared by the government for centuries.[77] However, in the sparsely populated southern provinces these considerations were irrelevant, and rational mercantile motives prompted the government to take a more tolerant view of Jewish settlement and commercial activities in general. In fact, Catherine II was so intent on attracting Jews to the newly conquered provinces that she entered into a secret understanding with a group of Jewish businessmen eager to settle in Riga and Smolensk—outside the boundaries of permissible Jewish settlement—allowing them to live where they wished on the condition that they encourage Jewish settlement to the south.[78]

Jewish participation in the region's economic life dated back several centuries. Polish and Ukrainian Jews had settled in the southern Ukraine in the sixteenth century, working among the Cossacks in the Zaporozhskaia Sech' as merchants, importers, and occasionally even as translators. They owned many of the stores and taverns in the region and were active in exporting goods from the Crimea to the Ukraine and Poland. Jews remained in the area despite the massacres of Jews in the Ukraine by the Khmelnitski forces in 1648. Jews tended to drift toward the newly established towns along the coastline after the disintegration of the Zaporozhskaia Sech' in 1775 and the consolidation of Russian control over the area.[79] Khazhibei's original Jewish population—remembered as vagabonds and adventurers by subsequent Jewish immigrants—was probably made up of these itinerant merchants.

Samuel Pen, the author of a brief but valuable study, *Evreiskaia starina v Odesse* (The Jewish Past in Odessa), wrote that Jews may have lived in Khazhibei since the mid-eighteenth century and that the oldest legible inscription in the Jewish cemetery dated from 1770. Some of Khazhibei's Jews, suggests Pen on the basis of his examination of local Jewish cemetery headstones, were born in the Crimea or even further east. Only six Jews were in the fortress when it was captured by the Russians, part of a colony of merchants made up mainly of Greeks and Albanians.[80]

By 1794 Odessa's Jewish population had risen to 240 (10 per cent of the total population), and five years later it was just over 310 (187 males and about 130 females). The institutions essential to the stable functioning of a Jewish community were now established, including a burial society, a synagogue (subsidized by the local authorities, who had offered to help build houses of worship as one of the incentives granted prospective settlers), a *Talmud Torah* (a school for the indigent and orphans), a *hekdesh* (a combination poorhouse and hospice), and a Kehillah.[81]

The new, remote community was heavily dependent upon immigration for its growth, and it experienced two distinct waves during its first two decades. Odessa's original Jewish settlers were, much like their non-Jewish counterparts, rugged, young, generally unmarried males, the sort of itinerant Jewish merchants and laborers who had worked in the southern steppe area for centuries.[82] The city was then "a lodestone for all riffraff, for all types of persons for whom it seemed good and nice to go to a place where they were not at all known, and to live a life of ease—a new life, free from the chains of tradition dragging alongside."[83]

Jews were important in Odessa commerce from its earliest years. A report from the *Odesskaia gorodskaia magistratura*, dated March 27, 1797, underscores the role Jews played in the city's commercial life, though their numbers had dropped to 135 from 1794's 240. Possessing much of the city's commercial capital, they dominated the trade in such commodities as silk, cotton, wool, hardware, iron, and shoes. Jews were also active in the exporting of salt. Nonetheless, very few were sufficiently wealthy to register under the mercantile category of *kuptsy* (in 1801 only two had done so), and the majority apparently worked as petty traders and artisans for the Russian soldiers stationed in the fortress.[84]

On the heels of this first wave of "nameless" and "depraved" settlers, as Jewish sources later referred to them, came still other immigrants from Volhynia, Podolia, and White Russia, who were keenly sensitive to changes in the grain market and aware of the potential importance of the Russian Black Sea port.[85] The community's growth was further augmented by the arrival of Jews from the newly established agricultural colonies in Kherson. By 1809, 1,691 Jewish families had settled in these colonies; the vast majority quickly became disenchanted (by 1819 only 417 families remained) because of the poor land they were allocated, inadequate supplies, the brutal regimen imposed by non-Jewish supervisors, and the attraction of pursuing traditional Jewish occupations in the southern cities. In contrast to the first wave of settlers, nearly all now came with families.[86]

This second wave coincided with a critical period in the new city's commercial and cultural development. Between 1803 and 1819 Odessa was transformed from a modest seaport into a city of international importance, offering Jewish residents a range of opportunities rarely encountered in the Pale of Settlement. Indeed, this combination—Odessa's frontier location and its role as both a commercial and cultural center—laid the foundations for the Jewish community's receptivity to modern institutions. Odessa's Jewish community must be examined against this background of diversity, change, and rawness.

Jews in frontier settings frequently observed religious ritual less scrupulously than those living in established centers, and in the absence of traditional institutions, powerful sanctions, and respected authorities, traditional values tended to weaken. The process of immigration often contributed to the erosion of such values, particularly since the more conservative elements were less likely to abandon established Jewish centers, leaving voluntary resettlement to the adventurous, young, and unattached.[87] The relative lack of traditional Jewish restraints in Odessa in its early years may be illustrated by the following incident: one evening in 1817 the city's rabbi, Berish ben Yisrael Usher of Nemirov, was beaten on the streets by several Jews because they were unhappy with his stringent approach to the observance of ritual law.[88]

Materialism also contributed to the erosion of traditional values and helped foster acculturation. In the first published historical sketch on Odessa Jewry (written for the *Odesskii vestnik* and translated later into German), J. L. Finkel underlined the threat that the passion for business posed to Jewish life and identity. Materialism, observed Finkel, quickly became an overriding passion for the city's Jewish immigrants, and this obsession prevented the emergence of strong communal ties. "All [Odessa Jews] came to live solely for themselves," wrote Finkel. In an effort to adapt their social positions to their new economic standing, some Jews, a decade before the Galician immigration, abandoned certain ritual practices and tried to make themselves appear less distinct and foreign to non-Jews. Their adaptation was at best superficial, Finkel observed, and the ambitious social climbers reverted to familiar social patterns whenever they found themselves among Jews. Nevertheless, some visible adaptation to the mores of the larger society did occur.[89]

Moreover, the degree to which Jews were valued in Odessa was reflected in their active involvement in local politics.* Permission for Russian Jews to participate in municipal affairs—a privilege first granted Belorussian Jews in 1783—was, after the second and third Polish partitions, extended to all but Lithuanian Jews. Participation, however, was almost immediately thwarted in most cities and soon restricted officially by imperial decree. Odessa emerged as one of a handful of towns and cities where it was permitted, and indeed encouraged. In Odessa's first elections, in 1796, Meir Elmanovich was one of ten candidates elected to mu-

*Jews elsewhere envied Odessa Jewry's involvement in politics. When in 1845, for instance, the Jewish community in nearby Kishinev petitioned the New Russian governor-general, Vorontsov, for permission to participate in municipal elections, they cited Odessa as a precedent. See Iulii I. Gessen [J. Hessen], *Evrei v Rossii* (St. Petersburg, 1906), pp. 261–62.

nicipal posts, from a list of twenty-one. He was chosen to serve as one of the two arbitrators of the *slovesnye sudy*, courts for the settlement of small civil suits, especially those concerning commerce. Three years later Tevel Lazarovich was elected a *glasnyi*, a councilman representing Odessa's second merchant guild. Jews continued to play a prominent role in political affairs, even after Jewish participation in municipal elections was drastically limited by St. Petersburg in 1835.[90]

This participation was linked to the esteem with which Jews, associated as they were with commercial activity, were held by New Russia authorities. In the absence of an indigenous middle class that Jewish business might threaten, regional officials treated Jews with consideration, sympathy, and tolerance. So warm was the relationship between Odessa's conqueror, DeRibas, and the Jewish community that a rumor, based probably on DeRibas's part-Spanish ancestry, circulated among Jews that he was in fact a Marrano. Richelieu's dealings with local Jews were no less friendly, and he was remembered for evenhandedness to all residents of the city, including Jews. A memoir published in the *Odesskii vestnik* many years after Richelieu's death recalled an incident in which a Jewish glazier complained that a prominent non-Jewish contractor, who was a close friend of Richelieu's, had commissioned him to work on a project and then refused to pay for the services. Richelieu arranged for both men to meet in his office, confronted his friend with the Jew's charges, and demanded compensation for the work.[91]

These good relations between Jews and local officials (continuing through the 1860's)—in contrast to relations with municipal and regional authorities elsewhere in the Pale—raise several intriguing questions: To what extent were these officials chosen because of their cosmopolitan breadth, tolerance toward foreigners, and positive view of commercial enterprise? To what extent did the commercial character of the city and its preoccupation with international rather than purely insular concerns help free the authorities and townspeople of traditional bigotries?

Though answers to these questions depend on as yet inaccessible archival material, one can offer some tentative suggestions. For instance, perhaps one reason for the city's tolerant attitudes toward Jews is that in Odessa, unlike elsewhere in Russia, Jewish policy was not framed with the implicit goal of minimizing Jewish economic competition and alleged exploitation. Indeed, the authors of the official history of the city, written on the occasion of Odessa's centennial, observed that life here was distinctly more liberal than in other Russian cities, noting that "a Russian could feel as if he were in Western Europe without ever leaving his native land. . . . Life here was easy; morals and manners [were] considerably freer than elsewhere in Russia; and in society one felt a certain cultural equality."[92] The authors suggested that the St. Petersburg authorities may have consciously treated Odessa differently in order not to interfere with its highly lucrative commercial activities. The implications of this policy for the government's treatment of the city's Jews are clear; indeed, the deterioration of relations between Jews and local officials in the last quarter of the nineteenth century may have resulted in part from the contraction of the grain market.[93]

Jewish residence patterns reflected the city's tolerance and also testified to the wealth of relatively large numbers of Odessa's Jews. In contrast to the often heatedly disputed attempts by Jews to settle in other Russian, Ukrainian, and Polish cities, in housing frequently located in outlying areas or in specially designated buildings, Jewish residence in Odessa was never restricted, although four of the five Jewish property owners in 1794 were allocated adjacent lots in the area which came to be known as Vorontsov hill.[94] Arriving in the city before neighborhoods were consolidated and patterns of residency set, Jews spread eventually throughout Odessa, the wealthier generally settling in the center of the city and the poorer concentrating in Moldavanka and eventually also Peresyp'.

In sum, whereas immigration to other frontier communities frequently engendered religious and ritual laxity, little potential existed in these settings for a cultural challenge of any sort, since in most cases the absence of Jewish cultural institutions reflected the general rawness of the city. In Odessa, however, traditional Jewish life was weak, and the attractions of the non-Jewish world were powerful. Jewish youth in Odessa were less likely to imbibe a well-integrated body of traditional teachings and were, at the same time, exposed to the newest cultural institutions and trends. The extent to which Jews participated formally in the larger cultural sphere before the 1820's—attending non-Jewish schools or making use of local cultural institutions such as the opera and libraries—cannot be determined on the basis of the available sources, but such activity was probably unlikely. The assumption, however, that the enlightened Galicians who came to Odessa in large numbers in the second decade of the nineteenth century encountered a cultural desert, which they subsequently transformed, is an exaggeration. Odessa, for reasons unrelated to the appearance of the Galicians, was fertile soil for Haskalah ideals and institutions. The receptivity of the local Jewish community to these innovations must be traced to factors predating the 1820's—to the city's remoteness, its heady materialism, and its rapid rise as a Russian cultural center.

Indeed, the factors that encouraged the community's receptivity to modernity remained relevant throughout the nineteenth century; whereas elsewhere Haskalah frequently came to be seen (even by disappointed maskilim themselves) as an irrelevant, impractical Western import prompting quixotic dreams and affecting the lives of only a few, reforms here grew out of widespread social concerns and needs. At first rather unimportant as a center of Jewish intellectual activity (since it lacked the well-established traditional educational institutions that provided the linguistic and substantive skills required by Jewish scholars, modern and traditional alike), Odessa rapidly became the center of the most successful progressive Jewish institutions in the Pale. These institutions—most importantly the city's modern Jewish schools and synagogues—were started by Galicians who settled in Odessa within two decades of the city's establishment. Chapter 2 explores how the Galicians' commitment to maskilic institutions, the local administration's favorable view of their efforts, and the relative receptiveness of the city's Jews all contributed to the success of Odessa's innovative Jewish institutional life.

TWO

Institutional Reform, Haskalah, and Cultural Change, 1826-1860

The Galician Immigration

Brody, "the rising star east of Lemberg," was seen by Russian maskilim as Galicia's cultural center and the home of its most sophisticated Jewish intellectuals. Here the Austrian government's campaign to transform Jewry through the promotion of primary and secondary schools seemed to yield the most visible rewards. Jews had lived in Brody since its founding at the end of the sixteenth century; its leaders were prominent in the Council of the Four Lands; and Brody's distinguished rabbis had attracted many students. Yet in some respects Brody's Jewish community was new and burgeoning, since only in the last quarter of the eighteenth century did Jews supplant Armenians as masters of Brody's commerce. By the first quarter of the nineteenth century, Jewish merchants were settling there in large numbers (1,134 were registered in 1820 alone); by 1826 Jews made up 89 percent of the city's population.[1]

Under Austrian rule, which began in 1772, Brody obtained the status of a free city, where in-transit merchandise was subject to no tax or duty. The Austrians thereby hoped to encourage Russian merchants to import German and Austrian finished products in exchange for raw materials from Russia. Later, during the Napoleonic blockade, Brody became a critical link in the transportation of goods and products from Leipzig and Breslau to Russia. Its contact with Odessa increased after the Napoleonic wars, when local merchants began to transport large quantities of goods to the Near East, in particular to Persia. An 1803 ukase permitted imported goods to be stored free in Odessa for an extended period. Recognizing the city's commercial potential, about three hundred Jewish merchants from Brody transferred their main offices here; later many of them made the move permanent.[2]

The Galicians fit well into intensely competitive Odessa. According to Joachim Tarnopol, they

> spare no effort in honorably earning their livings and in providing for their families' needs. Some of them are enlightened and have obtained comfortable positions in society by virtue of their abilities and *savoir faire*. The Galicians are generally employed as bankers, merchants, or brokers. They congregate in the commercial exchanges. . . . Their connections with St. Petersburg, Brody, and Berdichev, their extensive relations with some financial notables of Europe, as well as their care in punctually fulfilling their obligations, have placed them in a position to undertake all [of Odessa's] banking operations.[3]

By the 1830's Odessa's Galician Jews had come to dominate the functions of middleman, factor, and agent in the grain trade of this *pshenichnyi gorod* (wheat city), although export continued to be monopolized by Greeks and Italians. The middlemen spent much of the year in the countryside gathering information for exporters, maintaining contact with producers, negotiating agreements for the sale of harvests, and supervising the transportation of the produce. So greatly did exporters depend on the information collected by such middlemen that an Odessa resident who hoped to establish a Russian-language newspaper complained in 1821 that he could not interest more than seven kuptsy in the project; the rest felt that they obtained all the news they needed from their Jewish emissaries.[4]

Jews made fortunes, large and small, in this period. Indeed, Brody's Jewish merchants earned 2 million rubles from trade with Odessa in the first decade of the nineteenth century, 300,000 rubles in 1808 alone. (A character in Yekutiel Berman's 1877 Hebrew novel *Ha-Shododim ba-tsohora'im* [Plunderers in the Afternoon] comes to Odessa penniless in the first quarter of the nineteenth century; after working as a middleman for five years, he manages to amass a fortune of 15,000 rubles, whereupon he opens a retail store specializing in foreign delicacies.) By 1842 Jews owned 228 businesses in Odessa, including 67 factories and workshops, 26 crockery stores, and many fine-goods and tobacco stores. Between 1837 and 1844 the number of Jewish kuptsy rose from 169 to 221, while the number of Christian kuptsy dropped from 586 to 468. Jews constituted, by the 1850's, the fastest-growing commercial group in the city; of the 5,466 individuals engaged in trade in Odessa in 1851, 2,907 (53.2 percent) were Jewish. Several local guilds, including those of the furriers and glaziers, were dominated by Jews. Of the city's 17,000 Jews in 1855, 477 (2,908, including family members) now belonged to one of the merchant guilds.[5]

By the early 1830's, at the very latest, the Galicians, who had emerged as the wealthiest sector of the community, captured control of the local Kehillah and the curatorship of the institutions under its jurisdiction. Their efforts were supported by Governor General Vorontsov, who was impressed by their sophistication and wealth.[6] Odessa's Kehillah, like similar institutions in nearly all Jewish communities in the Pale, levied taxes and appointed judicial and religious functionaries. Before the Galicians appeared, it had been run in a particularly arbitrary and oligarchical fashion, in keeping, perhaps, with the city's frontier character (the municipal government before Richelieu's arrival was also controlled by an unresponsive, even corrupt, clique).[7] Indeed there was, as Pen found when he inspected the Kehillah archives, no record kept of the body's deliberations for nearly thirty-five years after its first meeting in 1795. When the Galicians assumed authority in the late 1820's, they standardized the Kehillah's structure and functions, recording and saving minutes of its meetings and holding elections at regular intervals. The Odessa Kehillah continued to act as a semiautonomous body even after the Russian government officially disbanded all Kehillot in 1844, although its decisions were then subject to ratification by municipal and regional government officials.[8]

In 1826, once the Galicians formed a sizable portion of the Jewish community, substantial enough to gain some prominence in communal affairs, they opened a modern Jewish elementary school. Its genesis and development, as reflected in the one fairly extensive body of material available on the cultural life of the community from the 1820's to the 1850's, reveal much about the relationship between social factors and the process of cultural change in the Pale.

The Modern Jewish School

Despite repeated efforts by maskilim, plans to establish Jewish elementary schools in the Pale designed along "modern" lines and offering instruction in secular as well as Jewish subjects were almost invariably obstructed until the 1840's. In this obstruction the Jewish masses, the Kehillot (all controlled by traditional Jews in the first half of the nineteenth century, save in Odessa), and the local Russian authorities all played a part.[9] When Hirsch Baer Hurwitz petitioned in 1822 to establish in Uman a modern Jewish school "based on the system of [Moses] Mendelssohn," for example, authorities objected because they were then holding in prison a Jew named Mendelssohn, and they felt that any system based on his teaching would be subversive.[10] Because such responses were commonplace, the 1804 ukase that permitted modern Jewish schools to be established and Jews to enter any school they wished, including the universities, in any faculty they chose (with medicine, surgery, physics, and mathematics listed explicitly), remained essentially a dead letter until much later in the century.[11]

Jewish enrollment in non-Jewish schools in the Pale was almost nonexistent before the 1840's and the campaign of Count S. S. Uvarov, who served as minister of education from 1833 to 1849. In 1833, 12 Jews were enrolled in gymnasiums in the eight western provinces of the Pale, out of a total of 2,105 students in attendance. In 1835, out of a total of 2,000 students in Russian universities, 11 were Jews. Even those few found their positions untenable. Simon Lev Wolf, for example, who completed a course in jurisprudence at the University of Dorpat in 1810, was denied his diploma unless he converted. When he appealed the decision to officials in St. Petersburg, they upheld the university's resolution on the grounds that jurisprudence was not among the areas specifically mentioned in the ukase of 1804.[12] Even with the removal of restrictions, secondary and higher schools remained inaccessible to most Jewish students because they lacked basic skills and because their cultural isolation had not prepared them for advanced instruction. With the exception of the Jews of New Russia and a small number living outside the Pale of Settlement and Poland, the Empire's Jews lived in formerly Polish areas that were still culturally dominated by Poles, and Jewish applicants found Russian schools doubly foreign. Furthermore, two-thirds of the schools in the Pale and Poland in the 1840's, according to the historian of Russian Jewish education S. Pozner, were Catholic, and the stress on Christianity increased in the first quarter of the century in state schools as well, a reflection of the mystical predilections of Tsar Alexander I.[13] Jews' fears that non-Jewish schools would be used to convert students seemed thereby substantiated. Lastly, perhaps the most important reason for the small number of Jewish students was the fundamental indifference of the Russian government until Count Uvarov's radical reversal of policy in the 1840's. The education of Jews (and, for the most part, of non-Jews as well, at least on a primary level) was of little interest to Russian officials.

In Odessa, however, authorities consistently supported modern Jewish education, and Jewish traditionalists were unable to oppose the reforms successfully. On October 2, 1826, representatives of the Galician Jews requested the permission of the acting governor-general, Fedor Petrovich Pahlen, to establish a Jewish school where secular as well as Jewish subjects might be taught. The request was signed by 4 prominent members of the Galician community and cosigned by 66 others, all members of one or another of the three merchant guilds. The petition, written in German, asked that funds for the school be obtained from the *korobka* tax (imposed mainly on kosher meat), as stipulated in the ukase of 1804. The petition requested that the following subjects be taught at the school: Hebrew, the Talmud ("according to the varying abilities of the boys"), calligraphy, arithmetic, German, and Russian. It stated that the signers were executing the will of the *obshchestvo*—an ambiguous term literally meaning "community," but implying, in this context, the support of a sizable segment of the city's Jews. Had the Galicians controlled the Kehillah at this stage, they probably would have stated so explicitly in the petition.[14]

The local government responded favorably. Only three days

after receiving the petition, Pahlen sent it to the minister of education, A. S. Shishkov, in St. Petersburg with his personal recommendation for its approval. Pahlen suggested, in addition, that the Jewish community be permitted to choose its own director and inspector for the school, with both subject to the confirmation of the governor-general. The Kehillah, he reported, would commit itself to spending 5,000 rubles annually for the maintenance of the school from funds collected by the korobka tax.[15] Without waiting for approval from St. Petersburg, Pahlen authorized the establishment of a commission to manage the school, composed of himself, Solomon Gurovich (an officially designated "learned Jew" attached to Pahlen's administration), Dr. Rosenblum, and Ber Bernshtein, the latter two among the signers of the petition. By the time the petition was approved by Shishkov on December 31, 1826, the school was already functioning.[16]

Pahlen's evident sympathy for the Jewish educational project, though uncharacteristic of Russian authorities, was not unusual in Odessa. S.O. Pototskii, curator of the Kharkov Educational District (which then included Odessa), warned the director of the newly established Odessa gymnasium in 1805 that Jewish enrollment should not be discouraged. Perhaps with this in mind, the curator appointed the German-born Jew Leon Elkan to teach history, geography, statistics, commerce, and German at the gymnasium. Elkan briefly served as its director in 1812, and he remained at the school for at least two decades.[17] Eager to attract more Jews to the school, Pototskii indicated in a memorandum that Elkan had agreed to establish a private school to prepare Jews for admission to the gymnasium.[18] There is no evidence, however, that such a school was started.

In 1826, 63 students enrolled in the Odessa school, and by 1827 the number had risen to 250.[19] Most of the school's teachers were, predictably, immigrants from Galicia. Students in the first year of the six-year program studied Genesis and Exodus with the Galician Zalman Balis. Samuel Kandel, a graduate of Joseph Perl's well-known modern Jewish school in Tarnopol (where Bezalel Stern, the director of the Odessa school from 1829 to 1852, had himself studied and taught), instructed students in German, Russian, and arithmetic. For the second, third, and fourth levels, Zalman Zinas, also from Tarnopol, taught Deuteronomy and the

Prophets. Eliezer Israel Kanigsharf offered instruction in Russian, and Max Hurwitz, a member of a distinguished Brody family, taught German, mathematics, biology, and handwriting. For the highest level, Bezalel Stern taught geography and history, and the archaeologist and historian Simha Pinsker (father of Leon Pinsker, author of the Zionist tract *Autoemanzipation*) taught the Latter Prophets, the Hagiographa, Hebrew grammar, and bookkeeping. Yitzhak Hurwitz offered a course in German and one in advanced bookkeeping; J. L. Finkel instructed the senior students in Russian, and Max Hurwitz taught French. The study of the Talmud was dropped from the curriculum in 1829 and replaced by readings from the works of Isaac Baer Levinsohn, Isaac Reggio, and Herz Homberg.[20]

Traditional Jews in Odessa resisted secular education with as much vehemence as their counterparts elsewhere, but less effectively. They responded to the proposal of the Galicians almost immediately, in a letter to Pahlen dated October 26, 1826. Signed by hundreds of local Jews, the letter invoked Odessa's community rabbi, Reuven mi-Zhitomir, as well as Moshe Tsvi, the *tsadik* (Hasidic leader) of the nearby townlet of Savran. (The opposition of the community rabbi is another indication that the Kehillah did not support the initiative.)[21] They criticized the request on two grounds: first, that among the supporters of the school were individuals who had no children themselves, and who were known for their callous attitude toward traditional practices; second, that anyone who wished to educate his children in foreign languages could already do so and did not need a new school. Moreover, they objected, many of the people who requested the establishment of the school already had tutors for their children. Pahlen sent them a sharply worded response, restating his emphatic support for the new institution.

The sources reveal that the leader of the opposition to the school was Moshe Tsvi, known as *Ha-rav mi-Savran*.[22] A member of an eminent family of Hasidim based in the townlet of Savran (about 120 miles northwest of Odessa), he was a charismatic leader with many followers and several eminent students.[23] Moshe Tsvi and the Hasidim of Odessa were blamed by maskilim for mounting the opposition to the school, though there does not seem to have been a large Hasidic community in Odessa at the time. A popular local figure, called affectionately *Hasid'l hayat* (the little Hasidic tailor, or simply the pious tailor), maintained a small prayer house, which may have functioned as a center for local Hasidism in the first decades of the nineteenth century.[24]

According to the poet Ilya Werbel, who began to teach at the Odessa Jewish community school several years after its establishment, and who was notably unfriendly to the critics, the opposition of the Hasidic rebbe of Savran went beyond the mere signing of the letter.

> And the cry of the people was great. The sound of strife and contention was heard in the home of the *Rebbe mi-Savran*, for it was to him the desperate hasidim, moneybags in their hands, came so that he might shelter them in their time of trouble. . . . And the rebbe's body shook vigorously in prayer. [He] clapped the palms of his hands, and did this for a long time, until he no longer had the strength to shout. After this, once his oppressed spirit was restrained, he spoke to his hasidim, comforting them with the following words: "You witnessed what level I reached in my prayers, in order to curse Satan. I struggled with him to the best of my abilities. Do not fear, for the wicked counsel will not prevail. This is what God showed me: A great fire and a valley of hell will blaze around the periphery of Odessa for seven *parsa'ot*, and beneath the feet of the wicked it will burn all day, and like Korach and his flock they will be lost."[25]

Though the maskilim clearly survived, so did the rebbe's imagery, and the popular saying that "hell burns seven miles around Odessa" may have originated with this incident.[26] Traditionalist opposition to the school continued despite lack of success: one Mordecai Feldman was arrested for conducting himself with disrespect in the presence of the Odessa gradonachal'nik during a heated discussion about the school; rocks were thrown at teachers and students of the school in its early days; and traditionalist opposition of a more civil form thwarted the efforts of the school's administration in 1831 to receive approval for an additional 15,000 rubles from korobka taxes to construct a school building.[27]

No further evidence exists, however, of effective opposition to the institution by traditional Jews. Indeed, the theme of traditionalist "oppression" of maskilim rarely appears in contemporary sources on Odessa. The absence should not be attributed to the reluctance of maskilim to write about oppression at the hands of traditionalists; the memoirs of their counterparts elsewhere in the Pale, Binyamin Mandelstamm, Abraham Baer Gottlober, and Moses Leib Lilienblum, abound in tales of traditionalist oppression and sordid political manipulation.[28] Traditionalist opposition in Odessa was indeed muted, even neutralized, a fact that, as we shall see, profoundly affected the course of local Jewish cultural history.

The differences between Odessa's cultural development and that of other Jewish communities in the Pale may be highlighted by comparing Odessa's modern school with the government-sponsored elementary schools for Jews, which were established in the 1840's. The contrast is particularly revealing in that the curriculum of the government school system, down to the smallest details, was modeled closely on that of the Odessa school. For instance, according to a report of the White Russia Educational District, dated July 29, 1848, vacations for the government schools were to be determined according to the precedents set by the Odessa school and the rabbinical seminaries.[29] Clearly, the Odessa school was the more successful, but why?

The origin of the government-sponsored schools was different, of course, from that of the Odessa school. The former were created by Uvarov, who assumed, correctly as it turned out, that Jewish students might more easily be drawn into Russian schools if these were established within an at least minimally Jewish framework. Instruction in the schools was in Yiddish (though officially in German), and about half the teachers were Jewish. These teachers, suggests Yehuda Slutsky, often behaved like "cossacks of enlightenment," antagonizing their already wary constituency with their impetuous attacks on Jewish ritual and communal life.[30] Non-Jews, often converts, held the directorships. The system was supported by a special tax on Sabbath and festival candles (which was bitterly resented by most Jews); a goal of the school (stated more or less clearly by government officials, and accepted, if halfheartedly, by their Jewish allies) was to weaken the hold of the Talmud on Jewish minds, since officials viewed the Talmud as the major obstacle to Jewish integration.[31]

The most frequent criticism leveled against the government-sponsored school system was that it attracted few students. By nearly all accounts, it was only in the 1860's that more than a negligible number of Jews enrolled. By 1873, when the system closed, barely 4,800 students had attended the schools, which numbered between 62 and 103, according to varying accounts. Even this low attendance figure is probably exaggerated, since school officials did not remove the names of students who had dropped out of the school.[32] In contrast, the Odessa school was praised, from its earliest establishment, for the large numbers of students enrolled; all sketches and articles treating the school never fail to note this fact. During its 26-year history—it was merged into the government school system in 1852—at least 2,500 students attended the school. When Uvarov's Jewish emissary, Max Lilienthal, visited the school in 1842, between 400 and 500 students were enrolled.[33]

Another difference was in the socioeconomic background of the students attending the respective institutions. The indigent, orphans, and sons of widows are reported to have made up a substantial part of the student body at the government-sponsored schools. Generally, the wealthier and more influential parents avoided sending their children to these reputedly unwholesome institutions, though the students in the rabbinical seminaries apparently were more heterogeneous in this respect than was the case in the network's other schools.[34]

The Odessa school drew from a broad spectrum of economic and religious-cultural backgrounds. The majority of its original 63 students, according to J. L. Finkel, were children of the kuptsy who had championed its establishment. Later, as the school grew, less wealthy Jews—and not primarily marginal, poor, and particularly vulnerable ones—were drawn to the school. The sources on the school consistently underline this point, though precise numbers and information on the backgrounds of individual students are not available.[35] Indeed, Ilya Werbel declared, probably with some exaggeration, that as soon as the school was created, students idling aimlessly over their Talmudic tomes in Odessa's arid *batei midrashim* (traditional study halls) abandoned this wasteful activity to enter the new school, drawn, in his words, "out of the darkness and into the light." Most of the city's Jewish children, to be sure, continued to receive a thoroughly traditional education until the 1870's, though an increasingly large number were introduced to secular study.[36]

Perhaps the most important difference between the institutions was the disparity in the level and quality of instruction. Professor Mykhlinskii, the inspector of the government-sponsored school in the city of Lubavich, in the Mogilev guberniia, reported, on the basis of an inspection conducted between 1852 and 1853, that the level of learning was deplorable. Only one of the 23 students demonstrated what Mykhlinskii felt was a substantial knowledge of either Russian or German, though translations into German of the Bible and the medieval philosopher Maimonides were a central part of the school curriculum.[37]

Mykhlinskii suggested that these inadequacies, as well as the high attrition rate, were largely caused by the unfamiliarity of the material. The languages drilled in school were rarely, if ever, heard outside its walls: "The students never hear from their parents at home the sounds of Russian; they do not understand a word of their teachers' explanation and study the subject in an entirely mechanical way. Thus, they tire of this useless work and give up school."[38]

Aside from the Odessa Jewish school's own conventional, self-laudatory assessments, at least two outside reports seriously examined the quality of instruction. The first was written by Max Lilienthal, who inspected the school during his tour of the Pale in 1842 to encourage support for Uvarov's educational project. The second report was prepared by a member of the local intelligentsia, M. Markevich, a non-Jew who visited the Jewish school as well as the newer school for Karaite children. (The Karaites, a Jewish sect of medieval origin, by modern times were completely separate from other Jews.) At the Karaite school the students' knowledge of Russian particularly impressed Markevich: "Children of eight to nine years recite by heart fables and parables; older students, entire odes by Lermontov, the works of Zhukovskii [and] Pushkin. . . . And amazingly, all of this is done with genuine Russian pronunciation and entirely correct diction, without any tinge of the provincial dialect characteristic of Odessa residents—although now and then, two or three times, one hears an incorrect word stress." He noted that the 48 students at the school also excelled in handwriting and geography.[39]

Students tested at the Jewish school, however, did not measure up to these standards. Markevich was especially disappointed by how poorly they spoke and understood Russian; he complained that "since at home they all speak German mixed with Hebrew, students cannot master clear pronunciation of Russian on the basis of a few lessons." Markevich acknowledged, nevertheless, that the Jewish school had a significant impact on the local community as well as on communities in the rest of the Pale. Many of its graduates were now teachers themselves in modern Jewish schools, he wrote, and Jews throughout Russia looked toward the Odessa school as a model, despite its shortcomings.[40]

Max Lilienthal's impressions of the Jewish school seven years earlier had been favorable, even enthusiastic. Lilienthal was by no means an inevitably friendly observer, and he was contemptuous of most Russian maskilim. When, for instance, as many as two hundred of them wrote to him asking for employment in the projected government school system, Lilienthal stated flatly that in all Russia only the Jewish educator Leon Salkind of Vilna was competent to teach. Russian maskilim, so Lilienthal wrote in a letter to the Ministry of Education, were in fact "dirty, bearded Jews who are barely touched by the rays of enlightenment." Russian Jewry, he observed, was ethically and morally inferior when compared with the Jews of the West. Lilienthal had additional reasons to feel ill-disposed to the Odessa school, since he and Bezalel Stern, the school's director, disliked one another intensely. Their relationship was so fraught with tension that Stern was persuaded to leave for an archaeological study-tour in the Crimea during Lilienthal's visit to Odessa. The high level of instruction at the Odessa school nonetheless impressed Lilienthal. He spent three days there, testing students in Russian, German, French, geography, history, arithmetic, bookkeeping, rhetoric, and literary history. Lilienthal was especially impressed by the skill of the teachers, who were able to make their subjects clear and accessible. The teachers responded carefully to all questions and encouraged thoughtful, rather than mechanical and spiritless, study. The school, he felt, should serve as a model for the government-sponsored system.[41]

Lilienthal's impressions of the school are a better gauge of its achievements than are those of Markevich because of the latter's inordinate emphasis on mastery of Russian. The students' poor knowledge of Russian in the Jewish school, noted by several observers, resulted from the school's emphasis on German, as well as the wide use of French and Italian.[42] Lilienthal, who did not know Russian, based his favorable assessment of the students' mastery of that language on the testimony of others and on their excellence in other subjects. Markevich's observations, moreover, were probably based on the ethnographic principle believed by most philosemitic non-Jewish intellectuals of the period, that Karaites were superior to Jews. These two groups were often compared to one another, particularly in Odessa, and Jews invariably were found morally and culturally inferior, since the Karaites were considered free of the evils of talmudic prejudices and economic greed.[43]

How are we to explain the differences between the Odessa school and Jewish schools elsewhere in the Pale? One factor that must be considered when comparing these institutions is the wealth of Odessa's Jewish community, which freed it from the economic restraints that often plagued other Kehillot, obstructing the establishment of modern schools and institutions and keeping them inadequate.

The Odessa school did in fact experience financial difficulty during the first decade of its existence, until its budget was stabilized and a school building constructed. The school functioned on a budget of 9,000 rubles, allocated by the government in 1826; these funds had to be supplemented by large private donations. The teachers' salaries were low, and the school lost several staff members as a result.

By 1835, however, the school was financially secure, with municipal funds covering the bulk of its expenses. According to the official history of Odessa, published in 1895, the institution's annual budget was now 21,846 rubles, and salaries had risen considerably.[44] Bezalel Stern now reportedly earned 4,000 rubles a year; senior teachers such as Simha Pinsker earned 2,400 rubles.[45] This was generous even when compared with the salaries at the prestigious Richelieu Lyceum—3,000 rubles to the director, 2,000 rubles to senior professors.[46] The average salary of teachers at the government-sponsored schools was 225 rubles.[47] Although the actual salaries at the Odessa school may have been somewhat lower than reported, they were surely substantial. They serve as the earliest example of a persistent motif in the cultural history of Odessa Jewry: the impact of the community's wealth on its ability to translate enlightenment ideals into reality. The communal functionaries of Odessa were granted generous financial sustenance and were envied throughout the Pale for their salaries and comfortable circumstances.[48]

The school's most persuasive attraction, more important than financial stability, was that it helped prepare students to meet future economic challenges. Participation in the city's commercial arena demanded a higher level of linguistic competence and technical skill than was necessary in most other settings in the Pale. Some knowledge of either French or Italian, the standard languages of local commercial life, was essential, as was a familiarity with mathematics and bookkeeping. The maskil Abraham Baer Gottlober recalled in his memoirs the frustration he felt when, upon his arrival in Odessa in 1831 at the age of 21, he began to consider how to pursue his livelihood and recognized that a commercial career was all but closed to him:

> If I was hired by a commercial house, would I know what to do? Would I know how to execute mathematical problems or to record items in ledgers? The youth who worked in the commercial houses in Odessa spoke the languages of the many different nations living in the city. And which languages could I understand? I knew only how to read German and could not either use the language for commercial purposes or even write it. And Russian was almost entirely foreign to me; of other languages, I had no knowledge at all.[49]

Thus a secular education fulfilled a distinct economic function. "Odessa had a wondrous effect on its Jews," Skal'kovskii noted wryly. "Here they quickly and eagerly pursued an education, recognizing in it material profit and esteem."[50] The Odessa school was profoundly conscious of its role in preparing graduates to find employment in commercial establishments. Upon his arrival in 1829, its director Bezalel Stern reorganized the school, placing special emphasis on commercial subjects and adding the study of French and bookkeeping to the curriculum. At least three hundred of its graduates became bankers, accountants, negotiators, merchants, speculators, agents, middlemen, and clerks. Graduates went into the professions as well, and a writer for *Razsvet* stated that among the former students were 200 teachers and 150 doctors. These numbers seem inflated, yet even the more sober calculations of J. L. Finkel are impressive: by 1843, 15 doctors or medical students and 10 pharmacists or pharmacology students had graduated.[51]

In this respect Odessa anticipated by decades the social, economic, and cultural changes that would alter Russian Jewish education in the last quarter of the nineteenth century. The building of railroads, the improvement of water transport, the expansion of the sugar and oil industries and of banking would open up previously unheard of economic possibilities for Jewish participation and investment,[52] and a recognition of the utility of a secular education would draw Russian Jews in increasing numbers into non-Jewish schools. For the masses of Jews, Haskalah would thereby be significantly transformed from an abstraction into a widely pursued practical necessity. "Jewish parents," wrote A. Kotik, "did not look upon the gymnasium as a way to educate their children, but entirely as a means by which to ensure them a good livelihood."[53]

The relative success of Odessa's Jewish school foreshadowed the triumph of a wide variety of progressive Jewish institutions in the city and anticipated developments that would later affect the course of Russian Jewish cultural life in general. In Odessa, since the city's earliest years, such institutions answered clearly discernible social needs. The international trade conducted here encouraged Jewish enlightenment for reasons that were concrete, so that in Odessa, in contrast to elsewhere in the Pale, Haskalah was not primarily the product of abstract ideals. The ineffectiveness of traditionalist opposition permitted Odessa maskilim to experiment with greater freedom and ease; local government officials maintained close and congenial relations with maskilim, acknowledging them as the natural leaders of Odessa Jewry; and the community's wealth (as well as its considerable social aspirations) helped to crystallize Haskalah into institutional reality. The school was not only the first such institution in the Pale but also a vivid and telling illustration of the potential for Jewish acculturation. The establishment in Odessa of two synagogues designed along modern lines demonstrated that by the 1850's Haskalah ideals had expanded beyond the confines of maskilic circles and had touched the lives of many other Jews in the city as well.

Synagogue Reform and Community Leadership

Synagogue reform was high among the priorities of Eastern European maskilim. The dignity of synagogue services was viewed as a barometer of the moral character of a community. Reform in the synagogue, maskilim hoped, would produce changes in Jewish behavior in the marketplace and in the home, since corruption of the true nature of prayer (exemplified by the sale of synagogal privileges such as *aliyot* and *mitzvot*, and by talking during services) was thought to indicate the corruption of everyday Jewish life. The progressive synagogue would serve not only as a temple of moral education but also as a school for language instruction, since it was considered incumbent upon a community to obtain the services of a preacher qualified to present his sermons in what maskilim called a living tongue, thus helping to broaden the flock's linguistic and intellectual horizons.[54]

Russian maskilim were, of course, mirroring the efforts in synagogue reform of their German predecessors; the emergence of the German Jewish enlightenment and the synagogal reforms that followed in its wake radically changed the nature of discourse about synagogue worship and decorum. In themselves the largely aesthetic alterations in Eastern Europe hardly seem radical. Indeed, they are easily justifiable under Jewish law, whereas the boisterous prayer services in traditional synagogues did not have their roots in religious law.

Eastern European traditionalists were acutely aware of developments in Germany and regarded the aesthetic reforms proposed by maskilim as merely the tip of the iceberg; proponents of change in the Pale, though generally critical of the more extreme manifestations of reform in Germany, felt some intellectual kinship with more moderate proponents of ritual reform, who were in the majority. Odessa's modern Brody Synagogue, for example, was described by a local maskil in the *Odesskii vestnik* as "maintained according to the model of German temples."[55] Both sides grew acutely aware of the symbolic importance of even the smallest alteration, viewing changes that seem in retrospect no more than minor matters of interior decoration as laden with extraordinary significance.

The Brody Synagogue, the first in Russia designed along what maskilim considered to be modern lines, was established in Odessa in 1841. Within a few years of its establishment it became the model for Jewish prayer in the city, and the older Beit Knesset Ha-Gadol was transformed in its image. This reversal contrasts vividly with the process of institutional change in other cities in the Pale, even in such a prominent center of Haskalah as Vilna, where the modern synagogue Taharat Ha-Kodesh (Purification of the Sacred) was established not long after the Brody Synagogue. The Vilna synagogue, however, remained fairly isolated, inspiring little in the way of imitation.

The Beit Knesset Ha-Gadol, eventually also known as the Glavnaia, was established in Odessa in 1795 or 1796.[56] By the 1820's, perhaps even earlier, the synagogue was located on one of the city's major arteries, Rishelevskaia ulitsa. The building in which it was housed was described in 1830 by a visiting English physician as "of plain construction and in bad repair—a circumstance attributable to the love of money which characterizes this sect."[57] As was common for traditional synagogues, the Beit Knesset Ha-Gadol employed no preacher on a regular basis, the official Odessa rabbi speaking on the Sabbath preceding Passover and on one or two other occasions during the year.[58]

The maskil Abraham Baer Gottlober attended services at the synagogue as a young man. He described the proceedings as dismal: "The building was filled with a mass of people from end to end, pushing one another, climbing onto the tables; the noise was great." Gottlober observed that the one bright spot in the service was the remarkable cantor Bezalel Shulsinger.[59] Shulsinger, according to Pincus Minkowski the "true genius" of classical Jewish cantorial music, was born in or around 1779 in Uman; he was the composer of many influential melodies, and among his students were Joshia Abras and Ya'akov Bakhman, who both succeeded him at the Odessa synagogue.[60]

Despite Shulsinger's presence, the Galician elite found the Beit Knesset Ha-Gadol an unpleasant setting in which to pray. Perhaps they also wished their dominance of communal affairs to be mirrored in the leadership of a synagogue. Their control, of the Kehillah, Jewish school, Talmud Torah, hospital, and other institutions was completely solidified by this time, and the Beit Knesset

Ha-Gadol was one of the few major institutions in the city that had withstood their considerable ambitions.[61]

In contrast to the community-sponsored Beit Knesset Ha-Gadol, the new synagogue that they established, which was often called simply the Brody, was self-supporting. As part of an effort to raise sufficient funding—as well as to control the behavior of worshipers—permanent seating was sold. The Galicians rented a small and narrow room. Here the sale of aliyot and mitzvot was abolished, and *piyyutim* (medieval lyrical compositions) were dropped from the service. The celebrated Nissan Blumenthal was hired as cantor. He would serve the synagogue from 1841 to 1903; his compositions, designed for a four-voice choir, would be based heavily on German classical patterns.[62]

Traditionalist opposition to the new institution was predictable. We know of it only through the responses of the synagogue's defenders. The local journalist and notary Osip Rabinovich, for example, in an 1847 article in *Odesskii vestnik* written upon the occasion of the Brody's move to larger quarters, dismissed the condemnations of traditionalists by saying they were "blinded by the ancient past, and they proclaimed that this House of God was a pagan temple and that its parishioners were apostates."[63] Defending the reforms, Rabinovich vigorously attacked the boisterous, unwholesome atmosphere of traditional synagogues. There, he wrote, ignorant, itinerant cantors shamelessly stood before the altar singing prayers to dance tunes picked up in taverns or inns. So ignorant were these cantors that they could not even understand the meaning of the Hebrew prayers they chanted. Amidst frenzied shouts and applause, hundreds of voices bellowed "Shah! Shah! Shah!" demanding quiet, all the while banging their prayer books on their chairs to emphasize the need for silence during prayer.[64]

Rabinovich found it less easy to dismiss the criticism of Jews he acknowledged as enlightened and who had not as a body abandoned the Beit Knesset Ha-Gadol. Indeed, the most prominent local maskil, Bezalel Stern, disagreed with the founders of the Brody Synagogue, who, he felt, were abdicating their responsibility to serve as guides and leaders for the untutored "Polish-Russian" Jews. Stern also scored the practice of selling permanent seating as exclusionary and elitist.[65] Rabinovich treated the sale of permanent seating in a tone emphatically different from the sardonic, taunting way he answered the traditionalists. At the Brody Synagogue, he argued, it was due solely to considerations of money and space. Even though the synagogue now had larger quarters, it still could not accommodate the hundreds of Jews wishing to worship in a proper and dignified manner.[66] But charges of elitism would continue to be leveled against the Brody Synagogue for decades to come.[67]

Although Isaac Baer Levinsohn, the most widely respected Russian maskilic leader, had been calling for synagogue reform since the 1820's, he responded ambivalently to the new synagogue. He learned about it in a letter from one of its leading members, Berish Trachtenberg, who had written Levinsohn hoping to win his approval for the Brody.[68] Trachtenberg had stated that in the new synagogue the only innovations that traditional Jews opposed were the prohibitions against speaking during the service, the installation of permanent seating—to protect the synagogue from being overcrowded—and aesthetically pleasing cantorial renditions accompanied by a choir. In his reply, Levinsohn praised these reforms as exemplary and discussed at some length the limits of acceptable synagogue reform, distinguishing between what was and what was not within the boundaries of rabbinically sanctioned change. Since the essential order of the service was maintained in the Brody Synagogue, changes there fell clearly within the boundaries of the permissible. Levinsohn nevertheless hesitated to give his approval to the synagogue. He was troubled by the fact that maskilim such as Bezalel Stern had not joined the Brody because they felt that the split was not justified. The reforms effected in the synagogue, he suggested, though theoretically permissible, were apparently unnecessary and precipitous, and he advised Odessa's maskilim to repair the divisions in their ranks.[69]

Since Levinsohn was not particularly familiar with Odessa affairs, his acute awareness of the bitter debates between maskilim and traditionalists elsewhere over the Uvarov campaign may have conditioned his advice that the Brody's leadership not weaken themselves by permitting divisions in their ranks.[70] Yet the enlightenment campaign initiated by the government in the 1840's did not lead to the consolidation of traditionalist forces in Odessa, as happened elsewhere. Quite to the contrary, it did not take long for the Beit Knesset Ha-Gadol to transform itself along the lines of the new institution. Stung by the Galicians' criticisms, the leaders of the older house of worship closed it within four years of the establishment of the Brody and raised money for the construction of a new synagogue building. Convinced now of the moral and aesthetic superiority of the Brody, in their plans for the new Beit Knesset Ha-Gadol they predictably allocated space for a choir.[71]

In erecting a new building, they wished to emulate the reforms initiated in the Brody Synagogue and to make Odessa's most visible Jewish institution reflect the increasingly prominent social and economic standing of the city's Jews. The article in the *Odesskii vestnik* on its dedication ceremony in 1850 alluded to the progress of the community: "The numerous class of Jews in Odessa did not until this time have a house of prayer corresponding to their wealth and level of enlightenment—which have greatly increased and expanded in recent years. . . . Synagogues and houses of prayer, now existing in various parts of the city, are distinguished neither by their comfort nor their elegance, and in most cases present an extremely poor appearance."[72]

Nissan Blumenthal participated in the dedication ceremony, leading a choir of 22 voices. Bezalel Stern delivered the major address in German before hundreds of listeners, including at least fifty non-Jewish officials. He opened the speech with a few general remarks about the history of the Jews, emphasizing the long ordeal between the Exile and the dawn of the modern period. He stressed inevitable Jewish progress to true citizenship and full participation in the lives of the countries in which they resided. Toward the conclusion of his remarks—delivered in the most graceful, learned German, according to the *Odesskii vestnik*—he spoke directly about the split between the Brody Synagogue and the Beit Knesset Ha-Gadol. Nearly ten years earlier, he said, a group of men of uncontested wisdom had decided to form a synagogue where they could pray by themselves. They remained separate to this day and small in number. Stern called upon them to rejoin the larger community in the new Beit Knesset Ha-Gadol and assured them that among the first goals of the reconstructed institution would be the hiring of a modern preacher.[73]

Negotiations between the leaders of the two synagogues were opened, continuing on and off for over ten years. On at least two or three occasions the Brody Synagogue was dissolved, and congregants rejoined the larger institution. The Brody Synagogue finally announced in 1863 that it, too, would build a new structure; 197 contributors gave 35,646 rubles to purchase a lot and erect a building on it.[74] The Brody Synagogue became a local landmark of Moorish architecture on Pushkinskaia ulitsa and the most prominent modern synagogue in the city. Here, by the turn of the century, services were accompanied by organ music.[75]

To appreciate how singular Odessa's situation was, it may be useful to consider the very different history of synagogue reform in Vilna, the major center of Russian Haskalah in this period. Founded in 1847, Vilna's Taharat Ha-Kodesh was the second modern synagogue in the Pale. The major published source on its early development is a long letter written by Binyamin Mandelstamm.[76] In this letter he promises to tell everything about the new institution, both its good and its bad points. His description opens with an apparent excursus. Instead of speaking directly about the establishment of the institution, Mandelstamm devotes several pages to the relations between the city's maskilim and traditionalists. In Vilna, he writes, maskilim grew like rare, endangered flowers, seemingly out of place in a hostile environment; their relationship with the larger community was a continuous tale of mutual recriminations and petty incidents, of denunciations and confrontations. The situation finally became intolerable, adds Mandelstamm, at the funeral of the eminent maskil Mordecai Aaron Guensburg. There the officiating traditionalist rabbi refused to eulogize Guensburg properly and mentioned his name only in passing in the rabbi's address, dwelling instead on the recent deaths of several traditionalists. Cooperation with the traditionalists, maskilim now decided, was impossible, and not long after Guensburg's funeral they established Taharat Ha-Kodesh.[77]

Strained relations between traditionalists and maskilim stunted reform in Vilna's modern synagogue, and its leaders' caution led to profound shortcomings. The poet Adam (or Avraham) Ha-Cohen Lebensohn, for instance, was chosen as its preacher. Lebensohn, according to Mandelstamm, could preach only in Hebrew and Yiddish; thus Vilna maskilim wasted an opportunity to instruct the community from the pulpit in foreign languages and to rid it of its disgraceful state of cultural and linguistic illiteracy.[78] Nor were substantial changes made in the structure of the services. A choir was not established because the leaders of the synagogue felt that this reform was "not in their power to accomplish." Aliyot and mitzvot were sold. The cantor picked up melodies from the theater, as was the practice in traditional synagogues. The very name of the institution, thought Mandelstamm, was better suited for a ritual bath than a synagogue.[79]

Petty as some of these criticisms are, the fundamental objection is cogent, being essentially that traditional society not only inhibited the behavior of those who functioned within it, but also distorted the character of the new institutions ostensibly established outside of it. Mandelstamm asks rhetorically:

> What expands the valor of a soldier's heart more than the trumpets of war? And what arouses and quickens a man to complete an action more than Satan standing on his right side condemning him and interfering with his work? And when the new generation heard what the fanatics thought of them, they gathered together as one to do battle against them. Some worked . . . in the disbursement of funds; others wrote petitions to judges; still others mediated with the officials whom they knew. [However,] they didn't cast their eyes and hearts upon the essential purpose of the affair [as they were] concerned only with the success of the endeavor.[80]

Since the synagogue was concerned primarily with survival, proper attention could not be paid to the structure of its services, the qualifications required for a proper preacher, or the implementation of enlightened reforms. The atmosphere in which the synagogue was established was so uncongenial and contentious that far-reaching reforms were viewed as impracticable.

Unlike their counterparts in Odessa, Vilna maskilim represented only a small portion of the community and were not in control of the local Kehillah; they were at best vying for equal status with traditionalists on certain occasions, such as the visit of the English philanthropist Moses Montefiore.[81] These intellectuals, who saw themselves as harbingers of a new era in Jewish history, felt a sense of powerlessness that pervaded their writings.[82] Indeed, they faced frustration in obtaining employment, establishing institutions, and achieving recognition from the Russian authorities.

This sense of powerlessness was somewhat ameliorated by the government-sponsored enlightenment campaign of the 1840's since maskilim now felt themselves allied with Russian officials.[83] The tenuous alliance, however, did not prevent officials from seeing where power truly rested in the Jewish community. Significantly, Count Pavel Dmitrievich Kiselev, chairman of the Committee for the Fundamental Transformation of the Jews, advised the authorities to ignore a proposal made by 23 Vilna Jews, who had suggested that the government prohibit the use of distinctive Jewish dress. These maskilim, he observed, act as if they speak in the name of the community at large, when, in fact, they represent only a tiny minority, shunned and despised by the majority of Jews.[84]

By contrast, the most distinctive indication of the central role maskilim played in Odessa was the prominence of Bezalel Stern in local Jewish affairs. His leadership, unparalleled in this period in any other large community in the Pale, anticipated the emergence later in the century of members of the free professions and the administrators of modern Jewish institutions as among the leaders of the Russian Jewish community. Stern's prominence is illustrated by his appointment to the Rabbinical Commission of St. Petersburg, on which he was the sole representative who was neither a rabbi nor a strictly traditional Jew. According to the *Odesskii vestnik*'s eulogy for Stern, in the Odessa Jewish community during his tenure as school director "nothing of major importance was done without his participation."[85]

His masterly knowledge of German, keen administrative abilities, and prodigious energy—his associates at the school were impressed by his long working hours, from eight in the morning to noon, and from two in the afternoon to seven in the evening—helped Stern rise to the top of Jewish communal affairs.[86] Ability alone, seldom the sole criterion for success in Imperial Russia in the first half of the nineteenth century, would not have propelled Stern to a comparable position in the communal life of Vilna. Though enlightened Jews were often imposed upon the community by Russian authorities as "learned Jews" or censors of Jewish books, Stern's standing as an enlightened communal leader with the confidence and esteem of broad segments of local Jewry was unparalleled. Long before Jews in other centers of the Pale would come to place their trust in Jewish leaders whose religious convictions or ritual practice they knew to be less than traditional, maskilim and acculturated Jews in Odessa were the standard-bearers of their community. Their institutions fulfilled clearly felt needs and therefore proved successful; enlightenment not only satisfied abstract moral or aesthetic criteria, but also prepared Jews for the singular conditions of the Odessa marketplace.

Moreover, a wish to partake in the city's cultural offerings seemed to follow naturally from the involvement of Jews in commerce, and many were eager to leave the narrow Jewish milieu for a larger setting. The progressive thrust of Jewish institutional life in Odessa also led some Jews to look toward the non-Jewish sphere to satisfy social and cultural, as well as economic, needs.

Since the city's earliest years, religious and ethnic differences tended to diminish in importance because of common commercial interests, though commercial competition also engendered a certain degree of enmity, as, for example, between Greeks and Jews.[87] Odessa's social elite, observed a French visitor in 1838, was strikingly heterogeneous, for "here side by side with a broker's wife [were] pure blood, mixed blood, all shades, all tones, all possible physiognomies." Nowhere outside the Italian commercial towns, he remarked, had he witnessed anything similar.[88] This was so in Odessa, suggested several observers, because religious differences—and spiritual matters in general—were not treated with seriousness. The first Orthodox archbishop of the Kherson province complained that church attendance in Odessa was abysmally low, and that at least one-third of Odessa's couples lived out of wedlock. An English missionary who visited the city in 1816 found Odessa's inhabitants completely indifferent to religion; as a merchant told him, "I have so much to do with the present world that I have no time to think of a future one."[89]

Jews were occasionally invited to the drawing rooms of the Odessa elite—a visiting kupets reported with dismay that local society's New Year's Eve party in 1800 included a Jewess among the guests—but such interaction was exceptional.[90] In Odessa, as elsewhere in Russia and outside of it, traditional patterns of social segregation proved resilient (except perhaps among the lower classes) despite accelerated Jewish acculturation. Nevertheless, although close friendships between Jews and non-Jews remained unusual on all levels of society, business partnerships and other less intimate relationships were common, and acculturation, or so it appeared to Jews, paid dividends in social as well as economic terms. Speaking French, German, and sometimes Russian, relatively unhampered by traditional Jewish institutions and constraints, Jews felt welcome (perhaps more than was warranted) in the liberal, ethnically heterogeneous society.*

A particularly vivid indication of the eagerness of Odessa Jewry—including even the fairly traditional element—to integrate non-Jewish cultural forms into their lives was the enthusiasm it displayed for opera, music, and theater. The opera, in particular, was the rave of Odessa society, and a monthly periodical devoted to it and to music in general appeared in the city six years before Odessa's first Russian-language newspaper. Local Jews, even those who had no knowledge of foreign languages, found the opera enjoyable, and for the mere price of a ticket (tickets were priced quite low) they could appreciate a sense of belonging to, and participating in, the larger cultural milieu. The Odessa Jew became, in the Italian phrase of a Russian visitor to the city in 1839, "fanatico per la musica."[91]

Jews flocked to the opera house and were said to nearly monop-

*Generally, Odessa's non-Jewish intellectuals had about the same attitude toward Jews as those in the two capitals had; and anti-Jewish sentiment among intellectuals in Odessa only began to soften somewhat once it had already softened in St. Petersburg and Moscow in the late 1850's. Before that, however, it was not uncommon for the city's intellectuals to be openly contemptuous of Jews. P. Morozov, for example, in "Odessa v 1830 g.," a sketch on contemporary Odessa life in the 1831 *Odesskii almanakh,* of which he was editor, complained that on Saturdays Odessa's boulevards swarmed with Jews, speaking their barbaric tongue. Odessa residents could nonetheless be comforted, added Morozov, because this happened only once a week—on all other days Jews were too occupied with their moneychanger stalls to walk the city streets in leisure. For an example of the anti-Jewish stance of another prominent local intellectual, see K. Smol'ianinov, *Istoriia Odessy* (Odessa, 1853), pp. 182–83. Despite escalating tensions between Greeks and Jews, it is likely that Odessa's non-Jewish intellectuals were considerably less well-inclined toward Jews than were local merchants, for whom economic considerations outweighed ideological determinants. On the attitude of the nineteenth-century Russian intelligentsia toward Jews, see Joshua Kunitz, *Russian Literature and the Jew: A Sociological Inquiry into the Nature and Origin of Literary Patterns* (New York, 1929).

olize its seats, usually those in the hall's least expensive sections, in the pit or high above the stage; by the 1860's many sat in the stalls. Even Jews with sidecurls attended. Russian observers in the 1840's complained that Jews ruined the performances by their unseemly fervor after every scene and for every singer.[92] This same enthusiasm for music was reflected in the interest that Odessa's Jews showed in giving their children music lessons. A Jewish music teacher who lived in the city in the 1840's did a brisk business, and several of his students demonstrated considerable talent.[93] The Odessa cantor Pincus Minkowski suggested that the reason why the city had been a leading center of cantorial music since as early as the 1820's—quickly gaining ascendancy over older centers like Vilna and Berdichev—was the pervasive influence of opera. Though the opera was responsible, in his opinion, for Odessa Jewry's attraction to what he called light and superficial "lemonade music," it also sensitized them to appreciate the best tenors.[94]

The manifestation of a widespread interest in, and even a gift for, music on the part of Odessa Jews in the first half of the nineteenth century is intriguing, particularly in view of the large number of famous Jewish violinists, such as Mischa Elman and David Oistrakh, to emerge from Odessa several decades later. No one has yet explained the proficiency of Russian Jews, and in particular Jews from Odessa, as violinists. But any future evaluation must take into account the extent to which both the enjoyment and the playing of music constituted for Odessa Jewry a link, however tenuous, with the larger society. In a setting in which music was highly appreciated and musical talent well rewarded, the enthusiasm and virtuosity of local Jews may be seen as reflecting the eager preoccupations of the parvenu.

In this period a conspicuous, though probably quite small, segment of the city's Jewish youth came to view European culture as their primary affiliation, eschewing the Jewish sphere (and even, according to local maskilim, Jewish institutions designed along modern lines) in favor of the non-Jewish cultural arena. This was said to be especially true of the Jewish students and graduates of the Richelieu Lyceum.[95] Indeed, according to an article published in the *Odesskii vestnik* in 1841 by Mark Rafalovich, who had graduated the year before, Odessa was the only place in Russia where

Jews were attempting to become entirely European. Abandoning the customs and mores ("nationalism," Rafalovich called these) that separated them from the larger society, Odessa Jewry was successfully emulating its non-Jewish neighbors.[96]

Rafalovich's own biography illustrates this trend. The son of Odessa's wealthiest Jewish kupets, Abram Rafalovich, he attended the Richelieu Lyceum and, after graduating, went abroad to study medicine. The highly accomplished young man was soon offered a professorship of forensic medicine at the Lyceum and returned to Odessa. Changing his name (although he almost certainly did not convert) to Artemii Alekseevich, he published in 1843 the essay *Meditsinskaia statistika Odessy za 1842 god*, a pioneering study on the occurrence of tuberculosis in Odessa. A recognized authority on disease and plagues, Rafalovich traveled extensively in the Middle East and published an account of his trips in 1851. He died the same year. Neither in his writings (Rafalovich published extensively in professional as well as popular journals) nor in his other activities did Rafalovich display any interest in Jewish matters whatsoever, with the sole exception of the *Odesskii vestnik* article quoted above.[97]

Rafalovich was not unique in this respect. In this period several intellectuals and prominent professionals emerged who seemed to lead lives quite independent of the Jewish community. Among them were Mark Finkel, a leading physician, staff member of the municipal hospital, and frequent contributor to the *Odesskii vestnik*; and the philosopher-writer Mark Wahltuch, who published in 1855 the first Italian translation of Pushkin's works.[98] The many poems, short stories, and feuilletons published by D. Fridman in the *Odesskii vestnik* in the 1850's were entirely free of all specifically Jewish content, his fantasy world a rural wonderland of rivers, swans, and distant hills. Although Fridman's work was unremarkable from a literary standpoint ("Poetry orchestrates the night / The sun is quiet and low / And now and again is just a hint / Of a lovely song in the breeze" opens one untitled poem published in the *Odesskii vestnik* in 1856), it contrasts dramatically with the work of his Jewish contemporaries elsewhere in the Pale in terms of both its subject matter and the author's facility with Russian.[99]

Nonetheless, it is not clear that Fridman and the other Jewish contributors to the *Vestnik* in the 1850's can unhesitatingly be classified as "russifiers," that is, as Jewish intellectuals who consciously promoted the use of Russian rather than German or Hebrew. During this period, the decision of any intellectual, Jewish or not, to write in Russian was influenced by the increasing emphasis on Russian rather than German or French in Russian literary circles as a whole. (Likewise, in the late 1850's and the 1860's such better-known Russian Jewish writers in Russian as Osip Rabinovich, Menasheh Morgulis, and Ilya Orshanskii reflected changes in the larger cultural world.) Whether or not young intellectuals such as Fridman or Rafalovich were as estranged from Jewish life as the communal leaders and the maskilim believed, the perception that they were led to communal action. When Max Lilienthal came to the city in 1842 to promote the new government school system, Kehillah leaders asked him to present a petition to Governor-General Vorontsov requesting the emancipation of Russian Jewry—the first of its kind to be submitted by a Russian Jewish community. The petition specifically linked the need for Jewish emancipation to the growing numbers of disaffected Jewish youth.

This phenomenon, the petition stated, made emancipation a particularly pressing necessity. The new school system would encourage still greater numbers of Jewish students to pursue a secular education, and many would find themselves frustrated because of their inability to pursue careers of their choice, limited as they would be by restrictions on Jewish mobility and other prohibitions. Unless civic emancipation were granted, well-educated Jews, who were capable of assuming positions of importance in Russian society and yet were thwarted by the present arrangements, might choose to abandon the Jewish community and convert.[100] (The willingness of Odessa Jewry's leaders to air these fears shows their confidence in local officials.) Vorontsov expressed his sympathy with the request in general terms, but it is unclear whether he supported it before the St. Petersburg authorities.[101]

Although they were concerned about "assimilated" youth, Odessa's Jewish leaders were considerably less preoccupied with the excesses of modern life than with encouraging and promoting modernity. Their optimism about Russian governmental policy reached its peak after the accession of Alexander II in 1855 and, particularly in the early 1860's, took center stage in Russian Jewish cultural life. The image of Odessa as a prototype for a modern Russian Jewish community was now formulated by local intellectuals; a wide range of institutions was created in the city, enhancing its reputation and distinction; and the tenor of its communal life was increasingly and self-consciously enlightened.

THREE

A Middle-Class Urban Paradigm: The Early 1860's

Before the mid-1850's, "enlightened" Jews thought of Odessa as merely an attractive commercial port with many Galician maskilim. Vilna, Berdichev, and perhaps Pinsk, not Odessa, were the centers of Haskalah in the Pale. Neither Max Lilienthal nor Isaac Baer Levinsohn, for instance, commenting in the 1840's on Jewish institutional reforms in Odessa, felt the city itself was especially suitable for experiments in modernization. Remote and lacking prominent leaders and scholars (with the exception of Bezalel Stern, Simha Pinsker, and one or two others), Odessa was generally seen as somewhat marginal in the intellectual universe of the Russian Haskalah.[1]

The city's image began to change only once highly visible Haskalah institutions—in particular the Hebrew, Yiddish, and Russian Jewish press—were established there in the 1860's, during the period of concerted "russification" that followed the first reforms of Alexander II. It then became widely felt that large segments of Odessa's Jewish community were quite receptive to modern trends. Even then, assessments of Odessa in maskilic circles were by no means uniformly favorable. Maskilim still faulted Odessa for the supposed vacuity of its intellectual life and the restless hedonism of its Jewish middle class. By the 1870's, the center of modern Jewish institutional life once again shifted away from Odessa, and many intellectuals assumed that the community would permanently revert to what was considered its previous state of cultural obsolescence. This belief persisted until the "epoch of Odessa," which, according to Jewish literary historians, began in the 1880's and continued until World War I. During this time many of the most prominent Jewish intellectuals in Eastern Europe moved to Odessa (along with tens of thousands of other settlers) for long, often highly creative, stays. But these intellectuals typically felt that they constituted a distinct colony on the fringes of the Jewish community and that the city was indifferent to scholarship and literature, being more concerned with the pursuit of frivolity than that of knowledge. Chapters 3 and 4 examine the relationship in the 1860's between these intellectuals, the community's openness to institutional innovation, and the continuing process of Jewish acculturation.

In the 1860's, according to the historian I. Sosis, Odessa indisputably came to be seen as the center of a modern Jewish intelligentsia that quite consciously modeled itself on the increasingly russified gentile intelligentsia of the period and turned its back on the linguistic cosmopolitanism of the past. Russian increasingly replaced German among these intellectuals, although the Odessa Jewish mercantile elite retained an attachment to German cultural patterns and to the German language. At the same time, Odessa came to be celebrated by russifiers as prefiguring the Jewish future; by increasing numbers of classical maskilim as a vibrant center of Hebrew and Yiddish publishing; and by Jewish philanthropists as a model of institutional vigor. The community's wealth and its good relations with local authorities reinforced these favorable perceptions.[2]

The commercial position of Odessa Jewry was strengthened by the Crimean War. Because of the disruption of trade and the blockage of Odessa's port, Odessa exports plummeted from 35,513,000 rubles in 1853 to 3,675,000 in 1855;[3] English importers turned to North American producers to supply their grain needs; and even when peace was concluded, the city was unable to recover all of its lost clients. Several of the city's Greek magnates, unable to absorb their immense losses, were forced to close their Odessa offices; Jewish merchants, on the other hand, accustomed to operating with a smaller margin of profit and better able to assess the market because of their close personal contact with the producers, managed to withstand the economic slump. Indeed, Jews rapidly began to supplant the Greeks in the export trade, and by 1875 over 60 percent of the city's commercial firms were in Jewish hands.[4] By contrast, in the 1851 annual commercial report in the *Odesskii vestnik*, not one Jew was listed among the six Odessa exporters who had reported at least one million rubles of trade.[5]

Jewish retailers also achieved remarkable success, and by the 1870's Jews owned most of the city's stores. Odessa's leading retailer, L. Rabinovich, who consistently managed to undersell his competitors, was responsible for slashing the price of tea in southern Russia in the 1860's from 2.5 to 1.25 kopecks per pound.[6] A French visitor to the city in this period claimed that Jews were at the bottom of a notorious white slavery market (with which some Jews were in fact associated) and that they sold Russian women to Turkish buyers for sums of up to 30 million francs.[7] The author of an 1863 study of Kherson province offered a fanciful explanation of the commercial aptitude of Odessa Jewry. Jewish parents, he wrote, lent their children small sums of money that they had to pay back with interest. Jews were thus initiated into the mysteries of commerce at an early age, so that when they entered the business world as adults they conducted themselves with natural confidence, ease, and success.[8]

Joachim Tarnopol's *Notices historiques et caractéristiques sur les israélites d'Odessa*, published in 1855, vividly attests to the standing of Odessa Jewry. Completed soon after Alexander II's rise to the throne, the book argues that a relaxation of the political and economic restrictions on Russia's Jews would permit the community as a whole to be as productive and receptive to cultural change as were the Jews of Odessa. Odessa was, in Tarnopol's view, a paradigm, and its history should be widely publicized so that all of Russian Jewry might emulate it. Jews here had achieved "a level of . . . public-spiritedness and cultivation that are in keeping with the imperial government's beneficent goals, and this bodes well for the future of the Russian Jewish community."[9]

Odessa Jewry did not cluster either in commerce or in a few typically Jewish crafts like tailoring, Tarnopol writes. Rather, Jews also worked as carpenters, locksmiths, and engravers, and even in the most strenuous trades, such as bricklaying and blacksmithing. The city's standing as a "commercial city par excellence" showed what Jewish enterprise and resolve could accomplish when unfettered by counterproductive restraints. In fact, Tarnopol continues, "Not only in Odessa, but in all the other ports and commercial cities of Russia as well, our coreligionists contribute significantly to the development of all branches of industry and speculation. Blessed with intelligence and a speculative spirit, they have spread out and settled in all places that favor lucrative commercial activity."[10] Now that Alexander II had indicated his readiness to permit all Russian Jews the privileges long enjoyed by those in Odessa, Tarnopol expected to see Jewish communities like Odessa throughout the empire.

Tarnopol's argument about the societal benefits of Jewry's unhampered participation in economic life was consistent with a long tradition of philosemitic polemics, including Pinto on Sephardic Jewry, Luzzatto on the Jews of Venice, and Dohm on those of Alsace. In fact, Russian maskilim had employed similar arguments for decades.[11] But never before in Russia had a particular Jewish community been singled out to substantiate such a claim. For all of Tarnopol's praise of Odessa, when his book was published local Jewish institutional life was at a particularly low ebb. The transformation in 1852 of the community's modern Jewish school into a government-sponsored one, followed by the resignation of its director, Bezalel Stern (and by his death soon afterward, in 1853), led to a decline in the school's standing and its enrollment. In 1855 the Jewish hospital had a mere 75 beds (only 15 more than in 1843), though the community had grown rapidly in the last decade. Religious instruction, even at the elementary levels, was so poor that when David Shlomo Slouschz, son of the chief Rabbi of Moldavanka, turned four, in 1856, his father sent him to study in Minsk. The rather ineffectual Yehiel Halperin was still the community's rabbi, despite efforts to attract someone more suitable (indeed, Lilienthal had been offered, and had tentatively accepted, the position soon before he decided to leave Russia for the United States).[12]

Within the next four years the community would begin to turn itself around decisively. A correspondent from Odessa for *Ha-Magid* reported in October 1859 that the Jewish hospital was finally being expanded; the local Talmud Torah had been revamped; a pension fund had been established for retired teachers of the Jewish community school; a plaque was being prepared to commemorate the thirtieth anniversary of the death of Ephraim Zittenfeld, the school's first director; and Dr. Shimon Aryeh Schwabacher was soon to arrive as the new official rabbi.[13] Indeed, by the late 1860's the hospital building would have 200 beds, the Beit Knesset Ha-Gadol would finally be finished, and the Brody Synagogue would, in turn, initiate an extensive building program. An orphanage would be attached to the Talmud Torah, and the following would also be established: a local yeshiva; a school of cabinetmaking, mechanics, and handicrafts; a branch of the St. Petersburg Society for the Promotion of Enlightenment Among Jews; and mutual aid societies for Jewish clerks and teachers. The city, moreover, would become a major center of Jewish publishing: newspapers in Hebrew, Yiddish, and Russian, as well as three publishers of Jewish books, would now be vying for an expanding market.[14] Looking back at this decade in 1870, an editor of the Odessa-based newspaper *Den'* observed: "If one can speak of a center of the Jewish intelligentsia where self-emancipation (*samoemantsipatsiia evreev*) is becoming a reality, this without doubt is Odessa. This populous and wealthy community not only commands a well-deserved position of authority as a center of commercial and brokerage activities, but serves as the 'nerve center' of all of Russian Jewry, exerting its influence throughout the land."[15]

The reforms initiated by Alexander II (the abolition of the cantonist system and the relaxation of residency laws for Jewish merchants, artisans, university graduates, students, and others), the appearance of editors and journalists in St. Petersburg with openly philosemitic views, and especially the emancipation of Russia's serfs—all seemed to suggest that Jewish emancipation would come soon. In this buoyant, confident period innovative Jewish cultural institutions emerged, as did a series of impressive periodicals and a generation of Jewish students confident of the value of their secular education. Previously, maskilim could merely hope, their dreams nourished by the progress of Jews further west, but now these dreams appeared vindicated by the direction of Jewish life under Alexander II. The quickened pace of commercial and industrial development affected non-Jewish attitudes toward financial speculation in general and toward Jewish commercial activity in particular. The liberalization of Russian public opinion in these years helped place the Jewish Question on the political agenda.[16] Jewish expectations seemed to crystallize into political reality, ideological commitments into social trends. Under the previous regime maskilim had been faced with a painful gap between expectation and reality: that gap now seemed to narrow dramatically, if briefly.

In Odessa the reform of the relatively inactive *shestiglasnaia duma* (composed of the mayor and six representatives from the merchant class) and the creation in 1863 of a general municipal duma—made up of representatives from the property-owning classes—injected a vigorous spirit into communal affairs. Problems such as street repair, lighting, and water supply were addressed seriously for the first time. Jews came to play a key role in the new government. In the wake of the municipal reforms, 37 of the 75 members elected to the local duma in 1863 were Jewish. From the 1860's to the 1880's, Yehuda Khari, the leader of Odessa's Kehillah, supervised the city's financial affairs. Such participation in civic affairs prompted Jewish leaders to turn their attention to communal institutions. Reforms, contemplated as well as realized, created a mood of limitless possibility.[17] The continued existence of Jewish begging in the streets, the dilapidated state of the community's hospital, and the large numbers of homeless Jewish orphans now seemed an affront to the Jewish community's leadership.[18]

The Jewish newspapers established in Odessa in this period offered these leaders and the Jewish intelligentsia a vehicle through which to influence the social and cultural life of the community and, perhaps, that of Russian Jewry as a whole. The community's acculturated segment now emerged as the self-avowed spokesmen for the city's middle-class Jews. The newspapers underscored Odessa's role as a model for Jewish communal development, so that Eastern European maskilim began to admit, if at times reluctantly, that its charms were not wholly illusionary. Young Jews were drawn here from elsewhere in the Pale, eager to participate in the cultural world of such publications as *Ha-Melits*, *Kol Mevasser*, *Razsvet*, *Sion'*, and *Den'*.

The Jewish Newspapers of Odessa

Alexander II's abolition, soon after his rise to the throne, of the notorious censorship bureau, the "Committee of April 2, 1848," was the first of several initiatives that the new monarch took to improve the quality and effectiveness of the Russian press. To be sure, Alexander II shared with Nicholas I a distrust of the free exchange of ideas—he once characterized intellectuals as "people with very dangerous tendencies and thoughts"[19]—but he hoped to use the press to shape public opinion in favor of his prospective reforms. Along with the easing of press restrictions, in line with Alexander's wish to encourage more extensive discussion of public affairs and support for his policies, many new periodicals were approved—60 new newspapers appeared between 1855 and 1867, nine times more than in the preceding decade.[20] The decision of May 1862 to permit the publication of advertisements gave periodicals added capital. In 1865 permission was granted for newspapers to be sold individually as well as by subscription (though they had, in fact, already been sold individually for several years). In 1866 the Russian Telegraphic Agency was opened, initially to gather foreign and commercial reports but eventually for domestic news as well. A wide variety of publications were now started. "Trade and economic journals were founded to defend the principle of free trade and propagate the businessman's point of view," writes David Balmuth. "Popular newspapers catering to literate city people, village teachers, and lower clergy began to appear." The government soon became aware, however, that the mental ferment caused by its promotion of the press was difficult to manipulate successfully.[21]

Since the Crimean War, Eastern European Jews had become increasingly interested in the larger world. In December 1856 Osip Rabinovich and Joachim Tarnopol asked the newly appointed curator of the Odessa Educational District, the physician and educator N. I. Pirogov (who was responsible for supervising censorship) for permission to establish a Jewish weekly newspaper in Russian called *Razsvet* (Dawn). Both Pirogov and Governor-General Stroganov approved their petition, but the censorship committee in Kiev, fearing the impact the newspaper could have on

Russian religious life, quashed it, suggesting that a journal published in either Hebrew or Yiddish would be acceptable. At the same time, several Jewish intellectuals in Odessa and elsewhere were in fact thinking of starting newspapers in either Russian or Hebrew. Soon after they first met in 1857, Alexander Tsederbaum told his future son-in-law, Dr. Aaron Goldenblum, of his plans for a Hebrew periodical. In 1858 the Vilna-based educator and writer Lev Levanda, unaware of the efforts to establish *Razsvet*, wrote to Osip Rabinovich to suggest that he start a Russian-language Jewish newspaper. That same year, the Tirasopol printer Moshe Beilinson, later a publisher of Jewish books in Odessa, circulated a letter to various communities in the Pale—sending copies to both Tsederbaum and Simha Pinsker—which underlined the need for a newspaper in Hebrew. In the letter to Tsederbaum, Beilinson noted that Odessa was particularly suitable for such a project since it was well served by telegraph and maintained close contact with the larger world through its busy port. It was the natural setting, he observed, for the gathering and dispensing of information and opinion.[22]

The newspapers established in the early 1860's—*Razsvet* and *Ha-Melits* in 1860; *Sion'*, which replaced *Razsvet*, in 1861; and *Kol Mevasser* in 1862—were stamped with the personalities of three men: Pirogov, Rabinovich, and Tsederbaum. I shall discuss Pirogov and Tsederbaum below and Rabinovich in the next chapter.

Pirogov, appointed curator of the Odessa Educational District in 1856, was precisely the sort of man acculturated Jewish intellectuals hoped would emerge from the Russian intelligentsia. Politically progressive but not radical, religiously tolerant but pious, he had become a philosemite shortly after his arrival in Odessa, when he had had his first sustained contact with Jews (thereby confirming these intellectuals in their belief that greater interaction between Jews and Gentiles would ultimately lead to increased tolerance—and even emancipation). His philosemitism, moreover, differed from that of other Russian intellectuals, as it was rooted less in what a liberated Jewry might achieve in the future than in a basic respect for Jews in the present. As Pirogov said in a speech before Jewish dignitaries in Berdichev, in 1861: "You have expressed your appreciation of me because of my own evident appreciation of the Jewish people. But I don't deserve praise. My feelings merely reflect my innermost nature, and one cannot act contrary to one's nature."[23]

Soon after his arrival in Odessa, Pirogov wrote the Ministry of Education to argue against the widespread assumption that Jews instinctively distrust secular education. Pirogov observed that Jews have always viewed their children's education as a sacred duty. He recommended that the district's Christian inspectors of the government-sponsored Jewish schools be replaced by Jews, and that Jewish teachers be treated on a par with Christian ones. On his own initiative, Pirogov appointed the Jew U. S. Rosensweig an inspector of the government-sponsored schools. He also appointed Dr. Aaron Goldenblum director of Odessa's Talmud Torah, despite the objections of Jewish traditionalists, who reminded Pirogov, and eventually also his superiors, that Aaron Goldenblum—who they believed held heretical views—was a foreign citizen and thus disqualified for the position. Their objections were overruled.[24]

Pirogov emerged as the guiding force behind the renovated *Odesskii vestnik*—now published independently of the governor-general's office—which affected the subsequent development of Odessa's Jewish press. In late 1857 Pirogov obtained permission to transfer responsibility for the periodical from the government to the Richelieu Lyceum. Two young professors, A. Bogdanskii and A. I. Georgievskii, were chosen as its editors, but Pirogov himself was its leading spokesman. Serving also as chairman of the district's censorship board, Pirogov combined the roles of unofficial editor and official supervisor. Under his conscientious, highly partisan supervision, the *Odesskii vestnik* became for a short while the empire's most impressive provincial newspaper. In contrast to the provincial press as a whole, the *Vestnik* sought out and defined new issues rather than echo the influential newspapers of the two capitals.[25]

Within the first ten weeks, the renovated *Odesskii vestnik*, much to Governor-General Stroganov's annoyance, tackled some highly controversial issues: the treatment of Podolian peasants, the productivity of free agricultural workers in New Russia as compared with that of enserfed workers elsewhere, and the extreme poverty of Odessa's working class. Later numbers included an exposé by name of corrupt officials in the city of Ekaterinoslav and a comprehensive analysis of the Russian judicial system.[26] The paper also adopted a new tone and approach in its treatment of the Jewish Question, publishing at least ten articles on this topic in 1858.

Since the 1840's and perhaps even earlier, the *Odesskii vestnik* had published articles on Jewish subjects as well as contributions by Jews on a wide range of topics. Under the aegis of the firmly philosemitic A. Troinitskii, editor from 1834 to 1857, the paper generally had represented Jews in a positive light.[27] Indeed, even after Pirogov's circle had lost control of the *Vestnik* late in 1858, it continued to serve through the 1860's as a forum for Jewish opinion. When Yehuda Slutsky charges that after Pirogov's exit the *Vestnik* became an "absolutely antisemitic newspaper," he is uncritically echoing what Jewish intellectuals said following the *Vestnik*'s insensitive treatment of the 1859 pogrom. In fact, the paper soon corrected this lapse and resumed its evenhanded, indeed sympathetic, coverage of Jewish events.[28]

What distinguished the 1858 *Odesskii vestnik* from both the earlier and the later versions of the newspaper was its preoccupation with social issues. In 1857, as John Klier observes, practically the only article on some topic other than commerce, finance, or literature was a feature on the cultivation of orchids.[29] Similarly, the articles on Jewish topics published before 1858—as well as most published afterward—were celebratory announcements of the establishment of progressive Jewish institutions.[30]

In 1858 the *Vestnik* published articles that treated the Jewish Question in a comprehensive, analytic fashion. For instance, the newspaper evaluated the need to ease the restrictions on the empire's Jews, and it called attention to the dilemma of the russified Jewish intelligentsia, who were caught between an insulated Jewish world and an indifferent, often hostile non-Jewish one. "Every article treating a Jewish theme caused a sensation among the Jewish intelligentsia. It was read and reread, its each word weighed, every thought commented upon," wrote Sosis of the *Vestnik*'s impact.[31]

Without doubt, the most sensational of such articles was Pirogov's own essay, "Odesskii Talmud-Tora," published on March 6, 1858.[32] To signal that despite its title, his essay was not another celebration of a renovated Jewish institution, Pirogov opens with the remark that "many readers of the *Odesskii vestnik* will say, 'Why should we care about a Jewish school when even our own Christian ones are of little interest to us?'" This general indifference toward education was precisely the problem Pirogov wished to explore; an evaluation of the local Talmud Torah was his point of departure. Describing the unwholesome atmosphere of the Talmud Torah before its reform, Pirogov presents a picture of poverty, irascible *melamdim* (teachers), and schoolrooms filled with the "broken noises" of Yiddish. Pirogov states that because of the contributions of several Jewish benefactors as well as his own intercession, the school was reformed. A recent inspection of the school—now financially secure and headed by Pirogov's appointee, Goldenblum—revealed that the rooms were clean and the children properly clothed and fed by female volunteers. Students in the higher classes spoke German rather than Yiddish; and some forty students even performed choral singing in "the purest German."

Pirogov did not want merely to show that because of their achievements Jews were worthy of non-Jewish approval. Rather he wished to set up the Jewish school as an example to be emulated by non-Jews, who, in this case, were less advanced than their Jewish brothers. According to Pirogov, a Jew, unlike a Russian, "considers it his holiest duty to teach his son reading and writing when he has barely begun to lisp, for the Jew is deeply convinced that reading and writing are the only means of learning the Law. . . . In the Jew's mind reading, writing, and knowledge of the Law flow together into one indissoluble whole. He has no disputes, no polemics, about the necessity of teaching his people to read and write." Thus, in decided contrast to other Russian liberals, Pirogov stressed that Jews were meritorious because of—not despite—the values of traditional Judaism.[33] "Feed and clothe the pupils of the parish school," he instructs his non-Jewish readers. "Send your wives to help distribute food and examine its quality. Choose a teacher carefully and support him. Then you will have your Goldenblum, and your parish school will equal the Talmud Torah."[34] This article provoked a barrage of responses in the press (much of it, not surprisingly, critical) and unfavorable comments by the St. Petersburg censors.[35]

Pirogov was transferred to the Kiev Educational District in July 1858, and by the end of the year the *Odesskii vestnik* returned to the jurisdiction of the governor-general. While under Pirogov's control, the paper had profoundly affected the city's educated Jews, especially those who wrote for it or were closely associated with it in some other way—men such as Osip Rabinovich, Peter Liakub, Arnold Dumashevskii, Joachim Tarnopol, Solomon Chudnovskii, and Faddei Berezkin. Its commitment, integrity, and rigorous analytical approach gave them a model of what journalism might be; and this same loosely structured group—centered around the energetic Rabinovich—later dominated *Razsvet*.[36] The impact of the *Odesskii vestnik*, as well as that of the Russian-Jewish press of the 1860's and early 1870's, was limited, however, since most of the city's Jews could read little if any Russian. Both *Razsvet* and *Sion'* eventually closed mainly for this reason.

In Odessa Alexander Tsederbaum published *Kol Mevasser*, Russia's only Yiddish-language newspaper of the period (as well as its best-regarded Hebrew paper, *Ha-Melits*). His was a practical approach, and his periodicals attempted to cater to the needs of both the masses and the intelligentsia. Sensationalist articles, "human interest" stories, and pieces on popular mechanics ran side by side in his periodicals with contributions by Haskalah luminaries.[37] Tsederbaum's *Ha-Melits* and *Kol Mevasser* encouraged secular study in order to prepare Jews for eventual civic emancipation. This policy did not differ from that of either of the Hebrew periodicals *Ha-Magid* (established in 1857 in Lyck, a Prussian border town) or *Ha-Karmel* (started in Vilna in 1860). Where his newspapers were different, however, was in their readiness to explore topics outside the rather narrow purview of the Haskalah.

Tsederbaum, according to his co-worker Reuven Brainin, looked upon writing as just another job, as no loftier an activity than, say, shoemaking or tailoring. (He had in fact worked as a tailor when he first arrived in Odessa in 1824 and later opened a retail store for women's clothing.) As even his harshest critics had to admit, he had an uncanny ability to sense what might interest his readership. For instance, he published Abraham Uri Kovner's abusive criticism of the work of the leading contemporary Jewish writers—among them several regular contributors to *Ha-Melits*—because he shrewdly sensed that the controversy it generated would attract attention and new subscribers.[38] But his decision to establish the Yiddish paper *Kol Mevasser* is surely the clearest expression of his audacity and openness to experimentation.

Although most Jews in Eastern Europe understood only Yiddish, maskilim generally viewed writing in Yiddish to promote enlightenment as a contradiction in terms. The Jewish masses, they believed, lacked not only information about the outside world but, more important, a broad cultural and aesthetic appreciation.[39] How could this appreciation be heightened by using what Moses Mendelssohn called "a corrupt and deformed language of stammerers"?[40] Furthermore, maskilim thought Hebrew intrinsically beautiful, perhaps the most beautiful language of all. As Dan Miron has perceptively observed, "If to them Yiddish was all earth and dross, Hebrew was 'heaven and divine.' A maskil who chose to write in Yiddish had not only to reconcile himself to the deformities of Caliban, but also to prefer them to the perfections of Ariel." Using Yiddish for public writing made an author feel "constrained, isolated, even degraded."[41]

Tsederbaum himself shared such an attitude toward Yiddish (indeed, through the mid-1860's, he tended to favor russification). However, he was able to transcend his own biases in order to exploit the one potentially large Jewish readership in Eastern Europe. (Even *Ha-Melits*, the most commercially successful Hebrew periodical in Russia, had fewer than 2,000 subscribers in 1865.)[42] This venture seemed especially attractive since in the southern provinces—which lacked formidable yeshivot and a firmly rooted classical Haskalah—familiarity with Hebrew was far less widespread than it was, say, in Lithuania. Tsederbaum initially directed the newspaper primarily at a female readership, already accustomed to reading religious works in Yiddish, but he soon began to court male readers as well. Less tendentious than *Ha-Melits*, *Kol Mevasser* focused on providing useful, basic information. It also offered a forum for new talent: in its pages appeared the first Yiddish writings of Abraham Baer Gottlober, Abraham Goldfaden, Shalom Yakov Abramovitsch, Judah Leib Gordon, Isaac Joel Linetsky, and Moses Leib Lilienblum.

Some maskilim viewed the Yiddish literary activity centered around *Kol Mevasser* as just another example of Odessa's unrestrained backwoods character. Here, Lilienblum complained, Hebrew scholarship was irrelevant; the children of the wealthy, the russified intelligentsia, and the masses were all indifferent to it.[43] But precisely because of this indifference, as Tsederbaum shrewdly realized, Odessa was the ideal place for an open celebration of the Yiddish tongue. As Ephraim Deinard wrote, Tsederbaum

> saw that every book written in Yiddish would be consumed like the first fruits because of the ignorance of Hebrew. In the city where Jews live better and more pleasantly than in any other in Russia, Tsederbaum was to make a nest for this jargon. He could not have done this in any of the cities of Lithuania, where people looked with contempt on every book written in Yiddish. . . . But Tsederbaum lived among the tailors and understood their thinking.[44]

Tsederbaum, whom Reuven Brainin called the first journalist in the modern Hebrew language, personified Jewish journalism's many shortcomings as well as its strengths—its often laughable pomposity, naive rationalism, and narcissism, together with its intense preoccupation with communal betterment and its unwillingness to be a dispassionate observer, especially in times of crisis.[45] The press helped groom a new generation of Jewish leaders, who would later dominate the Odessa branch of the Society for the Promotion of Enlightenment Among Jews, and who would emerge, after the pogroms of 1881, as the community's most effective spokesmen.

Other Enlightenment Institutions

Odessa also now attracted intellectuals by its increasing importance as a center of Jewish book publishing. Before 1862 the government restricted such publishing to certain printers in Vilna and Zhitomir, and until 1863 even *Ha-Melits* was edited in Odessa and sent weekly to Zhitomir for publication.[46] Within the next few years, however, three Odessa publishers (M. E. Beilinson, L. Nitzsche, and A. Tsederbaum) were issuing books regularly. By the end of the decade more than one hundred titles in Hebrew and Yiddish had been published. Most of these were in Hebrew, though after the publication of Linetsky's hugely popular *Dos poylishe yingl* (1869), the number of Yiddish titles increased (six between 1868 and 1870 alone). Publishers were particularly interested in Haskalah books (which presses outside Odessa had been reluctant to print): five works by Isaac Baer Levinsohn were published between 1863 and 1865; one of these, *Divrei tsadikim*, was released in a second edition in 1868; Perets Smolenskin's first novel, *Ha-Gemul*, appeared in 1867. Young authors peddling their books just off the press became a common sight in the city, as Abramovitsch described in his *Fishke der krumer*, itself published here in 1869.[47]

The community's role as a cultural center was enhanced by the establishment in 1867 of an Odessa branch of the St. Petersburg Society for the Promotion of Enlightenment Among Jews (ORPME), the only branch outside the capital. This organization—supported largely by contributions from Baron Joseph Yosel Guenzburg, the society's chairman, and Leon Rosenthal, its treasurer—took at face value the official assertion that Jewish civic emancipation was contingent upon cultural and educational reform. The organization's goals were threefold: to promote the spread of culture among Russian Jews, to lend support to Jewish literature, and to grant aid to Jewish students. Control of the Odessa branch quickly passed from the city's magnates (the financier Abram Brodskii, in particular) to its russified intelligentsia.[48] Emmanuel Soloveichik, M. G. Morgulis, and Leon Pinsker were especially active. Differences between the group in Odessa and the one in the capital soon became clear when the intellectuals in Odessa insisted that the branch's charter specify russification as the sole means for enlightenment. Indeed, the proposed platform of the Odessa branch included encouraging the use of Russian as the language of synagogue prayer. Such a radical goal—no less than an explicit challenge to traditional Jewish religious forms—made the St. Petersburg leadership uneasy, and they insisted on the removal of the objectionable clause.[49]

Prodigiousness and purposefulness, thought Binyamin Mandelstamm, who visited Odessa in 1862, were the city's most pronounced characteristics. Its very establishment on the steppe seemed, to Mandelstamm, to bolster one's belief in man's limitless capabilities for creation, renewal, and change. The atmosphere here of overwhelming purposefulness helped to moderate intergroup tensions and to give the city's inhabitants a heightened appreciation for toleration and freedom. Common commercial interests reduced to insignificance differences between maskilim and hasidim, young and old, progressives and conservatives.

Mandelstamm wrote, "I have been here about seven days, renewing myself, and as I go here and there in the city I marvel at the wonders and abilities of man. To build a city as large as this one, filled with buildings, many in number and enormous in size, within only eighty years."[50]

The city's geography seemed to reinforce the sense of purposefulness and freedom. The suburbs extended to the very steppe, underlining the drive and determination responsible for Odessa's prosperity. The Black Sea, nearly always the first large body of water that arriving Jews had ever seen, bounded the city on the south (observers swore that from the center of the city one could see the steppe on one side and the Black Sea on the other); its closeness, some maskilim felt, reminded one of the world's immensity and diversity and of the human spirit's limitless potential.[51] "If I was attracted to Odessa by its large, new enlightened Jewish community," recalled Moses Leib Lilienblum, who had come from a substantially smaller city, Vilkomir, and settled in Odessa in 1869, "I also sought to flee the filthy deprivation and the stench of generations in my town for the sea and sun of the South. And so I came. I knew very few persons. . . . I thought and wrote whatever I pleased and in the evenings would go out and walk along the boulevards and breathe fresh air smelling of greenery."[52]

The city's center was now dominated by Deribasovskaia ulitsa ("the world's king of streets," according to Vladimir Jabotinsky).[53] It ran from the fashionable Aleksandrovskii Park, which overlooked the harbor, to the southern edge of a poorer quarter, Moldavanka. Deribasovskaia ulitsa was intersected by the city's most impressive boulevards, including Pushkinskaia ulitsa, where the prestigious Brody Synagogue was located. The wide neighboring streets, many lined with acacias, dazzled Jewish visitors from smaller cities and hamlets. "A precious sight, a very lovely sight," exclaims a provincial Jewish visitor to Odessa in Reuven Braudes's novel *Shete ha-ketsavot*. "Here," the narrator tells us, "he saw beauty face to face; here splendor and order met; loveliness and regimen joined together. . . . It brought his soul down to the very depths and made his heart throb. The beauty of the city was beyond estimation."[54] The typical building in the city center was made of limestone and had two or three stories, a courtyard, and a roof of iron and painted wood. The middle class, according to an impressed English visitor in 1854, lived in homes almost identical to those of the English bourgeoisie.[55]

To be sure, the city's Jewish intellectuals were deeply concerned by the increasingly crowded Jewish slums in the outskirts of Odessa and by the inability of local philanthropic organizations to meet the needs of the poor. However, even the harshest critics of this state of affairs continued to assert that if only resources were properly allocated, such problems could be solved. Their criticisms (unlike those leveled against the communal authorities later in the decade) did not disturb the pervasive optimism of the city's Jewish intelligentsia and communal leadership.[56]

Perhaps one reason for this confidence was that leading traditionalists as well as nontraditionalists had come to accept enlightened views or, at least, terminology. Whether out of newfound conviction or out of pragmatism, even longtime critics of modern currents seemed to recognize that public discussion had to be framed in enlightened terms. A striking example of the effect of such terminology on the community is the conflict over Dr. Shimon Aryeh Schwabacher, appointed Odessa's official rabbi in 1860. Both the supporters and the opponents of the rabbi defended their positions by using arguments taken from the arsenal of the Haskalah, thus acknowledging that arguments from other sources were now obsolete.

The Conflict over Rabbi Schwabacher

From before his election as Odessa's official rabbi in 1860 until his death at the age of 69 in 1888, Shimon Aryeh Schwabacher aroused intense controversy in the city. Some viewed him as a preacher of unequaled eloquence and a communal worker of boundless energy and devotion; others saw him as an unoriginal thinker and a political anachronism. Schwabacher's preaching, linguistic preferences, politics, and attitude toward reform prompted opposition from a large and influential segment of the community. Some of his critics objected to the appointment of a German-born rabbi who knew no Russian and who seemed unwilling to learn it. Others found him too sympathetic to religious reform and insufficiently learned. His defenders, most importantly the city's Galician elite, saw him as a symbol of the German-Jewish enlightenment; since they still looked to Germany for intellectual sustenance, they welcomed the presence of a German rabbi in Odessa. Not surprisingly, Schwabacher's reelection every three years was challenged by formidable candidates with significant support.

Controversy surrounded the office of official rabbi throughout the second half of the nineteenth century in nearly every community in the Pale. Indeed, the Jewish press frequently declared, with some exaggeration, that this was the most pressing issue facing Russian Jewry.[57] In Odessa, however, the nature of the debate over Schwabacher differed in both tone and substance from debates elsewhere. For here, both the opposition to Schwabacher and the loyalists claimed to speak in the name of progress. They differed (submitted the opposition, somewhat defensively at times) merely in their conclusions, not in fundamental assumptions. Thus, while elsewhere the debates over official rabbis in the 1860's were waged between self-avowed traditionalists and the "enlightened," in Odessa all claimed to be enlightened, even when this obscured real differences.

Little in the origins of the institution of the official rabbi suggested it would arouse such vigorous debate. A decree of 1812 required that rabbis know either Russian, German, or Polish; another, of 1826, determined that the rabbi was responsible for keeping records of Jewish births and deaths.[58] As a result, a sort of double rabbinate came into being. The true, or "community," rabbi, trained to settle ritual questions, was usually ignorant of foreign languages and unwilling to learn them; the "official" rabbi was appointed, in addition to the "real" rabbi, in order to satisfy the government's requirement. In Odessa, as in some other communities, one rabbi typically fulfilled both functions: Reuven mi-Zhitomir served from the early 1820's until 1835, when he was succeeded by his son-in-law Yehiel Tsvi Halperin, who filled the dual position until 1860, when he in turn was replaced by Schwabacher.[59]

Even Nicholas I's ukase in 1835, which comprehensively defined the official rabbis' responsibilities and promised ample compensation (in the way of bureaucratic honors) for sustained, loyal work, did little to improve their standing in the Jewish community. There still remained, in the words of the Zionist publicist Shmarya Levin (later official rabbi of Grodno and then Ekaterinoslav), "One rabbi for the Jews, another—for the government, the distinction in the folk-mind was almost as sharp as between kosher and nonkosher meats. The State Rabbi became a ludicrous figure, a buffoon, almost, put up to distract the attention of the non-Jew."[60]

After the rabbinical seminaries in Vilna and Zhitomir were established, the government decreed, in 1850, that within twenty years all official rabbis would have to be graduates of these academies. In 1857 the government announced that this decree would be effective immediately.[61] Many communities evaded the ruling. Others in the 1860's became embroiled in an institutional conflict that would continue until 1917. Many Jews regarded the rabbinical election as part of the larger question of what constituted the qualifications of communal leadership. The elections, declared Osip Rabinovich rather grandly in 1860, "began to capture the central place in the Jewish world."[62]

Schwabacher was born in 1819 in Oberndorf, Württemberg, into a rabbinic family. It is not clear where he received his rabbinic training, though he was later tested and declared competent by a series of distinguished German rabbis. He graduated with a doctorate in philosophy from the University of Tübingen in 1842, at the age of 23.[63]

He served as a rabbi in Prague, Hamburg, and elsewhere. In 1857–58, he moved to Lemberg. During his visit to Odessa in the winter of 1859, the community invited him to preach on the seasonal festival of Hanukkah. The communal leaders were so impressed that upon his return to Lemberg, Schwabacher received a letter offering him the position of official rabbi of the community, which he accepted, pending confirmation of his appointment by the Russian authorities.[64]

In the first issue of *Razsvet*, on May 27, 1860, Osip Rabinovich devoted nearly the entire editorial to Schwabacher. The entire community, wrote Rabinovich, was abuzz with expectations of prompt governmental confirmation, and though some people assumed that Odessa Jewry was divided into progressives and conservatives, the fact that all Jews were excitedly awaiting the rabbi's arrival showed that such crude divisions did not exist here. The higher elements of society as well as the masses, he declared, were moving with the times.[65]

By the following week Rabinovich acknowledged that the problem was more complex. Though Schwabacher had by now, Rabinovich was certain, received the telegram from St. Petersburg confirming his appointment, he had not informed the community whether or not he would come. Furthermore, Schwabacher had received an anonymous letter, allegedly sent by a member of the Odessa Jewish community, urging him to forestall future problems by not coming to the city. Rabinovich refused to believe that an Odessa Jew would write such a letter, "the common weapon of cowards and informers." He advised the community leaders, who had invited the German rabbi to the city, to write him again and urge his prompt agreement. Only then would rumors of his vacillation be put to rest. Rabinovich also noted that Schwabacher had been appointed that week to the Rabbinical Commission in St. Petersburg, ostensibly to represent Odessa, although it was still uncertain whether he would assume the position there.[66]

Though Rabinovich preferred to believe that Odessa Jewry approved of Schwabacher unanimously, an anonymous letter that he printed in *Razsvet* three weeks later undermined his confidence. The letter criticized the St. Petersburg Rabbinical Commission because Schwabacher, who still had not arrived in Odessa and had previously spent only three or four weeks there, could not adequately represent the city's Jews on the influential commission. And since he did not know Russian, he could not easily overcome his limited knowledge of Odessa's communal affairs. (Raised here in print for the first time, this charge about Schwabacher's ignorance of Russian would be made frequently.) Despite Schwabacher's unquestioned sincerity and capabilities as a preacher, the letter continued, the commission's appointment was precipitous and an insult to Odessa Jewry, for it implied that no one in the city was capable of representing the community's needs.[67]

Rabinovich countered that Schwabacher more than compensated for his lack of Russian by his familiarity with Polish, Latin, German, and French; that an ignorance of Russian had not been an obstacle for either Max Lilienthal or Avram Neiman, the official rabbi of Riga, the latter then serving on the Rabbinical Commission; and that Schwabacher's appointment did not imply that no other enlightened Jews lived in the city, but simply that, with his particular qualifications, he was the best suited for the position.[68]

When Schwabacher finally arrived in Odessa, on December 28, 1860, a large group met him forty versts outside the city and escorted him into town with great pomp.[69] The rabbi found himself embroiled immediately in a controversy that divided the community into two warring factions. On one side were Schwabacher's allies, usually connected with the Brody Synagogue and supported by the local government.[70] On the other side was the leadership of the Beit Knesset Ha-Gadol (made up of traditional as well as self-consciously acculturated Jews) and most of the community.

From the start the community regarded the rabbi as the appointee of the Brody Synagogue, and for his first half year, according to some accounts, he prayed only there.[71] Though he purportedly never visited the city's major synagogue, the Beit Knesset Ha-Gadol, on either a Sabbath or a festival, he soon insisted that one of its traditions be altered: namely, that marriage ceremonies be conducted inside the synagogue rather than in its courtyard, as was the Ashkenazic custom. Schwabacher felt that this reform was so pressing that he insisted on its being carried out even before the community's celebration honoring his appointment.[72] This lack of tact and patience may have hurt him as much as did his ideological orientation.

The conflict over Schwabacher largely concerned the unsuccessful merger of the two synagogues. Members of the Brody Synagogue, among Odessa's wealthiest Jews, had contributed generously toward the construction of a new building for the Beit Knesset Ha-Gadol. Upon its completion in 1860, the two institutions began to discuss a possible merger.[73] The question of seating was the major stumbling block. The Beit Knesset Ha-Gadol, which had originally objected to the Brody's practice of selling permanent seating, now argued that its own permanent seating was inviolable and refused to allocate desirable places to the keenly status-conscious congregants of the Brody.[74]

Though this problem was not resolved, a merger was attempted. Matters quickly came to a head on the festival of Simhat Torah in 1861. Schwabacher arrived at the Beit Knesset Ha-Gadol to find Halperin presiding over the services and seated in the most prestigious spot, on the right side of the Torah Ark. Though Halperin's action ruffled Schwabacher, he did not object. One of his supporters from the Brody, however, made remarks that offended members of the Beit Knesset Ha-Gadol, and a fight broke out.[75]

A commission was appointed to solve the problem of seating. But when the commission, chaired by a leader of the Brody and presided over by Schwabacher himself, ordered that significant changes be made in the Beit Knesset Ha-Gadol's seating and structure, the merger fell apart.[76] Schwabacher remained the official rabbi for the entire community but prayed almost exclusively at the Brody, which now initiated a building project of its own. In 1862 Schwabacher celebrated the first confirmation service in a Russian synagogue, prompting criticism from russifiers and traditionalists, who both found the service inauthentic.[77]

Though the conflict between Schwabacher's supporters and his opponents became more involved over the years, the fundamental differences between them remained much the same. Significantly, though Schwabacher's opponents included traditional as well as progressive Jews, they used only "modern" arguments when criticizing him in print. This can be credited only in small measure to the fact that traditionalists may have felt constrained by the pro-Haskalah orientation of the Jewish press. Traditionalists elsewhere often aired their sentiments in such periodicals, and, indeed, some of the criticisms of Schwabacher reflected an antimaskilic bias. Thus it is striking that this bias was muted or explicitly denied in the ongoing debate. Attached to the February 23, 1862, issue of *Sion'*, for instance, was an eight-page supplement—entitled "Explanations of the Odessa Glavnaia Synagogue Affair"—which was signed by representatives of the synagogue. In a detailed, partisan account of the Schwabacher controversy, its authors refuted the charge that the conflict was between conservative and modern Jews:

> In bringing up children in the spirit of Russian education, we were the first to begin sending them to the government-run Jewish school and to the gymnasium. We were the first to bring to our synagogue preachers in

Russian and German (in 1856 and 1858); in matters of philanthropic and communal concern, we are not unknown to our brothers—the Christians; in a word, we do all that good sense demands for the good of ourselves and our land. And so, of course, we should not be condemned for not wishing to adopt some of the reforms accepted by foreign Jews, the bulk of which are too extreme. . . . [However,] when we ourselves spoke about our synagogue and its reforms we were not being boastful but citing the very editors of *Sion'* and the first number of *Razsvet*, where Mr. Rabinovich comments that the "Glavnaia Synagogue now presents the most comforting spectacle in its decorum and spiritual calm; silence and order are maintained with the utmost strictness." To repeat Rabinovich's words, "Who can now say that in our community there is a party of conservatives opposed to all innovations!"[78]

An 1863 *Odesskii vestnik* article expressed similar sentiments in responding to a pro-Schwabacher piece published a few months earlier. The anonymous author of the original article (a leading member of the local Jewish community, according to an editorial note) had described the entire dispute as a battle between the values of Western Europe and conservatism. Progressives had hoped, he said, that decorum would prevail in a united synagogue, but the conservative party—comprising the bulk of the community—had effectively blocked all reform of the earlier, more boisterous services. Rabbi Schwabacher's contributions were inestimable, although they had met with hostility and resistance.[79]

The author of the later article replied that the distinction between conservatives and progressives did not accurately reflect local conditions since the so-called conservatives sent their children to the gymnasium and Odessa Lyceum, prayed to the accompaniment of choral singing, and had helped oversee the progressive transformation of the Odessa Talmud Torah. Moreover, all worthwhile innovations in the community had been made by the Jewish school's directors, Ephraim Zittenfeld and Bezalel Stern, and not by Schwabacher; indeed, the sole "contribution" attributable to Schwabacher was the introduction of the confirmation ceremony, which was alien to Judaism and merely reproduced a Christian rite. Though the new rabbi, the writer continued, wished to supervise the Jewish educational institutions, he was incapable of doing so because he did not know Russian and Yiddish; he also lacked sufficient knowledge of the Talmud. In fact, one could fill an entire book just by listing Schwabacher's shortcomings; and though no one, concluded the writer, disputed the need for a rabbi with a Western education, must this preclude Jewish learning?[80]

Odesskii vestnik's editor observed in a note following the article that though the piece expressed the sentiments of a substantial portion of the local Jewish community, the "enlightened segment" was completely opposed to such opinions. Readers were asked to remember the favorable reception, only a few years ago, of the Hasidic rebbe Dovid Twersky upon his visit to the city. The editor implied that those who had welcomed the Hasid now opposed Schwabacher.[81]

The editor's charge was misleading. Traditionalists were, no doubt, opposed to Schwabacher, as were many russifiers, maskilim, and others who would not have considered walking through the streets of Odessa in a Hasidic procession. Moreover, some of those who had both applauded Dovid and loathed Schwabacher probably now recognized—whether out of conviction or self-interest—that it was useless to employ traditionalist arguments against the rabbi. In Odessa those who elsewhere might have participated in an Orthodox reaction modified their polemics (if not, perhaps, their practices and beliefs) according to the environment.

If Schwabacher's opponents did not view the controversy surrounding him as a battle between conservatives and progressives, how did they argue their case? The most sustained analysis from that camp appeared in *Sion'* under the title "The Right Side and the Wrong Side." This anonymous article was presumably written by one of the journal's editors, Emmanuel Solovcichik, Leon Pinsker, or A. A. Ornshtein.[82] They had good reason to oppose Schwabacher.[83] At a time of accelerated russification within the Jewish community and indeed the entire city, they considered it shortsighted to appoint a rabbi who did not know Russian. Though opposed to the German Haskalah, they were more profoundly antagonistic to religious fanaticism, and their bias in favor of the Beit Knesset Ha-Gadol was therefore evidence in itself that the opposition to Schwabacher by the leadership of the Glavnaia did not amount to categorical opposition to progress.

The issues discussed in the article, the author allowed, might at first seem of only local interest; however, since Odessa had already traveled the road that other Jewish communities in Russia would inevitably take, they could regard its history as a model and guide, and profit from an evaluation of its achievements and shortcomings, which they should study as carefully as would an "old, experienced merchant [reviewing] assets and liabilities, pluses and minuses, strengths and weaknesses."[84]

Odessa Jewry, the author went on, was divided, as were all communities, into two distinct groups, a small elite and the larger community. The elite in this case were the Austrian Jews, who had arrived in the city decades ago at a time of great material abundance and Jewish communal disorder. The Austrians functioned here, in the author's words, as the Varangians of Odessa Jewry, after the Norman founders and rulers of the Kievan state.[85] They had been responsible for the "incredible progress" in the following years, when the community was transformed in the image of these pioneers of enlightenment.[86]

In fact, the author observed, the Beit Knesset Ha-Gadol had been renovated according to the model of the Brody Synagogue, established by the Galicians. But divisions between the two congregations persisted, with differences now based more on social class and sophistication than on enlightenment principles. The key distinction was no longer one of geography, since the so-called Brody Jews, especially the younger ones, had undergone russification. The Brody continued to regard itself as the synagogue of the Jewish aristocracy, separated from the Beit Knesset Ha-Gadol by its cultural superiority over the synagogue of the masses. Though the leaders of the Beit Knesset did represent a broader constituency, they nevertheless found the Brody's haughtiness insulting, especially as they felt they had accepted all of the Brody's fundamental principles.[87]

The writer concluded that because Jews throughout the empire regarded Odessa as a model, this conflict had to be resolved, for however trivial the dispute might seem, the broader issues were crucial and included the allocation of the community's limited funds (for instance, whether the construction of the new Brody Synagogue was an unnecessary luxury in view of the sorry state of the Jewish hospital), the character of communal leadership, and the ability of "enlightened" Jews to work together successfully despite differences of class origins.[88]

In fact, not only was work begun on a new Brody Synagogue but funds were also found to renovate the Jewish hospital. This is not to suggest that the concerns of the editors of *Sion'* were merely fanciful. From its beginnings, the conflict over Rabbi Schwabacher was of wide-ranging significance. His tenure suggested to russifiers the limitations of the German Haskalah; to the leadership of the Glavnaia, the overbearing pretensions of the so-called Austrian elite; to many classical maskilim in the city, intellectually unimpressive leadership. Few, if any, Jewish communal leaders, however, faulted Schwabacher for being a progressive. The employment of a "modern" rabbi of one sort or another was by now taken for granted in Odessa.

FOUR

The "Enlightened" and the "Assimilated"

A Lithuanian maskil who visited Odessa in 1861 found the dignity and stateliness of its Jews even more impressive than the community's wealth and institutions. The calm way they walked the streets, conversed in the Café Richelieu, enjoyed music at the Italian opera house, and conducted religious services showed how at ease they felt.[1] During the early 1860's, this sense of security and confidence characterized the self-image of the city's Jewish intellectuals as well.

This chapter will consider their priorities, biases, and fundamental assumptions in order to understand how they integrated their abstract commitments into the fabric of their lives. It will evaluate the career of the most distinguished of Odessa's "men of the sixties," Osip Rabinovich, as well as the response of Odessa's Jewish intellectuals to the challenge they felt as posed by the community's *enfants terribles*, the so-called assimilated youth.[2]

Rabinovich (1817–69) was born in Kobeliaki, in Poltava province, a city with few Jews (not one was registered in 1805, and only 322 were registered in 1847).[3] His father, Aaron, a wealthy otkupshchik, saw to it that his son received a substantial secular education as well as a religious one (the father's acquaintance with one of the area's highly educated nobles may have motivated him to do so). A teacher brought from Kharkov tutored Osip in Latin,

Russian, French, German, mathematics, history, geography, drawing, and music; another instructed him in Hebrew grammar and the Talmud. More traditionalist neighbors warned in vain that this sort of education would only create future problems.[4]

People like Osip's father lived by a haphazard amalgam of traditional and modern values. Thus, after giving Osip a progressive education, he married him off at the traditionally prescribed age of eighteen.[5] Rabinovich's secular education did not come to an end, however, and at 23 he entered the University of Kharkov, in the faculty of medicine.

He would have preferred to study jurisprudence but chose medicine since a law career was generally closed to Jews until the judicial reforms enacted under Alexander II.[6] He remained in Kharkov for only a short period, as he was forced to return home to help his father, whose business had taken a sharp turn for the worse.[7] He felt profoundly frustrated at having to abandon his studies and enter business. Nearly two decades later, Rabinovich, now a leading Odessan notary, described how secularly educated Jews were thwarted by limited professional opportunities.

> No university department besides medicine offers young Jews the prospect of a career. In their enthusiasm for science most of these youths do not consider what is best for their careers. Moreover, after a while their enthusiasm cools, and they return to the bondage of the commercial sphere. Thus one meets among Jewish merchants people who, in different circumstances, would have joined the educated class, but whose talents have been wasted in financial speculation.[8]

Rabinovich passed into adulthood far more smoothly than did many contemporary Jewish intellectuals, perhaps because his childhood was remarkably happy. By contrast, such maskilim as Bogrov, Guensburg, and Lilienblum looked upon their childhood as a time of obscure, unresolved tensions and conflicts. Significantly, of all their autobiographies, only Lilienblum's went beyond adolescence. Unable to resolve these conflicts or to transcend this tortured period, emotionally or artistically, these intellectuals saw themselves as having remained frozen in childhood and portrayed even their fictional characters as queer men-children, fixated on the tensions of the young.[9] Rabinovich's far more harmonious upbringing surely had much to do with his ability to portray characters of varied backgrounds, religions, and ages in his fiction, with his vigorous self-confidence (in marked contrast to the chronic self-doubt of many of his counterparts).

Rabinovich was unsuccessful in business and left Kobeliaki in 1845, together with his wife and family, to settle in Odessa.[10] Within three years he obtained certification as a notary and the privilege of pleading cases before the local commercial court. Rabinovich quickly built up a large practice. Established professionally (among his clients were several of Odessa's largest Jewish commercial firms), he began to publish in Russian journals and newspapers.[11] The poet N. F. Shcherbina, an acquaintance from his days at Kharkov University, invited him to contribute to the first volume of the local annual *Literaturnye vechera*, where he published his short story "Istoriia torgovago doma Firlich i Ko." in 1849 and a second story, "Morits sefardi," in the following volume. The critics were unimpressed by the first piece, but Ia. Rozenblatt of the *Odesskii vestnik* considered "Morits sefardi"—published alongside the poems, fiction, and essays of Odessa's leading intellectuals—the finest item in the collection and devoted over half his review of *Literaturnye vechera* to the story.[12]

The two early stories depict the commercial world as crass, seductive, and personally disastrous—a view consistent with the antibourgeois attitude of much of the Russian intelligentsia, which was largely influenced by German Romanticism.[13] "Morits sefardi" examines the emotional development of Morits, a young Odessa Jew. It opens with Morits unhappily employed as a clerk in the office of a wealthy commercial negotiator and romantically involved with Margal, his landlady's daughter. Feverishly impatient to enter the world of Odessa high finance, he unexpectedly acquires a fortune, and, immediately transformed, he shuns Margal's company in order to better his image. For him, wrote Rozenblatt, "there remained only the precious 'I,' which everything had to satisfy."[14]

Morits eventually finds his existence has become meaningless. Wrestling with the moral emptiness of his self-absorbed life, he is helped by an upright gentile water-carrier and by a Jewish physician. The simple, unassuming man of the people and the decent professional are thus contrasted with the miserable, vacuous financier. Several of Rabinovich's later works, especially the novel *Kaleidoskop* (1858), contrast helpless people (often the poor and children) with the germanized Jewish merchant elite, thereby underlining the tension between ethical integrity and the moral corruption engendered by materialism.[15]

Soon after "Morits sefardi" appeared, Rabinovich translated into Russian Jacob Eichenbaum's Hebrew poem *Ha-Kerav* (The Battle), a celebration of the game of chess. He also wrote several articles for the *Odesskii vestnik*—one defending Jews against antisemitic charges, another praising a Russian journalist's pro-Jewish comments. His earliest article, published even before the stories, was "Novaia evreiskaia sinagoga v Odesse" (1847); this defense of the new Brody Synagogue so angered traditionalists that his friends, concerned for his safety, insisted that he remain at home for some time after it appeared.[16]

Between 1850 and 1858, Rabinovich published nothing, inhibited perhaps by the repressive cultural atmosphere of Nicholas I's last years.[17] With the appearance of the renovated *Odesskii vestnik*, Rabinovich began to appear frequently in print. In 1858 he published several pieces in the *Vestnik*, notably the essay "O Moshkakh i Ios'kakh," which explores the origins and development of Jewish names from Biblical times to the present.[18] He also published a more comprehensive and analytical essay on this subject in the following year.[19] In the first article in particular, Russian readers encountered a fresh and unusual voice, that of a Jewish writer apparently unconcerned about whether his essay might project an unfavorable image of his people, and displaying none of the usual defensiveness of Jews writing in Russian.[20] The details of Rabinovich's speculations on the Polish origins of Jewish diminutive names and the medieval Spanish roots of the traditional Jewish kaftan (he pointed to the costumes used in *The Barber of Seville* as proof)[21] are less noteworthy than the tone of the essay, which openly derided anachronistic Jewish customs. One's name is a treasure to be guarded, Rabinovich writes, not something to be transformed into maimed and indecent noises. How then did names like Moshka, Noshka, Ios'ka, Nonashko, and Maoirka come to be considered acceptable? "Please tell me, can one gain sympathy for anyone called Shlomka? Can one assume ability on the part of someone named Volka? Can one feel positive about a person who calls himself Berka?" All people call their children by endearing diminutives, but the common use of such forms for adults reflects self-contempt and engenders disdain. Either Jews stop this practice, or "they will remain Moshkas and Ios'kas." In any case, Rabinovich solemnly declares, "I will have done all I could."

Like his editorials in *Razsvet* later, "O Moshkakh" is cluttered with anecdotes, abrasive declamations, and ultimatums, yet informed by generosity and kindness. Again, like the editorials, this essay aroused widespread rage and bewilderment among both friends and foes. Arnold Dumashevskii, a 22-year-old student at the Richelieu Lyceum who would later graduate from the department of jurisprudence at the University of St. Petersburg and work at the Ministry of Justice, responded to "O Moshkakh" in a lengthy, widely quoted letter in the *Odesskii vestnik*.[22] Dumashevskii observed that anyone who encouraged Jews to become integrated into the larger society deserved gratitude, including Rabinovich. However, despite Rabinovich's "absolutely irreproachable advice," his article might give readers an impression of Jews and of their chances for eventual absorption that was entirely different from what the author intended. Rabinovich's essay asserted, Dumashevskii complained, that the mere correction of linguistic habits would alter the position of Russian Jews, that the "blinding bias that separates them from everything foreign and causes them to brand any book of non-Jewish origin as *tref posul*" (literally, nonkosher and out-of-bounds) would be eradicated as if by magic. Indeed, Dumashevskii remarked, the article's derisive tone no doubt prompted more than one reader to question whether the author of "O Moshkakh" could possibly be a Jew.[23]

Rabinovich would surely have agreed with Dumashevskii that more serious obstacles than the use of diminutives impeded Jewish integration into the larger society; yet his essay did in fact seem to suggest otherwise. This apparent contradiction reflects his unorthodox attitude toward his non-Jewish readership. Rabinovich was relatively free from the distrust of Russian society that prompted most other Russian Jewish writers to frame their criticisms of Jewish life in cautious, moderate terms. Indeed, Jewish intellectuals of the period, despite their belief that Jewish emancipation would accompany the spread of capitalism and political liberalism grudgingly recognized that the Russian intelligentsia retained anti-Jewish prejudices, despite the philosemitic tendencies of the late 1850's.[24] Rabinovich shared with other enlightened Jews a profound sense of responsibility for his people, but, unlike them, he was confident that Russian society was now prepared to accept Jews as equals. Because he saw himself as part of this larger community, he did not feel the need to be particularly cautious when treating the Jewish Question in the Russian press; nor, he believed, should any other Jew writing in Russian about this subject worry unduly about avoiding the objections or misunderstandings of non-Jewish readers. With little compunction about laying bare the most sensitive areas of Jewish concern, he approached his Russian audience not as a supplicant but as an equal. He did not hesitate either to demand rights for his people or to specify the responsibilities that those rights entailed.

Rabinovich's sense of security about the Jewish present did not make him insensitive to the tragedies of the past. His 1859 novel *Shtrafnoi*, which appeared in the *Russkii vestnik*, was the first sustained fictional treatment in Russian of the cantonists, Jewish children inducted into Nicholas I's army and often subjected to humiliations, tortures, and pressures to convert. The novel was eagerly read, even by Russian Jews who normally avoided fiction. According to several accounts, large sums were paid to rent a copy of the journal after the 4,800 copies of the issue in which the novel appeared had sold out in two weeks. Some Jewish readers were so moved by it that they made a practice of reading the novel at the Passover table as part of the annual celebration.[25]

Soon after Rabinovich and Joachim Tarnopol finally obtained permission to establish a Russian-language Jewish newspaper in Odessa, the first issue of *Razsvet* appeared, in May 1860.[26]

No period of Rabinovich's life has been studied as closely as the year between 1860 and 1861, when he served as the newspaper's editor. Since *Razsvet* was the only Jewish publication in Russia accessible to non-Jewish readers—with the exception of the tepid Russian supplement to Vilna's Hebrew weekly *Ha-Karmel*[27]—its editor naturally came under careful scrutiny by Jews, Russian society, and government authorities. From the publication of its first issue, even the most casual reader must have recognized that *Razsvet* provided an unusually opinionated, even acerbic, forum for Jewish news and affairs. Rabinovich's critics attributed his ironic, disdainful tone to a distance from everyday Jewish concerns and attachments; his supporters considered his approach beneficial and endorsed his conviction that Jews had "nothing to fear from the brightness of clear light. . . . Only through self-awareness . . . shall we gain respect for ourselves."[28]

Rabinovich did not believe that his newspaper's role was to mediate between a supplicant Jewish people and a potentially beneficent government. Confident that Jewish emancipation would occur inevitably in the political development of society, he thought that Jews did not have to prove they were worthy of legal rights in order to receive them. Rabinovich therefore felt he could be entirely frank about his people's shortcomings. This stance was consistent with his perception of the Russian intelligentsia as a community to which he himself belonged rather than a group to be petitioned and solicited, and with his belief that once Jews and Russians came to know one another, warm friendships would soon develop.[29] His view of himself as part of the larger intellectual community is perhaps best exemplified in his friendship with the poet N. F. Shcherbina.

Relations between Jews and non-Jews, especially in the areas of business and government, were not uncommon in Odessa. For example, both Bezalel Stern and later Alexander Tsederbaum prided themselves on their ability to represent Jewish interests and ensure gentile cooperation; and the *Odesskii vestnik*'s Troinitskii, a sympathetic non-Jewish intellectual, helped Stern gain permission to establish a girls' branch of the Jewish community school in 1835.[30] These relationships nevertheless clearly fell under the rubric of *shtadlanut*, the interaction in which a member of a vulnerable minority seeks favors from someone more powerful. Little notion of true parity, let alone emotional affinity, permanence, or closeness, entered into them.

Rabinovich's friendship with Shcherbina, then, was a highly unusual instance of a warm relationship between a non-Jew and a Jew—a Russian version, though Rabinovich did not suggest the analogy, of the celebrated friendship between Lessing and Moses Mendelssohn in eighteenth-century Germany. In a letter published in *Den'* soon after the poet's death and not long before his own, Rabinovich movingly describes his intimacy with this playful, moody, and creative man. Significantly, he expresses neither gratitude to Shcherbina for engaging in a friendship with him nor surprise at Shcherbina's ability to treat him as an equal. Although the two had met in Kharkov as students, their friendship had developed fully only after both men had settled in Odessa and Shcherbina had convinced Rabinovich to publish in the *Literaturnye vechera.* Shcherbina, Rabinovich recalls, was obsessed by the fear that his book of poetry *Grecheskiia stikhotvoreniia* would be poorly received by the St. Petersburg critics and was certain he could not withstand such a response. During this anxious period their friendship grew very close. The book was warmly received, and Shcherbina was propelled into literary fame.[31]

Rabinovich relates that he and Shcherbina were inseparable when, after an absence of several years, Shcherbina returned to Odessa in 1860 for a visit. The poet teased Rabinovich about his prominence in the Jewish community, telling him that he had heard that Odessa Jewry had not worried during the city's bombardment in the Crimean War because they believed that Osip Rabinovich would not permit them to be harmed.[32] The gently bantering tone of Rabinovich's memoir reflects his relaxed attitude toward non-Jewish society. So, in fact, do his editorials in *Razsvet,* which constitute the most extensive body of expository literature by a local Jewish intellectual of the period. Though these editorials have been examined only in relation to the history of Russian Jewish journalism, they are also a valuable guide to the attitudes of an important member of Odessa's russified intelligentsia.

Rabinovich's treatment of Odessa's Jewish merchant elite, Hasidim, and so-called Jewish assimilationists is particularly instructive.

In his editorial on Schwabacher's confirmation as official rabbi by the local ruling body of one hundred of the city's merchant elite, Rabinovich described how though the session was called for ten o'clock, the members began to arrive at eleven; by noon perhaps forty members were present; ten more arrived within the next hour. These "disrespectful" communal leaders, Rabinovich exclaims, belong to the "commercial class—a busy class. Without something to do they will not sit for even five minutes; why then deprive themselves, without any reason, of precious time when they are engaged in communal affairs? When will they finally recognize that time is indeed money, and not an empty, superfluous thing?"[33]

He found the *tsadikim* (Hasidic rebbes) and their followers far more reprehensible than the merchant elite. In *Razsvet*'s first editorial, Rabinovich declared that Hasidism represented the most extreme and complete perversion of Judaism, a mirror of the worst degradations of the Middle Ages. Since Jewry's isolation was breaking down—an isolation essential to Hasidism—this and similar perversions faced imminent extinction; Hasidism perhaps still flourished in tiny, isolated townlets, but not in large cities like Odessa. All of Jewish Odessa, he affirmed in his first editorial, had shown an unmistakable willingness to move forward with the times.[34]

Seven months after publishing this confident assessment, however, Rabinovich had to acknowledge that his predictions were somewhat premature: the pace of social development was invariably deceptive and complex, progress inevitably punctuated by retrogression, and every step forward interrupted by a step backward.[35] This uncharacteristically cautious view of the process of enlightenment stemmed from an event that profoundly shocked him—the boisterous, joyful welcome that Odessa had just given the *tsadik* Dovid Twersky.[36]

Rabinovich wrote that despite unmistakable evidence of enlightenment and progress through Russia—he pointed to the establishment of schools and charitable institutions, secular school attendance, and Jewish contributions to a fund for Syrian Christians—Hasidism had suddenly experienced a revival, and at no time in recent history had the movement gained so large a following. Recently he had received numerous letters from cities and towns in the provinces of Kiev, Podolia, and Volhynia confirming the persistence and growth of this "stubborn illness."[37]

Odessa and the New Russia region in general had not in the past been afflicted with this disease, contended Rabinovich. He admitted that Odessa had always possessed a widely diverse population, which included some Hasidim, but the latter "never dared to lift up their voices: they concealed themselves—hidden always in dirty *kapotes* [kaftans]—in alleyways and engaged in their orgies in silence, as if they themselves were aware of their own insignificance." In Odessa, Rabinovich wrote, Hasidic wonderworkers were isolated and scorned, approached only by the poorest, most unfortunate women; and so they viewed the city as the source of "neither gold nor fame," indeed as an "empire of hell."[38]

He found it ironic that in the same city where, only a few days earlier, the enlightened Schwabacher had been confirmed as official rabbi, Dovid Twersky was triumphantly conducted through its streets to speak at the Beit Knesset Ha-Gadol; there he addressed a crowd composed not only of petty grain contractors and idlers (*kablanim i batlanim*), but also of the better elements of Odessa Jewry; the tsadik left Odessa with 70 subscriptions for his new book.[39]

The reasons for the persistence of Hasidism did not concern Rabinovich. Still unswervingly confident of the shape of the future (even if the path was not as direct as he had formerly expected), he saw extreme traditionalists as pathetic relics and was entirely insensitive to the nature of their attachments. In contrast to Rabinovich's contemptuous attack on Hasidism, the local Jewish publicist Faddei Berezkin responded to the "wild flurry of journalistic activity" about Twersky's visit with a historical survey of Hasidism in the *Odesskii vestnik* as part of an effort to place contemporary events within a historical context.[40] Similarly, Joachim Tarnopol, though sharply critical of the "hysterical tenor" of Hasidic prayer, acknowledged that it reflected authentic religious feeling.[41]

Although Rabinovich disapproved of the excesses of those considered assimilationists, his criticism of this loosely defined group lacked the sharp edge of his denunciations of the merchants and the ultrareligious. In an editorial in the newspaper's fourth issue Rabinovich speculated that contemporary Jewish youth was made up of two radically different types: the enlightened young, who had basically ceased to be Jews, and pious young people who were entirely indifferent to enlightenment. Fortunately, Rabinovich added, there were many exceptions who were able to integrate modern and traditional values.[42]

The first group's basic premise—the incompatibility of religion and modern culture—was, Rabinovich maintained, mistaken though understandable. Youths thirsting for enlightenment attended gymnasiums and universities often far from their homes and the centers of Jewish settlement; upon completing their studies and leaving the university, they had only vague and dim memories of Jewish practices and found that the Jewish religion and tongue seemed quite alien. Their plight, he suggested, must be appreciated if the problem was to be treated seriously.[43]

Seemingly unaware of all the contradictions and tensions in his editorials, Rabinovich gave *Razsvet*'s readers the impression of a man with abundant self-confidence who was rarely willing to question his assumptions. In one editorial, for instance, he insisted that the community's leadership promptly write Schwabacher to urge him to become Odessa's spiritual guide. "I consider it unnecessary to dictate the contents of this letter," he added, evidently half thinking that perhaps he should.[44] Responding in another editorial to spirited criticism of his newspaper, he stated flatly that all but one of the charges brought against *Razsvet* were entirely groundless, and even this one—that Russian Jewry needed a popular newspaper more than a journal of opinion directed at a fairly limited audience—Rabinovich dismissed as well. He ended by quoting a well-known preacher who had told his audience that those who did not know why they were gathered together might just as well go home in peace: he had nothing to say to them.[45] Neither, obviously, did Rabinovich.

Rabinovich's self-confidence must have been reinforced by his surroundings. In Odessa he was applauded by an eager, fairly large readership that shared his optimism about the course of political reform. Nearly half of *Razsvet*'s readership lived in the city (approximately 250 of the total 640 readers), and Rabinovich viewed his literary and publicistic work as rooted in the Odessa environment; all his novels and stories (with the exception, not surprisingly, of the two subtitled "Tales from the Past") were set there.[46] Viewing Russian Jewry through the prism of his beloved Odessa, Rabinovich declared confidently in a letter of 1858 that the bulk of Jews were familiar with at least the rudiments of the Russian language. This was probably untrue of even the majority of Odessa's Jews, but such exaggerations were less fantastic here than elsewhere.[47]

Odessa, declared Rabinovich, was a "New Eldorado," where both Jews and non-Jews tended to display a flamboyant eccentricity in dress, speech, and all areas of life. The city attracted a great variety of types: model merchants together with desperate speculators, the abysmally ignorant with the highly sophisticated, skillful bankers with notorious rogues, dandies with miserable cripples. Though some residents now claimed that Odessa was no longer a "city of real specimens" (*gorod obrazchikov*), Rabinovich predicted that its potential for eccentricity was far from spent.[48]

Rabinovich was not alone in his concern about the city's assimilated youth. Indeed, since the 1840's Odessa's Jewish intellectuals and communal leaders had worried increasingly about this issue. By the early 1860's the assimilated—who were said to favor *sliianie* (fusion) with the larger world over the *sblizhenie* (rapprochement)—had become quite numerous and the problem more acute. Maskilim as well as traditional Jews described them harshly—indeed, the former were often the more abusive about the *mithakmim* (pseudo-intellectuals) or *maskilim le-maryit ayin* (maskilim for appearance's sake). Those youths, an Odessa maskilic correspondent to the *Jewish Chronicle* wrote in 1860, have only "a smattering of knowledge, principally of foreign languages, just enough to enable them to read the lesser works of French literature and to scoff at all that is venerated and held sacred. Had the Bible been written by Dumas, they would no doubt deem it worthy of perusal. But as it is only the word of an ancient Hebrew, it is a most insipid, worthless composition."[49] Similarly, Arnold Dumashevskii observed that they are "devoid of enlightenment, whether Jewish or European," as well as of community, convictions, and even a proper respect for the law.[50]

They drew attention to themselves by their behavior and intellectual preferences, but they were not in fact seen as an ideologically committed cadre or as exponents of an explicit assimilationist ideology. One can even question whether they deserved the term "assimilated," which in Eastern Europe was sometimes applied to those guilty of the mildest deviations. (Some young Jews in Berdichev were called assimilated because on Friday evening they ate dairy food instead of the traditional meat meal.)[51] It is interesting, then, that normally optimistic russifiers saw the assimilated as a disturbing portent. It was especially galling that traditionalists regarded the assimilated—with their European dress, their use of foreign languages, and their ritual laxity—as no more alien than the enlightened themselves. The distinction between the two groups was fluid, which contributed to the antagonism of the self-avowedly moderate maskil.[52]

Assimilation in contrast to acculturation, in Eastern Europe, was, on the whole, restricted to the commercial and intellectual elites. Russian and Polish Jewry—the relatively small upper and middle classes as well as the numerous poor—remained largely unmoved by the most radical social and ideological demands of modernization. In Odessa too, the wealthy commercial class showed little propensity for assimilation (significantly less than its counterpart in Warsaw, which maintained close commercial ties with non-Jewish financial circles in St. Petersburg).[53] In fact, the so-called assimilated in Odessa were mostly students in the city's non-Jewish schools.

Quite a few of Odessa's Jewish students attended these schools in the 1860's: in 1863, 252 of the 990 Jews in all the empire's gymnasiums were in Odessa, more than twice as many as in the preceding decade. In that same year 286 Jews attended the district's other secondary schools, constituting 11.7 percent of total enrollment. In 1886, 32.5 percent of the students in the district's gymnasiums and pro-gymnasiums were Jewish.[54] "All the schools," wrote Perets Smolenskin about Odessa in the early 1870's, "are filled with Jewish students from end to end, and, to be honest, the Jews are always at the head of the class."[55] That schools held regular sessions on Saturday did not bother these Jewish students, according to Tsederbaum; most missed only a few days a year—on Yom Kippur, the Jewish New Year, and the seasonal festivals.[56] On the primary school level, out of the 2,000–3,000 Jewish students in local elementary schools in 1866, 766 went to either non-Jewish or government-sponsored Jewish schools. Moreover, even those who graduated from the modern Jewish schools had received only rudimentary training in Jewish subjects and often could barely read Hebrew.[57]

Perets Smolenskin's *Simhat hanef* (The Joy of the Hypocrites) vividly portrayed Odessa's so-called assimilated in this period. The extremists in Smolenskin's novel are chiefly emigrants from the smaller Jewish towns, where a secular elementary education was unavailable. Once in Odessa, they find they lack the background to obtain the education they crave. The only avenue open to them is to earn their livings as Hebrew tutors, which they do despite an almost total indifference to things Jewish. Dreams of enlightenment and personal advancement turn into cynical resignation and hedonism, and the tutors settle down to a listless routine of cardplaying, drinking, and debauchery. Smolenskin describes their evenings: " 'Let us go to the tavern!' called Naftali, and everyone responded like soldiers to the command of their chief. They all went to the tavern, where they drank all night long, played cards, acted riotously, and went out finally in search of love."[58]

The characters of Smolenskin's novel are so contemptuous of religious observance that they eat nonkosher meat in restaurants and smoke cigarettes on the Sabbath. Disenchanted with the values of traditional Judaism, yet unable to claim a part of the new world because of ignorance of European languages or an insurmountable provincialism, they become alienated, cynical, and unashamedly self-seeking. The novel tells of an incident concerning a young man named Tsvi, who proposes to a Jewish family that he teach their son French, though he does not know the language. When the family calls in a Frenchman to examine the prospective tutor, Tsvi babbles nonsense words and then proclaims to the family in Yiddish that his examiner is a fraud. The family drives the confused Frenchman from the house, hires Tsvi, and gives him a sizable advance. He never appears to give the lessons.[59]

Smolenskin thought that females were particularly vulnerable to the threat of assimilation: generally given only a minimal Jewish education and permitted to be idle until they reached a marriageable age, girls became addicted to scandalmongering, luxury, and all that was chic, their morality undermined by French novels.[60]

Although "assimilated" youth led secular lives, there is little evidence either of close personal interaction between them and non-Jews or of a significant increase in conversions. Friendships between members of the two groups were unusual, as was social interaction of any kind. The banquet given by Odessa Jewry in honor of Pirogov's departure from Odessa to Kiev in 1858 was, according to the *Odesskii vestnik*, "the first time since the creation of the world that a Russian dignitary ever accepted an invitation for a public dinner given by the followers of Moses."[61]

Some social interaction nevertheless took place, and contemporary Hebrew novels depict balls in Odessa where Jews and non-Jews danced together and where love affairs were contemplated.[62] A club called *Beseda* (Conversation) was established by local Jews in 1864 in order to foster fellowship and understanding between the two groups. Membership was unrestricted, and Jews as well as non-Jews were encouraged to join, with each member required to pay annual dues of 25 rubles and to donate a book to the club's library. This would have been a steep price for the students described by Smolenskin but was only half the dues of the two other clubs catering to the middle class. Beseda was hailed in the Jewish press, and a notice about the club appeared in the *Odesskii vestnik*, but it probably closed within its first year, though it was eventually reestablished.[63] The Zionist leader Vladimir Jabotinsky observed in his autobiography that as a boy growing up in Odessa in the 1880's and 1890's he did not have one close non-Jewish friend, although his interests and those of his circle were entirely secular.[64]

Moses Leib Lilienblum, who had first encountered assimilated Jews when he arrived in Odessa in 1869, was astonished by how little they cared about reconciling tradition and modernity, for him the central concern of Jewish inquiry. Their total indifference to Jewish issues persuaded Lilienblum that he and other maskilim were as anachronistic and useless as the most hopeless obscurantists. He concluded in his autobiography *Hat'ot Neurim* that in taking up the cause of Haskalah after having rejected traditional Judaism, he had merely substituted one set of spurious assumptions for another: "Formerly I strove to comprehend the Talmud and its commentaries, and now I toil to comprehend the works of the new literature. . . . Formerly I strove to disseminate the religion (*dat*) of the Talmud, and today I strive to disseminate the opinions (*de'ot*) that I have adopted."[65] Lilienblum's disenchantment with Haskalah and his conversion to what he himself called a "seminihilist" position will be examined later in this study.[66]

Perhaps an even more telling instance of how the challenge posed by Odessa's assimilated compelled Jewish intellectuals to reexamine their convictions and priorities is Joachim Tarnopol's *Opyt' sovremennoi i osmotritel'noi reformy v oblasti iudaizma v Rossii*

(An Attempt at Careful, Contemporary Reform in the Sphere of Judaism), written in 1858 and published ten years later.[67] An attempt to examine, in under three hundred pages, the history of Judaism, the place of secular learning in Jewish tradition (including women's education), the role of the modern rabbinate, the need for a Russian Jewish press, Jewish economic life, and many other issues, Tarnopol's book is a provocative if disjointed mixture of scholarship, apologia, and social analysis. Its chapters on religious reform attracted particular attention, and forty years after its publication the book was still lauded for its treatment of this highly sensitive issue.[68]

An unlikely proponent of reform, Tarnopol was a conservative who regretted his intemperate youth, was meticulous in his ritual observance, and was appalled when Osip Rabinovich (with whom he had served as coeditor of *Razsvet*) permitted contributors to write approvingly about German reformers such as Samuel Holdheim and Abraham Geiger. (Writers for *Razsvet*, according to Tarnopol, promoted the desecration of the Sabbath and supported reforms even more radical than those carried out in the West.)[69] The literary historian Tsinberg was not incorrect when he characterized Tarnopol as "coldly cautious in the realm of religious questions."[70] Yet Tarnopol's book was the first comprehensive analysis in Russian of religious reform, calling for changes moderate by Western standards but far-reaching in an Eastern European context. What caused Tarnopol to overcome profound hesitations about reform (reflected even in the book's title) was his compelling sense of responsibility for the "numerous" modern Jews who might become permanently disenchanted with Judaism if religious reform was not implemented.[71] That Tarnopol regarded the modernized segment of Russian Jewry as a pressure group comparable to the traditionalists and as a group to which concessions must be made lest it be lost to the Jewish people illustrates the singular situation of Odessa Jewry. Nowhere else in the Pale could one plausibly describe such elements as numerous.

Basing his arguments on those of Western and Central European Jewish thinkers, especially the French orientalist Solomon Munk, Tarnopol maintains in his book that the problem of religious reform is a recurring theme in Jewish history. Those willing to accept the dynamism inherent in Judaism (the Pharisees, Maimonides, Mendelssohn) were pitted against those who saw the religion as immobile (the Saducees, Karaites, and Hasidim). But, Tarnopol contends, Jewish religious practices had never remained static, always changing and adapting themselves to contemporary needs. Prayer, for instance, at the time of the Patriarchs consisted of the recounting of family legends; Moses introduced the practice of sacrifices and the concept of communal festivity and celebration; and in the Middle Ages mournful liturgical hymns (*piyyutim*) were introduced into synagogue worship, reflecting Jewry's distress and misery at the time. Now that this anguished period was over, sorrowful prayers should give way to choral singing, edifying prayer, and preaching.[72]

Synagogue reform, Tarnopol points out, was a vitally important issue that had torn the Jewish community between the demands of its two largest and most vocal groups. On one side were the "conservatives," who were attached to the "pious disorder" of their prayerhouses and feared the slightest alteration, their anxiety reinforced by the radical experiments attempted in Germany; their services, despite the unwholesome atmosphere, reflected profound religious sentiment. On the other were the young, who would not enter the prayerhouse because its obsolete practices jarred their modern sensibilities. Despite the convictions of the conservatives, the needs of the modern youths could not be dismissed or ignored, and quiet, refined, harmonious prayer must be substituted for the distressing uproar of most synagogues.[73] Though Tarnopol partly shared the conservatives' suspicion that reform was now especially hazardous because of the disturbing developments in the West, his concern for the assimilated youth outweighed his fear of precipitous change.

Both the assimilated and their enlightened critics were convinced that Russia was moving inexorably toward liberalism and heightened tolerance. This assumption, which had dominated the thinking of the maskilim even during the reign of Nicholas I, gained strength under his successor. However, the Odessa pogrom of 1871, along with other factors increasingly apparent in this period, seriously challenged this belief as well as the optimism of the city's intelligentsia. Some Odessa Jews now acknowledged the widespread Russian antisemitism, which they had previously dismissed as anachronistic and irrelevant. In the pogrom's aftermath, antisemitic incidents began to assume a distinct pattern and coherence for certain local Jewish intellectuals, prompting them to reexamine the fundamental assumptions of enlightenment. The gap between expectation and reality—which in Odessa had seemed greatly narrowed—was once again visible and even, some believed, unbridgeable.

FIVE

The 1871 Pogrom: The City as Netherworld

The Changing Political Atmosphere

On May 27, 1871, a major pogrom erupted in Odessa. Within four days, 6 people were killed and 21 wounded, and 863 houses and 552 businesses were damaged or destroyed. Not a single street or square in the Jewish neighborhoods was left untouched, according to a report in the *Jewish Chronicle*, and thousands were rendered homeless. The damages came to 1.5 million rubles, twice as much as would be caused by Odessa's 1881 pogrom, which was part of a wave that would engulf the communities of the southwest after the assassination of Alexander II.[1]

The editor of *Den'*, Ilya Orshanskii, wrote of the 1871 pogrom that there are moments when the most secret and hidden feelings and aspirations are suddenly visible in all their undisguised nakedness.[2] Indeed, the pogrom caused some local intellectuals to fall prey to bewilderment and skepticism as they questioned the assumptions that had guided them for decades: in particular, their faith in the eventual enlightenment of the non-Jewish masses, in the benevolence of the Russian authorities, and perhaps most important, in the support of progressive opinion in the battle against Judeophobia. Although a new set of beliefs about the Jewish future was not clearly formulated until the widespread crisis of the 1880's, the process of reflection and reappraisal was under way after 1871.

With the 1871 pogrom, which has received only scant attention in the historical literature, the local intelligentsia began to lose their optimism about eventual Jewish acculturation. The pogrom seemed to bring out the most disquieting tendencies in Russian life and to foreshadow what some feared might be the shape of the Jewish future. It revealed the apprehensiveness lying just below the sanguine surface of Jewish cultural life in the 1860's.

The faith of Russian Jewish intellectuals in the prospect of improvement in the political and civic standing of the Jews had already been challenged in the first part of Alexander II's reign, when the 1863 Polish rebellion led to increased hostility toward all non-Russian nationalities. To the surprise of his Jewish admirers, even the eminent liberal journalist M. N. Katkov now began to air chauvinist sentiments. Suspicions of the patriotism of Russia's Jews grew common in this tense atmosphere.[3] Therefore, when in 1868 the Christian convert Jacob Brafman charged that Jews constituted a distinct state within a state, he struck a particularly sensitive nerve in Jews and non-Jews alike. Basing his observations on the minutes of the Kehillah of Minsk, Brafman argued that the Kehillot, though officially disbanded by the Russian authorities in 1844, still functioned as an invisible Jewish government. This invisible yet pervasive body—affiliated with the ORPME based in St. Petersburg, the English Brotherhood for the Assistance of Jewish Emigrants, and the Alliance Israélite Universelle—collected taxes, imposed its own court system, and through seemingly innocuous fraternal organizations, made its powerful will known in the everyday lives of Jews. Even rules about clothing and food were determined by the ubiquitous and omnipotent organization. Brafman argued that Jewish isolationism arose from the "Talmudic municipal republic," or the Kehillah, rather than from the teachings of the Talmud, as Russian antisemites had previously assumed. Brafman thereby redirected Russian concerns about the integration of the Jews from the religious to the political sphere. The book's impact was profound. Within two years of its publication, the governor-general of Kiev warned in his annual report to St. Petersburg that the "cause of every last Jew is also the cause of the worldwide Jewish Kahal . . . that powerful yet elusive association."[4]

Jewish economic life also came under increasing attack during the late 1860's. Several Jewish financiers, most notably Guenzburg and Poliakov, reached national prominence in these years by investing in the building of railroads—a burgeoning, highly promising area recently opened up by the government to private Russian investment—and these fabulously wealthy men acquired the dubious status of "Russian Rothschilds." Their visibility lent credence to Brafman's charge that Jewish economic success was the result of a tightly coordinated worldwide endeavor. Moreover, the spread of populist sentiment among the Russian intelligentsia reflected an increasingly hostile attitude toward capitalism and industrialization, both of which Jews were now conspicuously identified with. Populism also drew a strict demarcation between exploited and exploiters in rural areas. And broad segments of even the progressive intelligentsia came to view Jews as representing big capital in the cities and rapacious huckstering in the countryside.[5]

Despite the euphoria with which Jews greeted even the most minor reforms of Alexander II, by the early 1870's they could point to little more than an alleviation of the worst features of Nicholas I's rule. The cantonist system had been abolished, and a small number of Jews were permitted to enter the interior, including all merchants of the first and wealthiest guild (1859), holders of advanced degrees (1861), and certain craftsmen (1865). But the Pale had remained intact, and legislation after the Polish revolt suggested that the process of liberalization had already reached an abrupt, premature end. Jews as well as Poles were prohibited from buying real estate in Polish rural districts. The new municipal statute of 1870 limited the proportion of non-Christian councilmen to one-third, a particular blow for Odessa Jewry, which had enjoyed complete equality under local regulations enacted seven years earlier. In this same year, rumors spread of an edict that would prohibit traditional Jewish dress, sidecurls, and women's headcoverings, leading Jewish journalists abroad to speculate that the springtime of Russian liberalism might be at an end.[6]

For the majority of Jews social and economic conditions, rather than improving in the period of reform, appeared by the end of the 1860's to have deteriorated. The emancipation of the serfs, the confiscation of the property of Polish nobles after the revolt, and the new railway system, which eventually bypassed major

Jewish centers like Berdichev and Zhitomir, challenged the foundations of Jewish economic life, which was built upon the pre-emancipation system. Crop failures in the northwestern provinces in 1869 and the famine and outbreak of typhus that followed prompted the first serious discussion in the Jewish press of possible mass migration. Also for the first time, Jewish intellectuals criticized the growing concentration of Jews in the Pale's larger cities—cities that had for decades been associated with greater economic opportunity and broadened cultural horizons, and that now drew droves of impoverished Russian Jews fleeing the smaller cities and towns.[7]

Increasing more rapidly than that of any other Jewish community in the Pale, Odessa's Jewish population tripled from 17,000 in 1854 to nearly 52,000 (out of a total population of 193,000) in 1873. These immigrants generally crowded into the already overcrowded suburbs, especially into Moldavanka. Preobrazhenskaia ulitsa was the dividing line between the city center and the suburbs of Moldavanka, Peresyp', and Slobodka-Romanovka. Moldavanka spanned the vast area of the city's northern rim and was Odessa's most populous Jewish neighborhood and best-known suburb—celebrated in Isaak Babel's stories for its daring, wily Jewish hooligans.[8] The customs barrier on the suburb's west attracted thieves, many of them Jewish, who were eager to pirate goods over the unimposing wall and past the eyes of the tax collectors.*

According to one Jewish source in the 1860's, the majority of Jews in Moldavanka worked as laborers, tailors, wagoners, and hawkers of used clothing.[9] Its residents, Jews as well as non Jews, were by no means as uniformly poor as is frequently suggested in the secondary literature, though several decades later the poet Tchernikhovsky described it as a neighborhood of "small, wicked apartments, filled with the constant screaming and shrieking of children."[10] In the late 1860's and early 1870's, Moldavanka's poverty would begin to preoccupy local intellectuals, some of whom began to write about city life in a new vein. M. Dantsig observed sardonically in his poem "Der Litvak" (1869) that the city's poorest

*"Knaves learn their business at Pera and come to Odessa to practice it" was a local saying. Pera was a section of Constantinople. See Shirley Brooks, *The Russians of the South* (London, 1854), p. 32.

Jews were forced to do without ritual garments and even underwear:

> Odessa used to be a good place a few years ago.
> That was all in another time, all under another star.
> A city made exclusively of the wealthy,
> And no poor did you ever see.
> Now Odessa is entirely a city of the poor
> . . . all without undergarments . . . without *tzitzit* . . .
> without *talesim*.[11]

Dantsig's 1870 novel *Odeser voyle yungen* (Odessa Rascals) depicts a city more miserable than the worst shtetl. Immigrants came to Odessa believing they would find "diamonds in the streets," wrote Dantsig, but how could they possibly discover wealth and happiness beneath the filth and soot that covered the entire city? Odessa's celebrated intellectuals were in fact only ignorant and greedy *kugel lerers* (avaricious instructors); and contemporary life gave a new and particularly sinister meaning to the traditional expression "Seven miles around Odessa burn the fires of hell":

> In Odessa began the second period of my life, and this period was worse and even more unhappy than the previous one. When I now recall this time my hands and feet tremble, and it is extremely difficult to record the sort of troubles I experienced in Odessa. Every day we would sit down without any bread and no one had compassion for us. I know why Odessa is a Gehenna.[12]

By 1871 the expectations that had characterized the first years of Alexander II's reign had proved false, and the prospects facing Russian Jewry seemed distressing indeed. In the early 1870's the growing disenchantment with the ideals of enlightenment even led to new social or political views: some Jewish intellectuals (e.g., Smolenskin) rejected enlightenment as conducive to assimilation; others (e.g., Kovner and Lilienblum) eschewed its idealism and turned to materialism or nihilism; still others lost faith in the goodwill of the authorities (as was the case of the students at the Vilna Rabbinical Seminary who established a secret, socialist study group in 1872).[13]

The 1871 pogrom brought matters to a head for several of Odessa's leading Jewish intellectuals (and perhaps for others as well). Because of the dimensions and intensity of the pogrom, coupled with the refusal of the local non-Jewish intelligentsia to condemn it, they could not dismiss the disturbance as merely an anomaly in the essentially progressive direction of Russian life. After the pogrom, their belief that the relationship between Jews and the Russian authorities would continue to improve, that industrialization would advance the economic position of Russian Jewry, that the masses would gradually become more tolerant toward Jews, and that the Russian intelligentsia was a resolute ally all appeared less certain and defensible.

Odessa Pogroms Before 1871

The 1871 pogrom was not without precedent. In the competition among Odessa's many national groups, Greeks and Jews had long been particular rivals, and several times this antagonism had erupted in pogroms—widespread, violent attacks on Jews. Before 1871, however, government authorities put down these riots with great resolve. Anti-Jewish riots and scuffles had broken out almost annually in Odessa during Holy Week since 1821, for example. These disturbances were almost always initiated by Greek sailors and amounted to little more than fistfights between Jews and Greeks in front of the city's major Orthodox church. Jewish communal leaders and intellectuals minimized these scuffles and even dismissed the fairly serious riots of 1821 and 1859, in which some Jews were killed, others wounded, and Jewish homes and businesses were damaged.

The pogrom of 1821 grew directly out of anti-Jewish feeling fomented by the Greek revolution, during which Jews had tended to support the Ottoman rulers rather than the insurgents. Thousands of Jews were massacred as the revolt spread from Moldavia throughout European Greece, and killings and even accusations that Jews used Christian blood for ritual purposes continued after independence had been won.[14]

The pogrom broke out after the Turks, in an effort to check the revolution, had killed Gregory V, the Greek patriarch of Constantinople, cut off his head, and displayed it before a large and enthusiastic crowd. Gregory's remains were soon brought for burial to Odessa, which had been a major center of anti-Ottoman revolutionary activity for decades (the revolutionary Greek society

Hetairia Philiké was established in Odessa in 1814). Gregory V's funeral, on June 19, was attended by the city's large Greek community. Their numbers were substantially augmented by the Greek immigrants who had poured into the city from Constantinople after Gregory's killing, and who had spread the rumor that many Jews had participated in his death.[15]

Immediately after the ceremony, a group of Greeks attacked Jewish stores and homes. Concerned about the possibility of such a disturbance, the Russian authorities had warned Jews not to leave their homes, but the warnings apparently went unheeded. The well-coordinated riot began simultaneously in three different Jewish neighborhoods, where the rioters shattered windows, smashed doors, and beat Jews with wooden sticks. The German writer Johann Heinrich Zschokke, who was present during the pogrom, reported seeing several deaths. By the afternoon the authorities had crushed the pogrom.[16]

Gregory's martyrdom was eventually transformed into a widely accepted tale of his humiliation at the hands of Jews. The local historian K. Smol'ianinov omitted any mention of the pogrom in his *Istoriia Odessy* (1853), but recorded that in 1821 many Greeks had come to the city from Constantinople after Gregory had been decapitated and his body dragged through the streets by a "furious Jewish mob."[17] Indeed, the increasing prominence of Jews in the export trade—previously monopolized by Greeks—surely intensified Greek antipathy. Jewish magnates such as Efrusi, Trachtenberg, and Rabinovich owed their success partly to the bankruptcy of several Greek firms after the Crimean War; and these merchants, like their Greek predecessors, preferred to employ their own people as clerks and even stevedores (by 1884 there were 1,709 Jewish stevedores in the city).[18] As a result of these tensions, overt hatred of Jews reached a particularly dangerous level. The anti-Jewish outburst of 1858, for example, was serious enough that the authorities had to use firehoses to disperse the crowd.[19]

In the next year the report of a ritual murder set the stage for a full-scale pogrom. Greek sailors brought word to Odessa that Jews had killed a Christian child in Galati (Moldavia), where fifteen Jews had been arrested for the alleged deed, the synagogue destroyed, and all the Jewish homes in the city attacked.[20] A small group of Odessa Greeks joined about three hundred sailors carrying daggers and stilettos and began to attack people in one of the city's Jewish neighborhoods. The next morning the pogrom intensified. Many Jews were stabbed, and one was fatally wounded. The authorities' efforts to disperse the crowd met with resistance, and this time the pogromists turned the firehoses on the police and firemen themselves. Even the arrest of about forty rioters that day did not quell the disturbance. The pogrom continued into a third day. Jewish-owned wine cellars were broken into, and rioting spread throughout the entire city. Pogromists attacked all people in European dress (an indication of how many Jews had shed traditional garb). By the day's end the authorities had finally put down the disturbance.[21]

When Jewish intellectuals criticized the authorities' handling of the 1871 pogrom, they invariably referred to the pogrom of 1859, emphasizing how officials had then promptly, if at first unsuccessfully, come to the aid of the Jews.[22] Immediately after the 1859 pogrom, however, Jewish intellectuals had felt far from satisfied. The authorities, though cooperative and sympathetic, nevertheless had attempted to minimize the pogrom's severity; and the semiofficial *Odesskii vestnik* had described it as a minor scuffle between children, barely mentioning either the predominance of Greeks or its anti-Jewish character.[23] Such distortions of fact stemmed from the pressure of local Greek magnates on the authorities (and perhaps also from the connivance of Jewish leaders). The frustration felt by local Jewish intellectuals, who were unable to publish accurate news of the tragedy, motivated Rabinovich and Tarnopol once more to petition the authorities to permit the publication of a Jewish newspaper in Russian.[24] The riot nevertheless had seemed to them no more than an aberration; the events of 1871 would not be dismissed as easily.

The 1871 Pogrom

The immediate cause of the riot was the rumor, which began to circulate on the morning of May 27, that Jews had desecrated the Greek Orthodox church and cemetery. It was reported that they had stolen the cross from the church's roof, knocked over or broken the fence surrounding the building, vandalized the cemetery, and even defiled Christ's shroud.[25]

On the first day of the riot, the pogromists limited their attacks to the houses adjacent to the church. The next day, however, they divided into five groups and converged on the middle-class Jewish neighborhoods, shattering windows of houses and businesses. The Jewish and non-Jewish merchants of the Staryi Bazar successfully defended the square from attack. But the authorities offered no resistance at all, to the surprise of Jews and pogromists alike. "The armed guardians of the peace," reported New York's *Hebrew Leader*, "contented themselves with playing the part of silent spectators."[26]

By the third day the pogrom was citywide. Pogromists began to enter Jewish homes and to destroy property. The home of the financier David Rabinovich, located within view of the police station, suffered particularly extensive damage. The furniture was destroyed—most of it shattered into tiny pieces—and the study was plundered, and books, accounts, and papers thrown into the street. The neighborhood was so strewn with papers—according to reports widely reprinted in Jewish and non-Jewish newspapers abroad—that it looked as if it had suddenly snowed. All the windows of the Brody Synagogue were shattered. On Preobrazhenskaia alone, 50 apartments were broken into, and damage amounted to 105,000 rubles. Groups of as many as one hundred would now converge on a single house. The editorial offices of *Den'* were attacked, and the newspaper's staff was forced to take refuge in a back room. A tragic loss to Jewish literature occurred when the pogromists burned down the print shop that was then publishing the collected writings of the recently deceased Israel Aksenfeld and all his novels and short stories, with the exception of a handful of works published during his lifetime, were destroyed.[27]

On the morning of the third day, a delegation of local Jewish dignitaries, including Rabbi Schwabacher and the financier Brodskii, met with Governor-General Kotsebue and urged him to act with greater dispatch to put the disturbance down. As Schwabacher, the group's leader, was speaking, Kotsebue stood up and, without a word, abruptly ushered them out of his office. Just as they were leaving his chambers, Kotsebue remarked, "The Jews themselves are the guilty ones, but do not concern yourselves, for peace is now being restored."[28]

When the authorities finally resisted the rioters on the afternoon of the third day—perhaps in response to the intercession of the Jewish communal leaders—the pogromists abandoned the city center for Moldavanka. Rioting continued through the night and into the next morning. The pogromists completely demolished homes and apartments and in the suburbs broke into many taverns and public houses; they damaged or destroyed 217 apartments and buildings in Moldavanka and caused 136,288 rubles of damage. On the morning of the fourth and last day, the pogrom intensified, fueled by the rumor that the St. Petersburg authorities had condoned it so long as no bloodshed occurred. Several soldiers now joined the rioters, as did several artisans and merchants. Rioting broke out again in the city center; the walls of a large synagogue were torn down and the Torah scrolls desecrated. The pogromists burned many stores and homes to the ground and even began to attack small children. By the time the authorities finally quelled the pogrom, on the afternoon of its fourth day, thousands of Jews were left homeless. The Hebrew writer Yehoshua Ravnitsky recalled that as a boy of eleven he saw, immediately after the pogrom, crowds of homeless Jews gathered in front of the Glavnaia beseeching the more fortunate for help. Collections were taken up as far away as Frankfurt and London to aid the pogrom's victims.[29]

Once the pogrom had ended, local Jewish intellectuals began to evaluate it. The rioters had generally preferred to destroy property rather than steal, thereby revealing the depth of their antipathy toward Jews. Ilya Orshanskii argued in a much-quoted article that this hatred was a noxious but inevitable product of the anomalous legal and economic position of Russian Jewry. Though treated by law as pariahs, Jews nevertheless maintained a prominent role in the empire's economic life. Because Jews were at once legally vulnerable and conspicuously successful economically, the masses saw Jewish wealth as illegitimate and Jews as personally defenseless.[30]

The authorities' lack of support and protection during the pogrom had shocked Odessa's Jews, who placed the blame for this unprecedented behavior squarely on Kotsebue. The governor-general had assumed his position in 1863 after a distinguished 40-year career in the military, and he had no experience at all in municipal administration and little if any previous contact with Jews. They took solace in the rumor that Kotsebue's superiors were furious with him for his handling of the pogrom (reportedly one of them had even kicked his foot, so that he now limped) and that his dismissal was imminent.[31] Indeed, the following year he was temporarily reassigned to a military command and in 1874 was named governor-general of Warsaw. In view of the long history of positive relations between Odessa Jewry and local authorities, Jews reasonably expected that his dismissal would restore official goodwill.

But they could neither justify nor explain the way Russian intellectuals and society responded to the pogrom. Since 1859, when Russian intellectuals had protested against the antisemitic charges of the newspaper *Illiustratsiia*, maskilim and russified Jews had regarded the intellectuals as a barometer of the country's best instincts and a bulwark against reaction; and they were confident, at least publicly, that Russia would inevitably move in the direction of its enlightened, ostensibly philosemitic pioneers.[32] Abandonment by these gentiles seemed a particularly unsettling omen.

Even as the pogrom was raging, the city's non-Jewish intellectuals openly maintained that the Jews themselves were to blame for the uprising, since the Jewish community had created the oppressive economic atmosphere in which such action was the only avenue for self-defense (gymnasium teachers had even told this to their classes). The upper classes proved indifferent, and often openly hostile, to the plight of the Jews: one well-dressed woman was seen riding in a carriage in the midst of the pogromists, pointing out to the mob the houses of wealthy Jews. Friendships and business partnerships between Jews and non-Jews dissolved: one Jew, for instance, who had planned to hide his valuables in the apartment of a non-Jewish business associate during the pogrom was greeted by his acquaintance with violent curses and abuse.[33]

These disparate, perplexing incidents took on a more sinister aspect in light of the liberal *Sankt Peterburgskiia vedomosti*'s report on the pogrom. The newspaper, hitherto considered the epitome of philosemitic journalism, reported that the event proved that the Jewish Question was one of the most pressing problems facing Russian society; this problem was essentially economic rather than religious and stemmed from Jewish exploitation of non-Jews, which was so unbearably oppressive and fierce that open revolt was inevitable. Jews wielded such power, the newspaper maintained, because they functioned like a tightly organized *artel'* (a Russian cooperative of workmen or craftsmen), accumulating vast sums of capital and monopolizing the economy wherever they lived; their stranglehold was extremely severe in New Russia, and especially in Odessa, where Jewish economic domination had reached its height. The Pale must be abolished, the newspaper insisted, so that Jewish economic control might be dissolved and Jews themselves dispersed in small, relatively harmless numbers over the entire empire.[34]

In view of the accelerated industrialization drive of the 1860's, the Jewish intelligentsia was highly puzzled by the progressives' use of explicitly anticapitalist arguments to attack Jews and by the intensification of antisemitic sentiment in general. Jewish intellectuals had assumed that the expansion of Russian capitalism would lay the foundations for greater civil liberties for all Russians, including Jews. After all, in New Russia had not social and political tolerance accompanied economic liberalism? The anti-industrialism of the Russian intelligentsia and the use of anticapitalist arguments to justify vandalism against Jews introduced Jewish intellectuals to a new factor that they were ill-prepared to confront.

Perhaps local intellectuals were too deeply shocked to reply directly to the charges of the *Sankt Peterburgskiia vedomosti*, since they usually responded vigorously to antisemitic articles. In their role as communal leaders, however, several of these intellectuals reacted to the pogrom with customary energy and commitment. For instance, immediately after the pogrom Orshanskii and Morgulis attempted to persuade the Jewish community to sue the government for damages and thus emphasize its legal responsibilities to Jews, but more cautious communal leaders quashed the effort. Undaunted, they circulated a detailed description of the pogrom, written by Isaak Chatskin and Aleksandr Passover to several liberal newspapers in the capitals, but none would publish it.[35] Although such intellectuals disseminated information about the pogrom and encouraged a coordinated communal response, they did not offer a full-scale analysis of it.

Den', it is true, provided a detailed summary but little if any serious evaluation of the *Sankt Peterburgskiia vedomosti*'s coverage of the pogrom, and in an afterword the editors asked, "What is the reason for this sharp change in attitude by the press toward the Jews?" But they did not attempt to answer the question, stating that they awaited a reply from the St. Petersburg newspaper.[36] No response came, and probably none was expected. The unwillingness of the editors of the usually forthright Russian Jewish newspaper to criticize the *Vedomosti*'s reporting did not result from censorship restrictions (an interpretation that several historians have offered, but which John D. Klier has recently shown to be unlikely) or from sudden editorial prudence (which would have been surprising in view of the editors' activities in the communal sphere at this time).[37] Rather, their failure to respond was caused by sheer bewilderment. The fact that the empire's leading liberal newspaper had leveled these charges, and that they obviously mirrored the hostility of much of the local intelligentsia and society, challenged their fundamental certainties and left them, in fact, speechless.

This sense of doubt and confusion about long-cherished values and assumptions was evidenced by the rapid deterioration, immediately after the pogrom, of the two major institutions headed by the local Jewish intelligentsia. *Den'* ceased publishing soon after the pogrom, announcing a temporary pause, which in fact lasted indefinitely. (Several decades would elapse before another Russian-language Jewish newspaper appeared in Odessa.)[38] In March 1872 the Odessa ORPME formally announced its closure; actually it had ceased functioning in October 1871 and perhaps even earlier. Its secretary, Emmanuel Soloveichik, an ardent russifier, explained in a letter to the organization's St. Petersburg headquarters that "Odessa's anti-Jewish disorders last year completely destroyed the faith of the Odessa branch's leaders in the usefulness of their efforts and convinced them that all attempts to establish a rapprochement between Jews and Russians will remain unrealized as long as the Russians stagnate in ignorance and civic backwardness." The branch reopened only six years later.[39]

To be sure, despite Soloveichik's apparent pessimism, he remained convinced that antisemitism was, as the Haskalah affirmed, the product of ignorance and that it could be corrected by education. In the pogrom's aftermath, Odessa's Jewish intellectuals did not turn their backs decisively on such Haskalah beliefs. The Jewish authors of a 21-page pamphlet on the pogrom written and published in Odessa in 1871, for example, echoed these sentiments when they placed responsibility for the tragic event squarely on the shoulders of Christian fanatics; religious fanaticism of this sort had all but disappeared in Western Europe, the pamphlet affirmed, and it would soon vanish in Russia as well.[40] Yet, as the lawyer and journalist Mikhail Kulisher recalled years later, the pogrom altered the way he and other Odessa Jewish intellectuals understood antisemitism, however imperceptible the change might have been at the time. Try as they might to assure themselves that the disturbance was an isolated one, precipitated by the envy of local Greeks, the intellectuals felt they had "discovered something of enduring importance in Odessa's apparently fortuitous pogrom—namely, that Judeophobia was not a theoretical error of some kind [but] an attitude that reflected centuries upon centuries of hatred."[41] Because of the growing conviction that anti-Jewish sentiment was far more tenacious than they had previously assumed, several of Odessa's leading Jewish intellectuals lost confidence in institutions that they had established earlier on the basis of a more optimistic appraisal of the non-Jewish world. Ilya Orshanskii, who left Odessa soon after the closing of *Den'*, explained that, although he continued to believe in the efficacy of the russifiers' efforts, he had moved to St. Petersburg because he felt that Jewish publicists could best serve their community by writing for the non-Jewish press. The pogroms apparently also disillusioned Jewish intellectuals elsewhere in New Russia. The Bessarabian maskil and notary Joseph Rabinovich, later a convert and missionary, claimed that the 1871 pogrom undermined his Haskalah convictions. As the British journal *The Christian* reported in 1887, "The persecution which broke out at Odessa in 1871, together with the defeat of the French, convinced [Rabinovich] that his schemes of education would not lead to the emancipation of his people."[42]

This change in attitude marked the beginning of a new phase in the cultural history of Odessa Jewry during which Jewish intellectuals began to reevaluate their support of progress, enlightenment, and what they saw as modernity. The increasingly reactionary turn taken by contemporary Russian society was all the more difficult for these men to tolerate because they believed they had joined Russian bourgeois society decades earlier. Meanwhile local Jewish acculturation continued unabated in the 1870's. Ritual laxity became widespread; many Jews, previously hesitant to permit their sons to pursue secular educations, now relented; communal departures from tradition were increasingly radical and began to resemble those initiated by Jewish communities in the West. The next chapter will consider how the city's intelligentsia became increasingly suspicious of the benefits of russification, whereas increasingly broad segments of the community as a whole became sympathetic to the prospect of modernization.

SIX

Continuity and Reassessment, 1871-1881

Widespread Cultural Accommodation

In the 1870's the most revealing sign of the diffusion of modern trends in Odessa beyond the middle class and intellectuals was the rise of "pensions" and their consequent displacement of *hadarim* (traditional Jewish primary schools). In Odessa, declared an impressed visitor in 1876, "Hasidim learn the Torah and also study mathematics."[1] The decline of the local *heder*, elsewhere in the Pale a fairly stable institution, marked the deterioration of an effective bulwark against the intrusion of modernity.

Throughout Russia in this period there was a substantial rise in the number of Jewish children pursuing a secular education. In 1870, 2,045 Jews attended gymnasiums (5.6 percent of total enrollment); ten years later 7,004 did (12 percent). Even children from the most obscure hamlets were streaming into Russian schools.[2] The increase in Jewish enrollment stemmed from several factors, including the 1874 military reform (which caused many Orthodox Jews to relax their opposition to a Russian education, since holders of secondary and higher degrees could now enter the peacetime army as commissioned officers for significantly shortened terms), accelerated urbanization (which made schools less expensive and weakened traditional patterns resistant to such innovations), and a general increase in the number of

Russian schools. Yet the typical Jewish child continued to be educated in a heder, under the supervision of a *melamed* (a teacher of basic religious studies). In 1879 there were at least nine thousand melamdim in Russia teaching some fifty thousand children. In 1898–99, 53.8 percent of Jewish children still attended hadarim; and in Kiev province over 70 percent did.[3]

In Odessa, however, hadarim were experiencing a precipitous decline in enrollment by the 1870's, and secular education, at the primary level at least, was increasingly taken for granted by rich and poor, orthodox and nonorthodox alike. The city's maidservants no less than its bankers, claimed *Ha-Magid* in 1879, had decisively turned their backs on the old style of education.[4] Jewish-run pensions were especially popular. These primary schools integrated secular subjects into a Jewish curriculum (special tutors taught Russian and mathematics) in order that parents might give their children at least some "European" knowledge without having to abandon Jewish schools.[5]

Moreover, Jewish secondary students in Odessa far outnumbered those in any other Russian city. A Ministry of Education report stated that in Odessa in 1876–77 69.5 of every 10,000 Jews were students in Russian schools, as compared with 14.7 in Vilna and 13.7 in Kiev. In 1880, 1,377 Jews attended Odessa's secondary schools; of the 300 students in the second gymnasium 215 were Jewish (71.6 percent), and of the 368 students in the third gymnasium 265 were Jewish (72.0 percent). A local commercial school was fully 77.9 percent Jewish.[6] Students came from all segments of the population. Many were poor: in 1878 an Odessa district school inspector informed the local branch of ORPME that a "large" number of Jewish students were too poor to pay gymnasium tuition and would be expelled. The list of these students was so long that the society asked that the names be ranked according to academic promise.[7]

Russian school inspectors and the Jewish community's more acculturated elements faulted Odessa's pensions for being little more than haphazardly reformed hadarim. Students and teachers generally spoke in Yiddish and teachers sometimes barely knew Russian. Teaching techniques were primitive: memorization was stressed and beatings were common. Critics charged that the sole difference between pensions and hadarim was the price of tuition, since pensions might charge as much as seven rubles monthly (more than twice the cost of an average melamed in Odessa) and that pensions merely served to shield children from outside influence rather than introduce them to the larger society. Indeed, pensions were accused of hindering, rather than encouraging, educational reform and social progress.[8]

Some pensions, even the harshest critics admitted, were exemplary. Yet even the less satisfactory ones had a significant impact. The skills, linguistic and otherwise, acquired in such schools gave Jewish children from the city's most insulated and traditional homes greater access to, and more extensive opportunities in, the world beyond the Jewish sphere. The mere introduction of secular study into a primarily traditional curriculum constituted a potentially corrosive influence. Russian Jewry had not produced a neo-Orthodox ideology comparable with that espoused by Germany's Samson Raphael Hirsch, which reconciled the study of non-Jewish subjects (as well as other departures from tradition) with an Orthodox viewpoint. The absence of a more expansive form of Orthodoxy equipped to absorb and justify such reforms (coupled with the increasingly secular tenor of Jewish life in Odessa in the 1870's) ensured that the impact of even a rudimentary secular education could be significant.

Odessa Jewry was still nominally traditional, but the most sacred rituals were casually ignored and the most stringent prohibitions publicly transgressed. Ninety percent of the city's Jewish-owned shops were now, according to some accounts, open on the Sabbath; Jews carried money on Saturdays, chatted in cafés, and when rushing off to recite the mourner's prayer, put out their still-smoldering cigarettes on the synagogue's outer walls.[9] Neither fathers nor sons went to synagogue regularly; religious observance in general was erratic, and the same individual might fast on a minor holy day and then desecrate the Sabbath. The American labor leader Michael Zametkin, born in Odessa in 1859, noted in an autobiographical essay that his father "was an uneducated man, an artist, a hatter, a specialist on *popokhes* (fur hats) and a free-thinking man 'in the Odessa fashion.' That is, there was not a true vulgarity with which he was not associated; he loved to drink liquor and would go to the synagogue only on the more important holidays."[10] So notorious had Odessa become among the Pale's traditional Jews that the orthodox weekly *Ha-Lebanon* attributed the 1874 recession, which had a devastating impact on Odessa, to divine retribution.[11]

Jewish communal and institutional departures introduced in this period indicate an unprecedented openness to the larger world. For example, in Odessa in 1873 a nonsectarian Jewish-funded hospice (named after the philanthropist Kahane) was established; its charter committed it to serving the needs of all, irrespective of nationality or religion.[12] Other Jewish institutions now oriented themselves along similar lines: the Jewish hospital, which in 1868 still catered exclusively to Jews, provided beds for 337 Christians eleven years later.[13]

Russification continued unabated, especially among the well-educated and the wealthy. When the son of one communal leader died in his twenties in 1874, a Hebrew newspaper spoke approvingly of how different the deceased was from the other children of "the city's elite, who are generally complete 'Europeans' with no connection at all with the Torah and Jewish literature."[14] Rabbi Schwabacher complained the following year in a Purim sermon that most of the city's Jewish youth had never seen, let alone studied, the Talmud.[15] The occupational profile of the communal leadership changed in this period—by 1878, 20 of the 100 members of Odessa's Kehillah were physicians[16]—yet another reflection of the accelerated process of acculturation. The city's Jews, curiously, were not particularly prominent in populist groups, despite their disproportionately large representation in Odessa's gymnasiums and at the New Russian University, and few joined the Volkhovskii, Markevich, or Osinski circles. An exception was Solomon Wittenberg, condemned to death along with four co-conspirators in May 1874, during the wave of terrorist activity that engulfed many of Russia's larger cities. By the 1880's Jewish participation in such circles would be increasingly common.[17]

Jewish influence in municipal affairs was not substantially diminished by the 1870 legislation restricting Jewish representation in local Russian dumas to one-third. Odessa's Jews managed to fill their quota of 24 out of the 72 seats, and their influence far exceeded their numbers. The relative apathy of non-Jewish members and the organizational skills of the Jewish ones, especially of the financier Abram Brodskii, ensured them a leading role in municipal deliberations. So influential was Brodskii that the local British Consul held him personally responsible for a controversy that in 1873 threatened to lead to the liquidation of a partly British-owned waterworks firm.[18]

According to the *Jewish Chronicle*, many of Odessa's Jews joined the international Red Cross during the Russo-Turkish war (1877–78) and even collected donations door-to-door wearing the association's distinctive uniform.[19] That they did so suggests how far the community had gone in absorbing the cultural norms of the outside world and transcending the most durable traditional taboos. Another significant occurrence during the war was the introduction of organ music into the Hanukkah services of the Beit Knesset Ha-Gadol.[20] Though this departure did not technically break with rabbinic law as the service was held on Sunday, in traditional Judaism the playing of music as part of the synagogue service was considered unjustifiable until the rebuilding of the Temple in Jerusalem.

With the apparently irreversible decline in the position of the city's traditional Jews, local maskilim displayed an increasingly tolerant attitude toward their opponents and their opponents' institutions. Thus a journalist for *Ha-Tsefirah*, himself a Hebrew tutor in the modern mold, suggested in 1875 that melamdim be admitted into the Association of Jewish Teachers of New Russia and Bessarabia. (The organization was then restricted to those holding government certification, which required proof of Russian literacy.) The writer pleaded that the melamdim were desperately poor, and whereas Association members had collected a reserve fund of 70,000 rubles, the melamdim had managed to raise only 7,000 rubles. "Did [the high priest] Joshua ben Gamla have a certificate in his hands? If Moses himself had applied for membership, we would have turned him away for want of a certificate!"[21] A decade earlier, when control over local education was still contested and traditionalists still held influence in this sphere, such compassion would have been unlikely. Now the enemy seemed virtually subdued.

However, local traditionalists were not entirely intimidated. In 1876 the city's rabbinical court, headed by the formidable Moshe Ha-Dayyan, was at loggerheads with Rabbi Schwabacher, who had departed from local custom by permitting grain milled in

Odessa to be used for the baking of Passover matzo. Schwabacher prevailed despite spirited opposition.[22] The presence of Hasidic rebbes convalescing at the local salt-lake resort caused consternation among acculturated Jews, who feared that the wonderworkers' popularity was considerable even in Odessa.[23] In 1874, because of Lilienblum's widely known antitraditionalism, he was denied employment at a yeshiva established by orthodox Jews.[24] Yet Orthodox resistance was fitful and largely ineffective; and apart from occasional apprehensions, the acculturated could feel sure of their success.

Despite the tendency toward acculturation and the loosening of traditional restraints, there was little relaxation of the social barriers separating Jews and non-Jews. Gentile members appeared only rarely in the Jewish club Beseda, housed in luxurious quarters built originally for the Steamshippers' and Merchants' Club, but Jews were almost never invited to join non-Jewish associations.[25] Indeed, anti-Jewish sentiment intensified over the decade, especially in intellectual circles influenced by populist ideology. The ever-increasing numbers of Jewish students in Odessa schools aroused considerable hostility. In 1880 the director of a gymnasium who had been friendly toward Jews in the past suddenly refused to admit Jewish applicants, though he apparently accepted less-qualified non-Jewish ones. A secondary school inspector attempted to dissuade Jewish students from pursuing their education. One teacher was reported to have greeted students on the first day of school by insisting that Jews sit on the left side of the room, Christians on the right. Teachers in one of Odessa's gymnasiums taunted their Jewish students without mercy, urged them to abandon their studies, and declared repeatedly that the school had space only for the Russian Orthodox.[26]

The Rise of Other New Russia Cities and Economic Reversal in Odessa

The *Russkii evrei* observed in 1879 that a new type of Jew—pragmatic, sophisticated, and well equipped to deal with the problems of modern life—had appeared throughout New Russia. Though the region probably would not produce scholarly luminaries like Solomon Maimon or Isaac Baer Levinsohn, the paper conceded, its efficient, imposing, and highly acculturated men of affairs could not be lightly dismissed.[27]

Only in the 1870's did New Russia cities other than Odessa emerge as centers of commercial and, to a lesser extent, cultural importance, kept as they were until then under Odessa's thumb. Kherson in 1859 was "little more than a village," according to the British vice-consul there.[28] Until the mid-1870's agents of Odessa firms virtually controlled trade in Nikolaev, which would be Odessa's major regional competitor in the 1880's.[29]

These raw ports and commercial outposts had earlier provided meager attractions in the way of cultural or educational institutions. The political exile S. L. Chudnovskii, sent in 1869 to Kherson, which he characterized as "a remote provincial nook," was dismayed to find that there was no public library and only one, inadequate, bookstore.[30] Jewish communities tended to be small (Nikolaev had almost no Jews between 1829 and 1865, when residency restrictions were lifted) and culturally undistinguished, whether by traditional or modern standards. Jewish ritual observance in these cities was frequently lax. Communal institutions were primitive and uncreative and rabbinical authorities generally unimpressive. Even the wealthiest and most worldly Jews of Ekaterinoslav dismissed the value of a secular education, according to *Ha-Karmel* in 1866. Jews in the same city were stunned when a promising Talmud student, Ilya Orshanskii, chose in 1863 to study law at Kharkov University.[31]

The region's surge in economic growth during the 1870's was caused by the introduction of the railroad, a decline in Odessa's international importance, and extensive improvements, funded by St. Petersburg, of the port facilities of Nikolaev and other cities in the area. Nikolaev's grain exports increased from an average of 697,000 chetverts in the period 1869–73 to 1,502,000 in 1874–78. In 1893, 47.9 million poods (a pood is equal to about 36.1 pounds, or 16.4 kilos) of grain were exported through the city, and twenty export firms were now based here. Ports on the Sea of Azov, which first assumed major economic importance in the late 1860's, had, by the end of the century, captured 40 percent of the New Russia grain trade.[32]

This increased economic activity dramatically affected the region's Jews. Kherson's Jewish community grew from 9,500 in

1860 to 18,000 by the end of the century, increasing at a rate twice as fast as that of the city as a whole. Ekaterinoslav Jewry grew even more rapidly, with 5,462 Jews in 1866 and 41,240 thirty years later. By 1879 one quarter of Elizavetgrad's 40,000 residents were Jewish.[33] Jewish participation in New Russia commercial life had, of course, long been significant: an observer reported in 1859 that Jewish and Karaite merchants so dominated retail trade in Kherson that "on Saturdays, when [they] close their shops, [Kherson] reminds the resident of a place where cholera or some dreadful scourge is raging, so completely deserted are its streets.[34] Now, however, Jewish involvement in the more lucrative wholesale trade increased substantially, and a highly visible, wealthy stratum of Jews emerged. In Elizavetgrad in 1879, 120 of the 160 members of the city's first guild were Jews.[35]

Not all New Russia cities were affected equally by such commercial expansion, nor did it inevitably encourage modernizing trends. But in several cities Jewish upward mobility led to heightened social aspirations and a newfound interest in secular education. Before the 1860's there were no Jews in Elizavetgrad's gymnasium; by 1879, 104 of its 134 students were Jewish. When the first gymnasium in Nikolaev opened the same year, 105 Jews and 38 Christians were enrolled.[36] Russian-language instruction was introduced in the late 1860's into the curriculum of the Kherson Talmud Torah—previously run along typical traditional lines—and by 1874 ten of its graduates attended the local gymnasium.[37] Tiflis Jews were so eager to prepare their sons properly for a successful career in international trade that they took to hiring British tutors.[38] The lawyer Oscar O. Gruzenberg, born in 1866 to a wealthy Jewish merchant in Ekaterinoslav, stated in his memoirs that "the first word that reached my consciousness was Russian; songs, tales, nannies, childhood games with friends—all these were in Russian."[39] Favorable relations with local authorities, international commercial connections, and the absence of particularly strong traditional restraints contributed toward transforming these Jewish communities in the last quarter of the nineteenth century, much as Odessa had been transformed earlier.[40] Their expansion, however, could occur only at the expense of Odessa's longstanding status as the only significant Black Sea port.

The rise of these cities was accompanied by signs of Odessa's decline. In the 1870's a gradual process of economic deterioration began that would continue despite short periods of intense growth. The volume of grain exports had risen consistently in the second quarter of the nineteenth century, trebling between 1854 and 1858. In 1868, however, exports fell sharply and the volume was 2.5 times lower than that of the previous year. The situation was even worse in 1869. The next year saw an improvement in export trade owing to the introduction of the railway linking Odessa, Taganrog, and Rostov-on-Don with the hinterland. The disastrous continental harvest of 1871 contributed toward this brief recovery, and in that year South Russia ports exported 9 million chetverts of grain, shipped mostly through Odessa. At the same time, Odessa's standing was enhanced by municipal improvements that decisively removed the last stubborn vestiges of the city's frontier character. Its major boulevards were finally paved with granite and lit with gas lamps, the city's vexing water problem was resolved with the construction of a pipeline that supplied water from the Dniestr at a substantially reduced cost to consumers, and its cumbersome internal transportation system was improved considerably by the introduction of an elevated track connecting Odessa's warehouse district with the port.[41] The city's most influential and vocal merchants were nevertheless certain by the mid-1870's that Odessa was headed toward a serious, perhaps irredeemable slump.

Particularly ominous from their perspective (and with greater impact on Odessa than on other less-established and more innovative South Russian ports) was the fall in the price of grain that accompanied the particularly poor Russian harvest of 1874; bad harvests had previously always been followed by rises in grain prices. This latest development was largely the result of American competition. Russia's formidable competitor in the international grain trade since the late 1860's, America had repeatedly slashed prices and Russia had been reluctantly forced to follow. The United States, with its virtually unlimited virgin soil, efficient economic practices, and superb transportation system, seemed an almost impervious adversary in the eyes of envious Russian merchants. Indeed, since the end of the Civil War the United States had successfully cut into Russia's near monopoly in the supply of grain to Britain. In 1867 Russia satisfied 44 percent of Britain's grain needs, and the United States only 14 percent. In 1871 Russia's share dipped to 40 percent as against 28 percent for the United States; two years later it fell to 21 percent against 44 percent for the United States.[42] The introduction in America of the grain elevator reduced the cost of handling grain, made sorting and grading easier and more reliable, and assured uniform quality. With the continuous fall in grain prices (which would persist through the 1890's), money saved by the use of such elevators often made the difference between profit and loss.[43]

The local Committee on Trade and Manufacturing declared in its 1874 report that "not only has [Odessa] experienced a temporary crisis because of poor harvests, . . . but it is also entering into a period of definite decline." The Committee warned that unless drastic action was taken, "ruin will overtake Odessa; her streets will become empty, her houses valueless; capital will desert it."[44]

One hundred sixteen properties, valued at 2.6 million rubles, were forfeited in 1874; three banks closed between 1873 and 1876; the city's largest brewery went bankrupt, as did several large soap and stearine candle factories, linseed oil plants, and sawmills. A leading importer and the owner of a large wool-washing business both hanged themselves. The decline, the committee concluded, was reversible only if Odessa turned its back decisively on commerce and embraced industry. The city was admittedly less suited to such endeavors since local mineral deposits were poor and cheap energy was unavailable; but by virtue of its abundant capital, advantageous location, and large, hardworking population, it could successfully reorient itself and thereby avert disaster.[45]

The introduction of railway transportation had a largely unfavorable impact on Odessa's commercial development. The cost of transportation was not lowered until 1879, when the Russian Steamship and Trading Company, which owned the southern rail system and had an interest in keeping prices artificially high, relinquished control.[46] The linking by rail of Nikolaev, Sevastopol, and Rostov-on-Don with the interior made these cities better able to compete with Odessa, now less capable of resisting such encroachment because of its own weakened position. The railroad also encouraged the grain producers of Ekaterinoslav and Taurida to look toward ports east of Elizavetgrad for international transport.[47] The improvement of Odessa's port facilities helped check the rapidity of Odessa's decline, and the city was able to maintain its dominant position, despite increasingly vigorous competition, until the 1890's. The signs, however, were already disturbing.

This economic reversal naturally affected the city's Jews. Many wealthy Jews were ruined in 1874, and thousands of other Jews were thrown out of work. Nine thousand rubles were spent on Passover aid that same year, the highest figure to date.[48] One Odessa wag observed that local Jews were now in the habit of rushing through their Passover Seders, reciting under their breaths the traditional benediction inviting "all who are hungry" to come and eat, for fear that the numerous poor might actually take them at their word. Four hundred of the city's two thousand restaurants, many of them Jewish-owned, closed for lack of customers. The streets, reported a visitor, were deserted; once-thriving commercial houses were in apparently irreversible decline; Jewish workers were unemployed and dispirited; and there was clearly a "vast mass" of indigent Jews.[49]

The more restrictive communities, several Jewish newspapers observed, were usually the most generous in times of crisis; communities like Odessa, where Jewish behavior was largely unregulated, were far less helpful in providing necessary assistance. Lacking a cohesive bond, Odessa's Jews lived in a carefully circumscribed world. Preoccupied with their own affairs, they were not so much indifferent to misery as simply unaware of it. Being poor in Odessa was said to be particularly humiliating and painful.[50]

Ideological Reassessment and Moses Leib Lilienblum

This economic decline, occurring at a time when the educational profile of Odessa's Jews was improving, contradicted one of the Haskalah's most fundamental beliefs, the equation of enlightenment and education. Through education, the theory went, would come political and economic change. This prognosis seemed substantiated by events in the West, where widespread cultural accommodation had preceded political and economic change.[51]

In the 1870's the contraction of economic opportunities in Odessa—and the general economic decline of Russian and Polish Jewry in conjunction with the advent of industrialization—made Odessa's intellectuals even more doubtful about Haskalah's efficacy. The reevaluation of Haskalah assumptions was, of course, not limited to Odessa. In Vilna Lev Levanda, and in St. Petersburg the circle centered around the weekly *Razsvet*, gradually assumed a Jewish nationalist stance in the late 1870's. In Vienna Perets Smolenskin, editor of the influential journal *Ha-Shahar*, wrote spirited criticism of the enlightened solution to the Jewish problem.[52] But in Odessa the questioning of enlightenment ideals was particularly urgent. The 1871 pogrom; the sharp discrepancy between the increasing secularization of the city's Jews and their deteriorating economic prospects; and the inescapable awareness that the social distance between Jew and gentile had, far from contracting, only widened—these so perplexed Odessa intellectuals that they lapsed into uncharacteristic inactivity. Paradoxically perhaps, as Odessa's Jewish community was undergoing accelerated acculturation in the 1870's, much of its intelligentsia were experiencing a deepening sense of despair about acculturation itself.

When the Odessa ORPME was reestablished in 1878, its program was far more modest than it had been before its closing six years earlier. Then the organization's goals had been ambitious, even extravagant, since it had hoped to coordinate a comprehensive campaign for the russification of the empire's Jews. It now turned its attention exclusively to philanthropic concerns. It provided loans to needy students enrolled in Odessa's schools, awarded subsidies to scholars living in the city, and contemplated the building of a modern Talmud Torah in Moldavanka. The organization's new charter stated clearly that its sights were set only on local improvement.[53] Now a pale reflection of its once militant self, the Odessa ORPME showed how much the intellectuals' confidence in Haskalah solutions (and in their own abilities to address Jewry's problems) had diminished over the course of the decade.

Their disillusionment is difficult to document, since it was mainly reflected in a slackening of institutional activity and in an uncharacteristic reticence. In the 1870's—in contrast to the preceding decade and, indeed, the following one—Odessa's Jewish intelligentsia were too confused and unfocused to establish organizations with clearly defined goals or journals with carefully articulated editorial stances. Their inertia is shown in the paucity of documentary material concerning the ideological odyssey of the Odessa physician Leon Pinsker, who played a prominent role in Jewish cultural life in the 1860's and who, in 1882, would systematically outline, in his pamphlet *Autoemanzipation*, the idea of antisemitism as a psychic aberration, a notion widely discussed by Odessa's Jewish intelligentsia since the pogrom of 1871.[54] Pinsker, who at his most productive was not especially prolific, published nothing at all in the 1870's; he may have demonstrated an interest in a territorialist solution to the Jewish problem as early as 1877, but neither wrote on the theme nor prodded the Odessa ORPME, with which he was once again involved when the branch was reestablished, to move in this direction.[55] His eventual conversion to Zionism—which in the movement's historiography became emblematic of the conversion of his entire generation—was probably less sudden than is generally assumed; the precise nature of the doubts that led to this change is obscure and will most likely remain so.[56]

There is, however, one local intellectual who both merits close attention and whose work provides sufficient, even abundant, autobiographical detail—Moses Leib Lilienblum.[57] A maskil of fairly conventional opinions in the late 1860's and early 1870's—when he came to be associated with *Kol Mevasser*—he would later be Pinsker's lieutenant in the Odessa-based *Hibbat Zion* (Love of Zion) as well as perhaps the most compelling Zionist ideologue of the 1880's.

The taciturn, self-absorbed melamed-turned-maskil admitted on several occasions that he felt awkward with bourgeois intellectuals such as Pinsker, and an apparently unbridgeable distance separated the two even after a common commitment to a proto-Zionist solution encouraged them to pool their energies. Moreover, Lilienblum's intense talmudic training was markedly different from the more secular upbringing of Pinsker, Tarnopol, Rabinovich, or even Morgulis. The fundamental levelheadedness of these intellectuals was alien to Lilienblum, who within a decade would move from an intense commitment to rabbinic Judaism to an equally resolute belief in Haskalah, and, subsequently, to radical positivism. Yet it is instructive to analyze his writings during the 1870's since they provide a detailed, though idiosyncratic, account of an intellectual's disenchantment with Haskalah—a process that Lilienblum himself attributes largely to the influence of Odessa. A study of his development in this period offers a useful framework within which to examine how environment affected ideology.

For Lilienblum, when he arrived in Odessa in October 1869, religious reform was the most pressing issue facing Jewry. His first articles in *Ha-Melits*, when he was still a teacher in a small Lithuanian yeshiva, had caused a considerable stir and made his life in the city where he lived unbearable. Some maskilim in nearby Kovno urged him to settle in Odessa, where he might prepare to enter a gymnasium with the help of the city's wealthy, enlightened Jews.[58] He arrived armed with letters of introduction and eager to achieve the distinction he had felt was rightfully his since the time of the highly lauded scholastic successes of his youth.

He was soon bitterly disillusioned. Odessa intellectuals were courteous and vaguely encouraging but essentially uninterested in the untutored, rather somber Lithuanian. Odessa ORPME gave him small grants, but he found the long search for employment demoralizing. It took him six months to find a handful of boys to tutor in Hebrew. Poor and without any foreseeable prospects, he was acutely aware that his interests, his plans for talmudic reform, and even his demeanor were alien. Religious reform, so controversial an issue elsewhere in the Pale, seemed irrelevant in the "new city" (as Lilienblum called Odessa), where talmudic law itself no longer assumed a prominent role in Jews' lives.[59]

He soon avoided religious polemics in his writings. (The eminent Hebrew poet J. L. Gordon, with whom Lilienblum corresponded in this period, helped move him in this direction.)[60] He still continued to promote the standard Haskalah program. The major issues facing Russia's Jews, he argued in an 1870 essay, were education, rabbinical reform, and economic reorganization. By becoming better informed, Jews could resolve these issues, he insisted, echoing the Haskalah's belief in the redemptive influence of learning: "If you read newspapers, with their analysis of life's most fundamental concerns, your horizons will expand and you will no longer walk in darkness."[61]

He began to doubt whether one could reconcile traditional values with modern beliefs. The local Spinozist Abraham Krochmol, son of the Jewish philosopher Nahman Krochmol, helped persuade Lilienblum that the Bible was composed largely by priests in the time of Jeremiah rather than presented to Israel in one piece on Mt. Sinai. Soon he ceased to believe in the divinity of the Scriptures and the existence of God: "All the treasures that I had inherited and cherished since birth suddenly became contemptible." Despite his newfound atheism, he continued for a time to observe orthodox Jewish practice, but by July 1871, when his pious wife came to join him in Odessa, he had passed so far beyond the limits of traditional Judaism that his transgressions made her faint.[62]

When he encountered Russian nihilism, his doubts gained focus and scope. Nihilism, as propounded by Chernyshevskii, Dobroliubov, and Pisarev, stressed philosophical materialism, scientism, and utilitarianism. In contrast to earlier Russian radicals, the nihilists (in particular Pisarev) were less preoccupied with the relationship of man and society than with the transformation of human nature. This, they believed, could be achieved once the "human sciences" followed the model of the natural ones; the most pressing problems could be solved once idealism was abandoned and "anthropologism," as Chernyshevskii called the study of man, was permitted to chart the future. Nihilism never fully reconciled with its social concerns either the quietism inherent in its commitment to philosophical materialism or its belief that pleasure is the chief motivator. Moreover, nihilism somehow embraced both scientism and complete human freedom—though as Philip Pomper suggests, scientism served the movement mainly as a way to dissociate itself from the philosophical categories of the past. In fact, nihilism was compelling, despite its philosophical inconsistencies, because it offered a radically new outlook in its rejection of bourgeois propriety and gradualism and of philosophical idealism.[63] Russia's university students were especially susceptible to nihilism's message of elitism, social alienation, and civic duty.[64]

Lilienblum found nihilism personally and philosophically satisfying. Personally, it enabled him to gratify his deep sense of specialness and his need, first felt in his Haskalah period, to improve society.[65] As he himself acknowledged, his first years in Odessa were so painful mainly because of the city's indifference toward him (as well as because of hunger and the irksome visits of his shallow, unlettered wife). He believed that in Odessa he had come face to face with the future, and the prospect he had thus glimpsed—that of being left behind or made peripheral—challenged both his social commitments and his considerable personal ambitions. Nihilism's anti-idealism not only seemed better suited than Haskalah to this pragmatic city but also offered a basis from which to criticize that movement.[66] Echoing Pisarev, whose essays had deeply disturbed him when he first read them in August 1871, Lilienblum promoted the egotism of all, rich and poor, educated and illiterate; ultimately all men were motivated by self-interest, he argued, but this force could be harnessed to fashion the perfect society. Lilienblum still believed in the great power of ideas, but only when they served utilitarian goals and were applied to practical rather than abstract problems.[67] He rejoiced when he was able to abandon his work as a melamed and take a clerical job, moving finally from a world of "abstract illusions" into the hurly-burly of the Odessa marketplace.[68]

When nearly 30, Lilienblum set his sights on a medical career: not, he insisted, for prestige (after all, doctors mended bodies, cobblers repaired shoes—both served equally important functions), but because he could thereby harness the eternal truths of science and apply them directly to human needs.[69] Science, he contended, was the supreme source of knowledge: "Since nature has never changed or altered, scientific knowledge, designed to probe nature, is the master of all wisdom."[70] Yet instead of studying medicine, he concentrated on writing rather tendentious literary criticism. In his long analysis of Abraham Mapu's Hebrew novel *Ayit Tsavua* (The Hypocrite), Lilienblum challenged the Haskalah by attempting to undermine its first major literary figure.[71]

The artist's function, Lilienblum asserts in this article, is to clarify the difference between good and bad, and between real and illusionary. The artist must describe evil, envy, sloth, and ennui, but only in order to warn readers of their perils. Jewish writers are unfortunately particularly ill-equipped to make such distinctions. How can they see clearly when they belong to a people that has been alienated since exile from the everyday world and consigned to a cultural and social ghetto in which it has been both humiliated by, and shielded from, the external world? No wonder contemporary Hebrew literature is so full of biblical commentary, obscure poetry, and similarly useless nonsense. Though avowedly modernist, this literature has proved so resistant to outside influence that such unfortunate tendencies have only been reinforced over the last century.[72] Indeed, the supposed European influence in Mapu's novel, Lilienblum observes, is merely superficial.

Lilienblum is concerned with the book's "real defects" rather than its aesthetic shortcomings. The most serious defect is the author's inability to distinguish between real and flawed heroes, and therefore to provide the readers with models both to emulate and to avoid. The pathetic, aimless "superficial man" deserves a place in literature, he admits, but only as a foil for the positive, forceful hero. Mapu, however, clearly sympathizes with his tragic protagonists and uncritically ascribes to their nebulous beliefs. "This is a major defect. Since the novel . . . is inaccurate and unrealistic in its depiction of everyday reality, it cannot be useful to its readers, no matter what its intentions."[73]

Mapu's supposedly enlightened and modern characters solemnly rehearse discredited, hopelessly old-fashioned ideas. They identify with Haskalah, which, as they explain, encourages Jews to speak Russian. But what connection, asks Lilienblum, does mere linguistic knowledge have with enlightenment? What effect would even widespread literacy have on Russian Jewry? Mapu, unable to view Jewry's problems from a broader perspective, unthinkingly repeats slogans without subjecting them to critical appraisal.[74]

What problems should Mapu's heroes address? The same ones that preoccupy Europe's best novelists: poverty and unemployment. Once poverty is overcome, literacy will follow in its wake; to think that cultural questions can be successfully resolved before this occurs is sheer fantasy. The efforts of even the sincerest maskilim are utterly trivial. Jews must realize that their situation is intertwined with the larger problems facing society. Literature can either help awaken this sense of social responsibility or reinforce harmful entrenched attitudes.[75]

The values espoused by Mapu jar the sensibilities of cosmopolitan youth, for "vacuous poetry, florid declamations, meaningless phrases and commentaries" fall flat on modern ears. Only unsophisticated youths from the hamlets and small cities will still be swayed by his contention that the demands of "religion and life" can be reconciled. Had Mapu been more closely in touch with modern trends, as Lilienblum was now in Odessa, he would have recognized that religion has been thoroughly discredited and contemporary man is indifferent to its call. "Judaism can no easier coexist with the needs of life than can water coexist with fire."[76]

Though Haskalah's goals and tactics had been criticized before, they had rarely been challenged so comprehensively.[77] Lilienblum ridiculed Haskalah's equation of enlightenment with education, its self-consciously Maimonidean attempt to reconcile faith and reason, its belief that cultural change would result in a thoroughgoing socioeconomic reconstruction of Jewish life, and, perhaps most important, its assumption that Jews themselves, acting exclusively within the context of Jewish society, could remedy contemporary ills. In February 1871 he reached the conclusion, according to his autobiography, that there was no longer any reason for the continued existence of the Jewish people and that their assimilation would be preferable to Haskalah's woolly vision of the future.[78] Jewry was powerless to resolve its own dilemmas—its cultural obscurantism and its economic deprivation—and only a force from outside the community could help redeem it. Publishing in the Hebrew, Yiddish, or even Russian-Jewish press, Lilienblum decided, was of doubtful value since only the powerless and uninfluential read such newspapers. "All Jewish collective activity is inevitably deceptive since there is no action that our people can realistically take that would be useful in any way."[79]

Earlier the Jewish nihilist A. U. Kovner had reached similar conclusions (he found himself virtually unemployable in Odessa because of his vituperative attacks on former patrons); he abandoned Judaism entirely and much later converted to Russian Orthodoxy. His protégé, Joseph Yehuda Lerner, may have later converted as well.[80] They rejected the Jewish community as being unworthy of their efforts. By the mid-1870's Lilienblum had come to agree with their assessment of Jewish politics. Though he became interested in socialism in this period, he did not stray very far in that direction.[81] He published little in the Jewish press between 1874 and 1878; despite his age, he spent most of his free time preparing for gymnasium entrance examinations that he never took. Unlike Kovner, he could not bring himself to renounce the Jewish sphere entirely.

Earlier, he had attributed his intermittent despair to his decision to settle in Odessa. Wandering the city streets and sitting alone in its parks, he had fumed at its vacuous intellectuals, uncaring communal leaders, and foppish youth. The city's easygoing atmosphere had grated on the reserved, puritanical autodidact; its preoccupation with commercial affairs had alienated him, concerned as he was with more abstract issues. Penniless, unable to find decent work or to pursue a systematic secular education, miserable without his children but in despair when they and their mother joined him, he had even contemplated suicide.[82] He cursed the day that he arrived in Odessa and recalled with anguish the sense of anticipation he had then felt.[83]

Once he became persuaded, however, that Jewry's problems resulted from its unwillingness to embrace reality on its own terms, his attitude toward the city changed appreciably. When he first arrived in Odessa, he wrote, he was "pure of heart, a dreamer, full of fantasies and illusions, a man consumed with burning desires. . . . During my first year [in Odessa] I recognized that there was no room for such feelings and dreams here, and this awareness culminated in a moment of crisis and transition, a transition from faith to common sense."[84] The indifference to human beings and their problems that he encountered in Odessa merely reflected, he now decided, the freedom it permitted its residents; and its feverish pursuit of money and pleasure grew out of its healthy pragmatism. Its lack of sympathy for abstract ideals such as Haskalah showed the city's wholesome involvement in the affairs of the world.[85] Lilienblum stated in his diary in October 1871:

> Illusions have lost their value in my eyes; truth has vanquished falsehood; and knowledge has displaced dreams. My attachment to the illusions of religion weakens daily, and I now find myself transgressing laws that I never would have even imagined transgressing in the past. . . . All

these are, of course, positive changes. . . . Best of all, I am no longer employed as a melamed, nor do I support myself from literary work. Though in the past I heaped curses on the day that I arrived in Odessa, I now appreciate that this change opened for me a new epoch, a bright and vibrant epoch.[86]

He would soon work as a poorly paid tutor again and, despite his attempts at optimism, would remain dispirited, disoriented, and unhappy with his still-alien surroundings. Despite his atheism, he would feel empty when he let Jewish festivals, which had once filled him with awe, pass unobserved.[87]

His autobiography, *Hat'ot Neurim* (The Sins of My Youth), focuses on the tragedies of his life: his traditional education, his prearranged marriage, his pursuit of Haskalah, and his platonic love for a young woman in Vilkomir who had remained attached to him and whose life he felt he had ruined along with his own. "Today," he wrote in November 1872, "I have begun to write my biography. . . . I decided to take stock of the 30 years and one month of my life, and how my heart sinks when I am confronted with an existence that amounts to zero."[88] The most he could expect, he remarks, is that his readers might avoid the same fate once they were acquainted with his wretched affairs.

Until the early 1880's Lilienblum remained torn between his newfound nihilist views and his deep and persistent attachment to Judaism. He continued to live almost entirely within the Jewish sphere, but as a militant atheist who doubted that Jews should continue to exist as a separate people. He spent his leisure moments with maskilim such as the Lithuanian Tzvi Shereshevsky and earned his living as either a melamed or as a clerk for a Jewish firm; he would later be hired as secretary of the local Jewish burial society.[89] Yet perhaps his most prized possession was the collected writings of the nihilist Pisarev (which he was eventually forced to sell for want of money). His apparent lack of self-confidence, his inescapable provinciality, his dry, almost morose, bearing all militated against his entry into a different world.[90]

Lilienblum clearly showed his inability to abandon the Jewish sphere in his unwillingness to divorce his wife forcibly. Theirs was a loveless marriage, as Lilienblum repeatedly stresses in his autobiography in order to warn readers of the evils of prearranged marriage.[91] (His true love was the sensitive, inaccessible Feige Novokhovich, the "N" to whom his autobiography is dedicated.) He could not stand having his wife with him in Odessa, tormented her by desecrating the Sabbath in her presence, and wrote of her with contempt in *Hat'ot Neurim*, which was published when she was still in her prime. He begged her more than once to agree to a divorce, but he could not abandon her. And he was appalled when Schwabacher, soon after Lilienblum's arrival in Odessa, suggested that he leave her to pursue his studies abroad.[92]

By 1878 Lilienblum was again actively concerned with Jewish issues, publishing articles on the need for Jewish agricultural colonies in Russia, the inequity of Jewish divorce laws, and even the necessity of religious reform.[93] He rejoiced when he heard of attempts in the West to secure land for Jewish use in Palestine. And in December 1878 he wrote in a letter that although religious and national affiliation was merely an accident of birth, "ultimately I am a Jew, and I will remain one until I am buried."[94]

The pogroms of 1881 compelled him to reexamine and resolve his various, often contradictory attachments. In *Razsvet* in October 1881, he set forth his Zionist beliefs in a seminal essay, "The General Jewish Question and Palestine." Stripping the Jewish nationalist argument of all romantic trappings, the article makes its case on the basis of utilitarianist criteria. The pogroms, Lilienblum contends, were neither aberrations nor merely a reflection of age-old and ingrained prejudice. They resulted from Jewry's status as a distinct minority permitted to reside only on sufferance and when fulfilling certain useful functions. In rigidly stratified medieval Europe, Jewish access to liquid capital had benefited stagnant economies; however, once an indigenous middle class had developed, Jews were resented, persecuted, and expelled. In the modern world, argued Lilienblum, Jews were more vulnerable than ever because increased mobility enabled others to compete with the Jewish middle class in fulfilling Jews' traditional economic functions. Pogroms were inevitable under such circumstances, in which Jews' very usefulness to the larger society made them targets of rivalry and attack. "In advancing this thesis," writes Jonathan Frankel, "Lilienblum had not simply cast doubt on the central assumption which had motivated two generations of maskilim in Russia. He had reversed it entirely, stood it on its head. The belief had been that the more useful the Jews became to society, the more they would win acceptance. Now Lilienblum argued that the opposite was true. To be useful at any level meant to be successful and success was dangerous."[95] The only practical options left were Palestinian settlement and a general evacuation of Europe. Of all the articles inspired by the pogroms, Lilienblum's essay was the most influential.[96]

Lilienblum's conversion to Zionism was the culmination of a long, painful reassessment of the idealist presuppositions of the Haskalah, presuppositions that his experiences in Odessa had convinced him were untenable. The Haskalah's belief in the power of ideas and its idealistic understanding of the nature of social and cultural change were, to his mind, anachronistic and even harmful. Nihilism's purportedly sober realism attracted him because he felt a need for an ideology that did not turn its back on life's practical and mundane sides. Lilienblum, then, became convinced by the utilitarian tenor of Odessa life that ideas played a limited role in motivating change. His nihilism was in large part an attempt to embrace (and even to celebrate) the practical ethos of his city, a city apparently indifferent to the ideologies of the modernizers and yet so patently modern.

Conclusion

A combination of factors—including economic incentives, the prospect of social mobility, a vibrant and westernized cultural life, a relatively tolerant political atmosphere for much of the century, and the absence of a particularly restrictive traditional Jewish communal structure—made Odessa Jewry susceptible to acculturation along distinctly European lines. By the 1870's, many Odessa Jews had integrated into their lives changes considered to be highly suspect and innovative by Jews elsewhere in the Pale. The increasingly widespread use of the Russian language by local Jews, the degree to which the more extreme Orthodox elements were marginalized in communal affairs, the ritual laxity of many nominally traditional Jews, all marked this community off as distinctly modern. Even in the 1830's pious Jews were spotted in the local opera house, despite the religious prohibition against listening to women sing, and large numbers of Jewish children were in attendance at the modern Jewish school newly established by the Galicians, despite widespread Russian Jewish fear of secular education. By the 1850's, prayer in the city's major synagogue was designed along self-consciously maskilic and "Germanic" lines.

In this ethnically heterogeneous, commercially preoccupied city, Jewish economic enterprise was encouraged, and many Jews took advantage of the extensive economic opportunities open to them. Jewish commercial energy—frequently checked elsewhere in the Pale by officials fearful of Jewish economic exploitation—

was encouraged here, and, curiously, Jews were valued in Odessa for many of the same reasons that they were inhibited and restricted in other Russian cities. The extensive economic opportunities open to Jews in this remote but culturally vibrant port city, with its large foreign-born and westernized population, encouraged them to learn foreign languages, to send their children to Russian schools, to emulate western cultural patterns, and to modernize Jewish religious life.

Nevertheless, few local Jews who learned to speak Russian or enjoyed listening to an edifying German-language sermon or dressed in European clothes viewed themselves as maskilim. Nor did most of the young, brash Odessa Jews who so shocked Moses Leib Lilienblum by smoking openly on the Sabbath. Only intellectuals saw modernity as presenting a set of ideological problems that demanded social, political, and religious responses; most Jews who did not consciously resist the new trends simply absorbed them without reflection, integrating them into an otherwise traditional framework. In this respect, ideology did not create the impetus for cultural change.

Russian Jewish intellectuals, who tended to associate cultural change exclusively with a self-conscious, ideological transformation and who assumed (or at least hoped) that modern society would produce large numbers of Jews committed to an avowedly modernist ideology, maskilic or otherwise, could not adequately explain a social setting where traditional Jewish practices were more often neglected than deliberately discarded. According to the Hebrew essayist Elhanan Levinsky, this could only be because Odessa was a frivolous city, whose libraries were deserted and whose cafes were filled with vacuous chatter.[1] Young provincials drawn into its orbit were said typically to be overwhelmed less by its intellectual attractions than by the frenetic activity of its streets, the gaiety of its theaters, the grace of its women, and the earnest secularity of its men.[2]

The Russian Haskalah had hoped that Jews might reconcile modern and traditional demands without relinquishing what it saw as Judaism's distinctive characteristics—its use of the Hebrew language, its religious attachments (modified along maskilic lines), and its allegiance to a Jewish intellectual leadership (in the future, maskilic rather than rabbinic). Maskilim, who had settled in Odessa since the 1820's, were attracted to the city by its fine Jewish and Russian schools, its newspapers and book publishers, its maskilic communal institutions, and its increasingly large and acculturated Jewish community. They came seeking jobs, stipends, education, a readership, a publisher, and often also a less restrictive Jewish communal atmosphere.

Local maskilim did provide an institutional framework and a terminology that helped contribute to widespread cultural change, even when these factors did not primarily motivate change. This is most apparent in the history of the modern Jewish school, started in 1826. Established by maskilim and wealthy Galician patrons, it was supported and attended almost from its inception by large numbers of local Jews because they recognized that it provided them and their children with useful linguistic and technical skills. Along similar lines, the priorities of local maskilim clearly influenced the city's Jewish communal leadership, at least by the 1830's. The maskilic orientation—sometimes tacit, sometimes explicit—won the support of a sizable segment of the community, which saw in it the most feasible and realistic defense of local interests.

The city's intellectuals, though often ill at ease with what they considered to be the materialistic tenor of the city, frequently found themselves and their work profoundly affected by it and by what they believed to be its up-to-the-minute trends, which they felt they could ignore only at the risk of losing touch with important new developments. The impact of this milieu on the work of Osip Rabinovich, Joachim Tarnopol, and Moses Leib Lilienblum—as Rabinovich and Lilienblum both readily admitted—was profound, and their careers cannot be fully understood without reference to it. The images that Odessa provided them and many others—most importantly, perhaps, the image of a society almost haphazardly embracing aspects of modernity without systematically evaluating it—gave them a unique and, in the minds of some, also a profoundly disturbing perspective on modern Jewish society.

In Jewish historiography Odessa never achieved the revered status of a "city that is a mother in Israel." Indeed its deficiencies were most often noticed: its lack of communal solidarity, its indifference to spiritual concerns, and its unabashed materialism. Yet

Odessa offered its Jews a dual opportunity, rare indeed in Russia, to live with relative well-being and freedom in the present and to contemplate with somewhat less inhibition (even if not necessarily with greater clarity) the shape of the future. Of all the cities of the Pale, Odessa most closely resembled the discordant, individualistic modern metropolis that for the vast majority of Western and East European Jews would soon supplant the familiar European Jewish communities of the past.

Reference Matter

❖

Glossary

The entries listed below give only the particular meaning of a term as used in the text.

aliyah (aliyot) The honor of being called up to read from or to bless the reading of the Torah during the synagogue service.

artel' A Russian cooperative of workmen or craftsmen.

Ashkenazim The Jews of Northern, Central, and Eastern Europe, in contrast to the Sephardim, concentrated in the Mediterranean region and North Africa.

cantonists Jewish children inducted into special battalions during the reign of Nicholas I.

chernozem The agriculturally rich Black Earth belt of the Ukraine.

chetvert A liquid measure, equivalent to 3 liters or 5.25 pints.

desiatina A measure of area, equivalent to about 3.7 acres.

gradonachal'nik An official with the status of a governor; responsible for the administration of a city and its surrounding area.

guberniia Province.

Hanukkah The winter festival commemorating the victory of the Maccabees in 164 B.C.E. over Antiochus of Syria.

Hasid (Hasidim) A follower of Hasidism, a religious movement of East European derivation stressing mysticism and prayer.

Haskalah The Jewish Enlightenment movement.

heder (hadarim) A traditional Jewish primary school, in which the curriculum consists primarily of the study of the Bible and commentaries, and some rabbinic texts.

Karaite A follower of a Jewish sect of medieval origin that denies the talmudic-rabbinic tradition. In modern times, Karaites disassociated themselves completely from normative Jews.

Kehillah (Kehillot) The executive committee of a Jewish community; responsible for administration of communal affairs.

korobka A government tax, mainly on kosher meat; some of it went to finance Jewish communal institutions.

kupets (kuptsy) A member of a Russian merchant guild.

maskil (maskilim) An adherent of the Haskalah.

maskilim le-maryit ayin Maskilim for appearance's sake.

melamed (melamdim) A teacher of basic religious studies, generally in a heder.

mithakmim Pseudo-intellectuals.

mitzvah (mitzvot) Religious duties and honors that constitute a part of the synagogue service.

otkupshchik (otkupshchiki) The holders of government concessions for distilling and selling liquor.

parsah (parsa'ot) A linear measure, equivalent to about four miles.

pood A measure of weight, equivalent to 36 pounds.

rebbe A Hasidic leader.

Simhat Torah The day just after the Sukkot, or the autumn festival, when the annual reading of the Scriptures in the synagogue is concluded and begun again.

talit (in Yiddish: tales, talesim) A ritual garment with fringes worn by men at morning prayer.

tsadik (tsadikim) A rebbe.

tzitzit A ritual garment with fringes worn by men outside the synagogue as well as during prayer.

verst 3,500 feet, or 1.06 kilometers.

Wissenschaft des Judenthums The "Science of Judaism" school of Jewish scholarship, which first appeared in Germany between 1810 and 1820.

yeshiva (yeshivot) A school for advanced study of the Talmud and related texts.

Notes

Complete authors' names, titles, and publication data for the works cited in short form are given in the Bibliography, pp. 187–204. The abbreviations CZA and PRO stand for Central Zionist Archives (Jerusalem) and Public Record Office (Kew).

Introduction

1. See Simon; Seltzer; Tchernowitz, *Masekhet zikhronot*; Orbach; Slutsky; Tsinberg, *Istoriia*; and Pearlmann. The book most closely resembling a history of the community is Lerner, *Evrei v Novorossiiskom krae*. Based on the archives of Governor-General Mikhail Semenovich Vorontsov, this work offers valuable and otherwise inaccessible material on the New Russia region. But though it focuses on local government policy, it does not analyze either what motivated the authorities to make this policy or the interaction between those authorities and the region's Jews. Pen, *Evreiskaia starina v Odesse*, is an account of Odessa Jewry's first few decades, based largely on the study of Jewish cemetery tombstones.

2. Shohat, *Im hilufei tekufot*; J. Katz, *Tradition and Crisis* and *Out of the Ghetto*.

3. Endelman, p. 4.

Chapter One

1. The most reliable survey of modern Jewish history is Shmuel Ettinger's section on "The Modern Period" in *A History of the Jewish People*, ed. H. H. Ben-Sasson (Cambridge, Mass., 1976), pp. 727–1096. For a more

synthetic approach see Baron, *A Social and Religious History of the Jews*, 2: 164–462; and J. Katz, *Out of the Ghetto*.

2. For a list of the numerous works on these movements, see Frankel's bibliography.

3. Among the standard studies on the Russian Haskalah are Raisin; Meisl; Tsinberg, *Di geshikhte*, vols. 8 and 9; Erik; and Slutsky, chap. 1.

4. The only sustained analysis of the social underpinnings of this historical process is to be found in the work of Soviet-Jewish historians writing in the 1920's (in particular, Sosis, Margolis, and Yuditski) and the Israeli Mahler. This body of scholarship, though tendentious and mechanistic, provides useful guidelines for the study of the transformation of Russian Jewry in the nineteenth century, especially in terms of its documentation. Greenbaum evaluates the Soviet-Jewish scholars. Sosis, the most talented (and least doctrinaire) of them, describes his historiographical approach in *Tsu der ontviklung*. See *Yivo Bleter*, 19 (1942), for a perceptive analysis of Mahler.

5. On the laws pertaining to the formation of the Pale of Settlement, see Gessen's essay "Zhitel'stvo i peredvizhenie evreev po russkomy zakondatel'stvu," in the *Evreiskaia entsiklopediia*. Also see the articles by Ettinger and Maor in *He-Avar*, 19 (Sept. 1972).

6. See Dubnow, *Ob izuchenii istorii russkikh evreev*, pp. 19–57. Graetz's impact on Dubnow is examined in Seltzer, pp. 142–74.

7. Lestchinsky, *Dos yidishe folk*, pp. 31–38, 43–50; Yuditski, pp. 103–4.

8. "Gramotnost' evreev v Rossii," *Evreiskaia entsiklopediia*; Rashin, p. 308; Anderson, pp. 33–36; Marek, p. 169.

9. Lestchinsky, *Dos yidishe folk*, pp. 71–72.

10. Fedor, p. 122.

11. Lestchinsky, *Dos yidishe folk*, pp. 21–25; Margolis, pp. 37–38; Yakhinson, p. 15.

12. Mahler, *Ha-hasidut*, p. 49; Lerner, pp. 60–66.

13. B. Katz, 2: 134, 162–63; Reuven Brainin, *Avraham Mapu* (Piotrikow, 1900), pp. 37–38; Yakov Shatski, "Haskole in zamosc," pp. 24–34; Tsinberg, *Istoriia*, pp. 8–9; Lachower, 2: 74–76. See also Green's discussion of Nahman of Bratslav's stay in Lemberg and Uman, pp. 221–66.

14. On Russia's canal system see Blackwell, pp. 266–67. Between 1802 and 1855, 718 versts of new canals were built in Russia, mostly within the Pale (see Margolis, p. 57). On the railway's impact, see Falk, pp. 44–55.

15. Weisbrem, chap. 2.

16. Ginzburg, *Otechestvennaia voina*, pp. 51–53; Mevorakh, pp. 173–89; B. Katz, 2: 183. The Napoleonic invasion did have some effect on Jewish cultural life: the first modern Jewish school in Warsaw—the first of its kind in the Russian Empire—was established in 1818 as a direct result of the French occupation. Moreover, some scholars regard the inva-

sion as a turning point in the literary history of the Haskalah. See Rabinovitz, p. 82; Lachower, 2: 76–77.

17. This work was published in the *Evreiskaia biblioteka*, vol. 7 (1879). The quotations are from pp. 13–14.

18. "Armiia v Rossii," *Evreiskaia entsiklopediia*.

19. Tsinberg, *Di geshikhte*, 9: 19.

20. Braudes, p. 41.

21. See Philipson, p. 33; Markgraf, pp. 24–35. On the number of Jewish members of the first merchant guild, see Margolis, pp. 62, 196–97; and Ilya Orshanskii, pp. 24–25.

22. Lestchinsky, *Ha-Tefutsah ha-yehudit*, pp. 94–95; Nadav, p. 252; Slutsky, p. 16.

23. Margolis, pp. 46, 58, 62; Yuditski, p. 81; Kleinman, pp. 15–16.

24. This novel is included in Abramovitsch, *Kol kitvey*, p. 234. For a summary of maskilic reactions to otkupshchiki, see M. Levin, pp. 96–97.

25. M. Levin, p. 88.

26. Tsinberg, *Di geshikhte*, 8: 85.

27. Quoted in Rabinovitz, p. 100.

28. Slutsky, pp. 26–29; Pozner, pp. 54–61; Marek, p. 167.

29. Stampfer, pp. 132–33.

30. Kahan, "Economic Opportunities and Some Pilgrims' Progress," p. 236.

31. Quoted in *Odessa 1794–1894*, p. 145.

32. Saul, pp. 8–9; Druzhinina, *Severnoe prichernomorie*, p. 4; Orlov, p. xi; Skinner, p. 23; Herlihy, "Russian Grain Trade," pp. 80–81.

33. Zagoruiko, 1: 19–23; Polons'ka-Vasylenko, p. 250; Mirov, p. 134.

34. Grigorii Petrovich Danilevskii, *Beglye v Novorossii* (St. Petersburg, 1901), quoted in Allen, p. 262; Druzhinina, *Iuzhnaia Ukraina*, pp. 76–79; see also Herlihy's review of Druzhinina's study in *Kritika*, 10 (Spring 1974). On the expansion of the barshchina system in New Russia after the 1840's, see Herlihy, "Russian Grain Trade," pp. 128–29.

35. Saul, p. 19; Allen, p. 262; Herlihy, "Russian Grain Trade," p. 122; Iakovkina, pp. 168–74.

36. Druzhinina, *Iuzhnaia Ukraina*, p. 199. Zagoruiko, 1: 59–61; Herlihy, "Russian Grain Trade," pp. 123–26; Bartlett, pp. 109–42.

37. Polons'ka-Vasylenko, p. 243; Druzhinina, *Iuzhnaia Ukraina*, p. 357.

38. Druzhinina, *Iuzhnaia Ukraina*, pp. 59–60. For a detailed description of the harbors of the Black Sea and the Sea of Azov, see Herlihy, "Russian Grain Trade," pp. 69–82.

39. Skal'kovskii, *Pervoe tridtsatiletie*, p. 132; Orlov, p. xii.

40. Skal'kovskii, *Pervoe tridtsatiletie*, pp. 119–20. Druzhinina, *Severnoe prichernomorie*, p. 256; Bremner, p. 484; Skinner, p. 118.

41. An apparent comparison to the achievements of the Polish King

Casimir III, who, according to the popular Polish saying, "found a Poland of wood and left behind a Poland constructed of stone." Norman Davies, *God's Playground: A History of Poland* (Oxford, 1981), 1: 95–98.

42. Skal'kovskii, *Pervoe tridtsatiletie*, pp. 129–30; Smol'ianinov, *Istoriia*, pp. 166–67; "Richelieu, Duc Emanuel Osipovich," *Russkii biograficheskii slovar*; *Odessa, 1794–1894*, pp. 174–79.

43. Druzhinina, *Iuzhnaia Ukraina*, p. 195; *Odessa, 1794–1894*, p. xxx; Skinner, p. 124.

44. Vigel', *Vospominaniia*, 2: 107.

45. Skal'kovskii, "Iz portfelia," p. 237.

46. Batiushkov, *Sochineniia*, 3: 512–13.

47. Morozov, p. 72.

48. Smol'ianinov, *Istoriia*, pp. 172–80; Lyall, *Travels*, 1: 168–70; see also Herlihy, "Odessa Staple Trade," pp. 184–86.

49. Druzhinina, *Iuzhnaia Ukraina*, pp. 153, 196; Skal'kovskii, "Iz portfelia," p. 238.

50. Lyall, 1: 171. "The freedom of its port draws to it Russian and Polish ladies—Odessa is their Paris, which they are all bent on visiting at least once in their lives" (Hommaire de Hell, p. 7).

51. Druzhinina, *Iuzhnaia Ukraina*, p. 203; Smol'ianinov, *Istoriia*, pp. 171–72; Iakovkina, p. 171.

52. *Odessa, 1794–1894*, pp. 179–82.

53. Smol'ianinov, *Istoriia*, p. 173.

54. Borovoi, *Kredit*, p. 261.

55. Skal'kovskii, "Iz portfelia," pp. 239–40; *Odessa, 1794–1894*, p. 182; Skinner, pp. 147–48. For a detailed description of the significance of Odessa's free-port status, see Hagemeister, pp. 14–16.

56. Kohl, p. 429; Hommaire de Hell, p. 7; Herlihy, "Odessa Staple Trade," p. 188. The English traveler Bremner observed that in the 1820's about eight thousand Poles traveled to Odessa annually, most of them to do seasonal labor at the docks (p. 486).

57. Smol'ianinov, *Istoriia*, pp. 180–86; Subbotin, 2: 196–97.

58. Hommaire de Hell, pp. 2–3.

59. Bremner, p. 496; Smol'ianinov, *Istoriia*, p. 216.

60. Lestchinsky, "Odessa," p. 810; *Odessa, 1794–1894*, p. 188; Herlihy, "Greek Merchants," p. 402.

61. Haxthausen, 2: 58–59. See also Hagemeister, p. 219.

62. Kohl, pp. 419–20.

63. *Odessa, 1794–1894*, p. 190; Herlihy, "Odessa Staple Trade," p. 185; Puryear, p. 197; Skinner, p. 157.

64. Kohl, p. 426.

65. Brooks, pp. 35–36; Hommaire de Hell, p. 19; *Odessa, 1794–1894*, pp. 188–89.

66. Guernsey, p. 9.

67. Iakovkina, p. 167; Herlihy, "Russian Grain Trade," p. 89. See chap. 6, pp. 135–39.

68. Zagoruiko, 1: 74; Smol'ianinov, *Istoriia*, p. 161; Skinner, p. 124; Herlihy, "Death in Odessa," pp. 417–42.

69. "Odessa," *Entsiklopedicheskii slovar*.

70. Lestchinsky, "Odessa," p. 810.

71. *Ibid.* This compares with 43.6 percent for city's overall population in 1897; see Herlihy, "Ethnic Composition," p. 55.

72. Baron, *A Social and Religious History*, 2: 170–71; Dinur, *Be-Mifneh ha-dorot*, p. 39; Subbotin, 2: 230; Rashin, p. 147. By 1897 the population of Odessa was about 500,000. On the growth of the Jewish population of New Russia, see Margolis, p. 35. On Jewish immigration to the South in the 1860's, see *Ha-Melits*, May 11, 1868, pp. 151–52; Kuznets, p. 52; and Kabuzan, p. 249.

73. S. Levin, pp. 190–91.

74. See, for instance, *Biuletin*, pp. 1–2; Kahane, "Zikaron," p. 789.

75. *Israelitische Annalen*, July 30, 1841, p. 246; Tarnopol, *Notices*, pp. 61–64, 75; *Ha-Melits*, Aug. 22, 1863, pp. 497–502; Sosis, "Obshchestvennyia," p. 22; Kleinman, p. 36.

76. Levanda, no. 28, p. 23; no. 42, pp. 36–37.

77. Dubnow, *History of the Jews in Russia and Poland*, 1: 306–34; Rogger, "Government, Jews, Peasants, and Land in Post-Emancipation Russia," pp. 5–11; Ettinger, pp. 20–34.

78. Gessen, *Istoriia*, 1: 57–63; Pipes, p. 6.

79. Borovoi, "Evrei v Zaporozhskoi Sechi," pp. 151–58; Druzhinina, *Iuzhnaia Ukraina*, pp. 361–62; Baron, *The Russian Jew*, pp. 77–78.

80. Pen, p. 12.

81. "Odessa," *Evreiskaia entsiklopediia*; Lestchinsky, "Odessa," p. 809; Natanson, "Zikhronot," p. 229; Pen, p. 19.

82. Pen, p. 20; Kahane, "Zikaron," p. 789; Borovoi, "Evrei v Zaporozhskoi Sechi," pp. 151–58.

83. Minkowski, 1 (1918): 140–41.

84. Skal'kovskii, *Pervoe tridtsatiletie*, p. 277; Druzhinina, *Iuzhnaia Ukraina*, pp. 152–53; Pen, pp. 14, 28–30.

85. See Werbel's letter in Gottlober, 2: 82; see also Lyall, 1: 165, and *Odessa, 1794–1894*, p. 624.

86. Borovoi, *Evreiskaia zemledelcheskaia kolonizatsiia*, pp. 83–84.

87. Weinryb, *The Jews of Poland*, pp. 87–91.

88. Kahane, "Zikaron," p. 789.

89. Finkel, "Zur Geschichte der Juden in Odessa," p. 240.

90. Smol'ianinov, "Pervye gorodskie vybory v Odesse," pp. 1–2; Orlov, p. 45.

91. Trivush, p. 58; *Odesskii vestnik*, Aug. 6, 1859, p. 365.

92. *Odessa, 1794–1894*, p. 185.

93. Herlihy, "Odessa Staple Trade," p. 188. See chap. 5, pp. 122–24.

94. On the fluid boundaries of what constituted the Jewish quarter of Odessa during Richelieu's administration, see Pen, p. 21. A. Umanski suggests in his article on Odessa in *Die Judenpogrome in Russland*, ed. Leo Motzkin (Cologne, 1910), 2: 109, that a ghetto existed in Odessa's early years but offers no evidence to substantiate his assertion. On Jewish residence patterns in 1792–94, see "Zastroenie goroda Gadzhibeia," pp. 591–92. According to Arsh, p. 148, since the 1790's Greeks had also concentrated voluntarily in certain neighborhoods of the city.

Chapter Two

1. Yisroel Vaynlez in *Yosef Perles yidishe kesovim* (Warsaw, 1937), pp. ix–x; "Brody," *Evreiskaia entsiklopediia*, pp. 25–26.

2. Borovoi, "Odessa," p. 41; Skal'kovskii, *Pervoe tridtsatiletie*, p. 143; Wishnitzer, pp. 113–23. Lyall (1: 162) reports a settlement of three hundred Galician-Jewish families.

3. Tarnopol, *Notices*, p. 65.

4. Margolis, p. 69; Shohetman, p. 64; Bliumenfeld, Apr. 1884, p. 2; *Razsvet*, June 10, 1860, p. 35; Ianson, pp. 70–80; Tarnopol, *Notices*, pp. 137–42, 148–52; Nadav, pp. 227–35; Skal'kovskii, "O periodicheskikh izdaniiakh v Odesse," p. 4.

5. Borovoi, "Yisroel Aksenfeld," p. 179; Tarnopol, *Notices*, pp. 141–48, 182; Finkel, "Zur Geschichte der Juden in Odessa," p. 223; Herlihy, "Ethnic Composition," p. 65; Lestchinsky, "Odessa," p. 814. In the same period several Greeks, who reputedly had arrived in Odessa not long before with little if any capital, became leading commercial figures. See Arsh, p. 142.

6. Tarnopol, *Notices*, p. 66.

7. Finkel, "Zur Geschichte der Juden in Odessa," p. 246.

8. Shohat, "Ha-hanhagah be-kehillot rusiah," p. 200. See pp. 197–207 for a review of Odessa's Kehillah and Kehillot in other Russian Jewish communities. Also see Pen, pp. 22–23.

9. On the control of the Kehillot, see Levitats, p. 71.

10. Stanislavskii, p. 132.

11. Pozner, p. 8.

12. Ginzburg's Introduction to Lozinskii, p. viii; Pozner, pp. 3–4, 8.

13. Pozner, p. 5; McConnell, pp. 172–73; Vakar, p. 67.

14. Smol'ianinov, *Istoriia*, p. 197; *Odessa, 1794–1894*, p. 649; Stanislavskii, pp. 130–34; Zilbershtein, pp. 317–19; Beletskii, pp. 8–9; Finkel, "Zur Geschichte der Juden in Odessa," pp. 245–47.

15. Lerner, pp. 11–12. Elementary schools for Italian, Armenian, German, and Greek children already existed in the city, according to Kohl, p. 429. Two particularly impressive Greek private schools were opened in 1811, and a distinguished Greek commercial school was established in 1817. See Arsh, p. 212.

16. Lerner, pp. 7–8.

17. *Odessa, 1794–1894*, p. 624; "Elkan, Leon," *Evreiskaia entsiklopediia*. In the former source—the 1895 official history of Odessa—it is not clear whether Pototskii hoped Elkan's presence would attract Jews or Germans, since he is quoted as saying that he hoped Elkan would draw to the Odessa gymnasium the teacher's *edinozemtsy*, literally countrymen, rather than his *edinovertsy*, or coreligionists. It is therefore possible that Pototskii was referring to the by now fairly large German community.

18. *Odessa, 1794–1894*, p. 633. For several decades, local authorities would, like Pahlen and Pototskii, show their benevolence toward the city's Jewish community. This is particularly true of two governors-general: Mikhail Semenovich Vorontsov (1822–55) and Count Aleksandr Grigor'evich Stroganov (1855–62). When in 1843 the Ministry of the Interior began to consider distinguishing between "useful" and "useless" Jews on the basis of their occupation, Vorontsov submitted a memorandum stating that "one cannot help wondering how these numerous tradesmen can be regarded as useless and consequently as detrimental if one bears in mind that by their petty and frequently maligned pursuits they promote not only rural but also commercial life." The proposal, he insisted, was "cruel and unjust," and Jewish economic activity, whether wholesale or retail, was beneficial. As for Stroganov, when in 1856 the governors in the Pale were questioned by the Minister of the Interior about their attitude toward the proposed liberalization of residence restrictions for Jewish artisans, he urged that all restraints on Jewish residence and employment be ended because they were "not in accord with the spirit and tendency of the age." Stroganov's memorandum, the first call for complete Jewish emancipation by a high Russian official, was all the more remarkable since the governor-general tended to be conservative politically. See Dubnow, *History of the Jews in Russia and Poland*, 2: 64–65, 168–69. There is evidence that Stroganov looked briefly to local traditionalists to lead the community. See Bernstein, pp. 84–85.

19. Zilbershtein, pp. 317–19.

20. See Gottlober, 2: 93–95.

21. *Odessa, 1794–1894*, p. 649. See also Bonaventura Mayer, *Die Juden unserer Zeit* (Regensburg, 1842), p. 28. This work was pointed out to me by Michael Silber of the Hebrew University, Jerusalem.

22. See Tsederbaum, *Keter kehunah*, p. 138. The most neglected area in nineteenth-century Eastern European Jewish historiography is the his-

tory of traditionalists. The educational history of traditional Jewry, the transformation of Jewish folk religion into Orthodoxy, the community's response to the challenge of Haskalah, all of these still await systematic treatment. Traditionalists constituted the vast majority of Jews, but often we know of their activities only through the reports of their ideological adversaries, who produced the major primary and secondary sources. In the last few years, however, there have been signs of a nascent interest in the subject. (Of the handful of recent studies, those by Green, Etkes, and Stampfer are among the most impressive.) In his *Tradition* (London, 1981) Edward Shils considers why historians and sociologists have preferred to study modern rather than conservative trends (see especially pp. 1–33).

23. Alfasi, p. 82.

24. *Ziunim mezuyanim*, p. 23. Tarnopol observes that since the city's earliest years itinerant rebbes had "encouraged a spirit of fanaticism among certain elements of the community." See *Notices*, pp. 73–74.

25. Quoted in Gottlober, 2: 86.

26. A list of sayings about Odessa Jewry is in Joffe and Mark, p. 45.

27. Lerner, pp. 12–14; Gottlober, 2: 87.

28. In 1835 Odessa's traditionalists tried to stop the establishment of the modern school for girls, and two decades later the appointment of Dr. Aaron Goldenblum as director of the Talmud Torah, but their opposition was short-lived and ineffective. See Avner Tenenbaum, "Odessa," *Otsar Yisrael*, p. 146. For a summary of the conflicts between maskilim and their opponents elsewhere in this period, see Lachower, *Toledot*, 2: 192–210.

29. "Kazennye uchilishcha," file no. 1, YIVO Institute for Jewish Research.

30. Slutsky, p. 22.

31. "Prosveshcheniie," *Evreiskaia entsiklopediia*; Pozner, p. 15; Marek, p. 92; Scharfstein, 1: 281–85.

32. Scharfstein, 1: 279; Marek, p. 86; Stanislawski, pp. 98–100. See the estimated enrollment figures in Marek, pp. 80–87, and in *He-Avar*, 7 (1960): 34.

33. Finkel, "Zur Geschichte der Juden in Odessa," p. 247. Finkel, who taught Russian at the Jewish community school and was later the school's director, states that by 1843, 1,440 boys and 450 girls had attended the institution. Also see *Razsvet*, Oct. 7, 1860, pp. 317–18. On the girls' school, see Tarnopol, *Notices*, pp. 125–30.

34. Marek, p. 80; Scharfstein, 1: 285–86. Stanislawski disputes the assumption that the students in the government-sponsored schools were generally poor, though he admits that a "large percentage" may have been. Yet he offers little new data to substantiate his argument. He is on

much more solid ground when he examines how the schools affected the careers of their teachers, several of whom were leading maskilim, for the system offered them, he suggests, a steady, if perhaps not generous, income and thus helped solidify the standing of the Russian Haskalah. See Stanislawski, pp. 106–9.

35. The eulogy for Bezalel Stern, the school's director from 1829 to 1852, in the city's newspaper states that "the wealthy classes of the Jewish community as well as the poor" sent their children to the school, *Odesskii vestnik*, Aug. 10, 1853, p. 1; see also Gottlober, 2: 87–88.

36. *Ibid.*, p. 87.

37. Marek, pp. 105–9.

38. *Ibid.*, p. 108.

39. *Odesskii vestnik*, Aug. 15, 1849, pp. 1–2.

40. *Ibid.*, p. 2.

41. Morgulis, *Dor ha-haskalah be-rusiah*, pp. 44–46; Gessen, "Smena obshchestvennykh techenii," p. 22. See also Kahane, "Lilienthal," p. 550.

42. The school's largely Galician-born faculty was, of course, better acquainted with German than Russian. As late as the 1860's the community's Galician elite was still most comfortable with German. This, suggests Orbach, may help explain why before the appearance of Odessa's Yiddish newspaper, *Kol Mevasser*, articles in German were published in the Hebrew paper *Ha-Melits*. See Orbach, pp. 79–80.

43. According to Skal'kovskii, for instance, in *Opyt'*, 1: 308–16, three different types of Jews lived in New Russia: Karaites; Krimchaks (Crimean Jews); and Polish Jews, or "Talmudists." He described the Karaites as being very pleasing in appearance despite their Jewish ancestry; as having a gentle and humble disposition; and as working as craftsmen, farmers, sheepherders, and wine growers. Moreover, in Odessa (where about 220 Karaites lived in 1850) and Eupatoria they were engaged in trade with Turkey. According to Skal'kovskii, the Krimchaks, who resembled the Karaites in dress, language, and disposition, were far superior to the Polish Jews, though they shared with the latter a belief in the sanctity of the Talmud. The Krimchaks worked as artisans and conducted their economic and domestic lives in an orderly fashion, in contrast to the Polish Jews. The Karaites were held in such high esteem in Odessa largely because of the Karaite archaeologist Abraham Firkovich, whose work was sponsored by scholarly institutions in the city. On the debate over Firkovich's work, much of which was subsequently found to be based on forgeries, see Ha-Cohen, 1: 78–79. Simha Pinsker's *Likute kadmoniot* (1860), itself based in part on Firkovich's findings, caused considerable discussion among Jewish circles in Odessa, especially its provocative espousal of a possible union between Judaism and Karaitism. See Bernstein, p. 87.

44. *Odessa, 1794–1894*, p. 703.

45. *Ibid.* Druianov found this information improbable, noting that according to several sources, Simha Pinsker had difficulty raising money to buy books for his research. See his *Pinsker u-zemano*, pp. 208–9.

46. *Odessa, 1794–1894*, pp. 703–4.

47. Marek, p. 66; Scharfstein, 1: 281. In 1836 the average salary for an employee of the Ministry of the Interior was 260 rubles; in 1837 it fell to 212 rubles. See Lincoln, "The Daily Life of St. Petersburg Officials," pp. 97–98.

48. In 1850, for example, the community allocated 35,000 rubles for the building of the Beit Knesset Ha-Gadol—an enormous sum at the time. Pincus Minkowski, later cantor of the Brody Synagogue, commented in his memoirs on the sumptuous life led by Cantor Abras of the Beit Knesset Ha-Gadol. Rabbi Schwabacher, elected community rabbi in 1860, earned a salary of 5,000 rubles; his critics observed that the Chief Rabbi of the French Consistory earned only 9,000 francs, or the equivalent of 2,300 rubles. When Schwabacher arrived in Odessa, he asked that a carriage be put at his disposal—after all, the local Russian Orthodox archbishop had one. The communal leader, A. Brodskii, a powerful and stubborn opponent of the German rabbi, answered that he would only grant his request if Schwabacher was willing to forgo other pleasures denied the archbishop, such as a wife. Yet even though Schwabacher's request was breezily dismissed, it was not entirely absurd in view of the community's wealth. See Minkowski, 5: 141–47, 6: 79; Beilinson, pp. 72–73; "Poiasneniia," p. 7.

49. Gottlober, 1: 261.

50. *Odessa, 1794–1894*, p. 648. Writing in the 1860's, the inspector of a government-sponsored Jewish school in Berdichev credited the school's increasing enrollment to new economic incentives. Quoted in Marek, p. 159.

51. Gottlober, 2: 92; *Razsvet*, Oct. 7, 1860, p. 318; Stanislavskii, p. 145; Natanson, *Sefer ha-zikhronot*, p. 229; Finkel, "Zur Geschichte der Juden in Odessa," p. 247.

52. Lestchinsky, *Ha-Tefutsah ha-yehudit*, p. 116; Yuditski, pp. 8–9; Sosis, *Di geshikhte*, pp. 128–47.

53. Kotik, *Dos lebn*, pp. 26–27; Slutsky, p. 27.

54. Etkes, "*Teudah be-yisrael*," p. 7.

55. Finkel, "Zur Geschichte der Juden in Odessa," p. 224.

56. *Ibid.*

57. Morton, p. 275.

58. On the role of rabbis in Eastern European synagogues of the period, see Levitats, p. 158.

59. Gottlober, 2: 172.

60. Minkowski, 5: 140; "Abras, Ioshia," *Evreiskaia entsiklopediia*.

61. See chap. 3 for a discussion of the communal conflict in the 1860's between Odessa's so-called Galician and Polish-Russian Jews.

62. "Blumenthal, Nissan," *Evreiskaia entsiklopediia*; Natanson, *Sefer ha-zikhronot*, pp. 68–69.

63. Rabinovich, *Sochineniia*, 3: 373.

64. *Ibid.*, p. 377.

65. Natanson, *Sefer ha-zikhronot*, p. 69.

66. Rabinovich, *Sochineniia*, 3: 379.

67. See chap. 3.

68. On the Trachtenberg brothers—Berish, Moshe, Abraham, and Yehezhiel—see Klausner, *Historiah*, 2: 374.

69. Natanson, *Sefer ha-zikhronot*, pp. 67–69.

70. Etkes, "Parashat," pp. 285–313; Breiman, "Pulmus ha-tikunim ba-da'at," pp. 115–21.

71. *Odesskii vestnik*, Aug. 23, 1850.

72. *Ibid.* See Tarnopol's description of the synagogue's interior, *Notices*, pp. 104–5.

73. Alexander Tsederbaum, *Zikhron mikrah kodesh* (Odessa, 1850), pp. 4–7; *Odesskii vestnik*, Aug. 23, 1850. Tsederbaum's eight-page pamphlet describing this event was lithographed because before 1863 the printing of Jewish books was prohibited in Odessa (see chap. 4). According to bibliographer Moses Marx, it was the first Jewish publication produced in Odessa. See Marx's handwritten, untitled, and undated catalog of Jewish books printed in Odessa in the nineteenth century, Hebrew Union College–Jewish Institute of Religion, Klau Library, Cincinnati, Ohio.

74. See chap. 3.

75. Lefkowitz, p. 9. On the Odessa Jewish Clerk's Association Synagogue, in which an organ (as well as a female choir) was eventually introduced, see "Odessa," *Jewish Encyclopedia*, p. 381.

76. Mandelstamm, pt. 2, pp. 76–90. See also Etkes, "Parashat," esp. pp. 303–13, for a somewhat different account of these events. Etkes bases his argument primarily on a letter written by the conservative maskil Yehuda Leib Katznellenbogen, who, as Etkes himself admits, had good reason to minimize the contentious atmosphere in Vilna at the time. In "Parashat," moreover, Etkes neglects Mandelstamm's criticisms of Jewish institutional change in Vilna and elsewhere in this period as well as other indications of the enduring sense of powerlessness felt by Russian maskilim.

77. Mandelstamm, pt. 2, pp. 76–80. On the conflict over Guensburg's funeral, see also Paperna, "Zikhronot u-shemu'ot," pp. 151–54.

78. Mandelstamm, pt. 2, pp. 78–90. On the often bitter relations between Adam Ha-Cohen Lebensohn and other Vilna maskilim, see *Kitvey Y. L. Gordon* (Tel Aviv, 1928), pp. 38–42. On Lebensohn, see Kleinman, p. 42. According to Mahler, that Lebensohn, perhaps Vilna's most prominent maskil, knew no continental language shows how provincial and intellectually isolated Russian maskilim of this period were. See *Divrei yemei yisrael*, 2: 91–92.

79. Mandelstamm, pt. 2, pp. 78–82.

80. *Ibid.*, p. 81.

81. Etkes, "Parashat," p. 302; Ginzburg, *Historishe verk*, 2: 294.

82. M. Levin, pp. 89–90.

83. See Etkes, "Parashat," pp. 311–13.

84. M. Levin, p. 81.

85. *Odesskii vestnik*, Aug. 18, 1853, p. 1.

86. Gottlober, 2: 92.

87. See chap. 5.

88. Hommaire de Hell, p. 6.

89. Skal'kovskii, "Iz portfelia," p. 243; Pinkerton, p. 139.

90. Kirpichnikov, p. 394; Pen, p. 29.

91. Vsevolozhskii, 1: 100.

92. *Ibid.* The actress A. I. Shubert, who appeared on the Odessa stage in the 1860's, commented on the enthusiasm of Odessa Jews for the theater; Shubert, p. 226. See also Borovoi, "Yisroel Aksenfeld," p. 181.

93. See the summary of J. L. Finkel's 1842 *Odesskii vestnik* article in "Odesskie evrei," p. 346. Several young Jewish portrait painters achieved considerable local recognition in the 1850's and 1860's, and two of them, Werbel (son of Ilya Werbel, the Jewish community school teacher) and Shklovskii, were granted scholarships by local organizations so that they could pursue their studies in Italy. See Natanson, "Zikhronot," p. 190.

94. Minkowski, 5: 135.

95. Mikhnevich lists at the end of his book the names of the school's graduates, the dates of their graduations, and their occupations. The names, however, are listed without the patronymic, making it often impossible to identify the Jewish students, who frequently changed their first names. (In addition, some names, like Iaakob, were commonly used by Ukrainians as well as Jews.) Despite these problems, the list does indicate a large Jewish enrollment. At least three Jews graduated out of a class of twelve in 1840, two Jews in 1843, three in 1844 (including Leon Pinsker), perhaps as many as five in 1845, four in 1846, one in 1847, three in 1848, and two in 1849. According to the article on Odessa in *Otsar Yisrael*, eight Jews attended the Richelieu Lyceum in 1835; see p. 146. In comparison, the first Jewish student to attend the gymnasium at Eka-

terinoslav began his studies in 1851. See Harkavi and Goldberg, p. 23.

96. Quoted in Druianov, *Pinsker u-zemano*, p. 18.

97. On Rafalovich, see Mikhnevich, under the heading for graduates of 1840. See also "Rafalovich, Artemi A.," *Entsiklopedicheskii slovar*.

98. "Wahltuch, Mark," *Evreiskaia entsiklopediia*; Tarnopol, *Notices*, p. 183. See also A. Frenkel's article in the *Odesskii vestnik*, Feb. 19, 1853; and Mark Finkel's examination of local health facilities, *Odesskii vestnik*, Oct. 13, 1853.

99. D. Fridman published frequently in 1856 in the *Odesskii vestnik*. See May 31, pp. 313–14; July 28, p. 415; and Dec. 15, p. 703.

100. Lerner, pp. 40–41. Tarnopol contended, perhaps largely for polemical purposes, that most of the young Jews who had grown indifferent to Judaism had come from traditional, even obscurantist, homes and had been overwhelmed when they had encountered the larger world. A few, he admitted, had come from the community's "classe aisée"; see *Notices*, p. 96.

101. Lerner, pp. 42–43.

Chapter Three

1. See chap. 2, pp. 53, 58–59.

2. Sosis, "Obshchestvennyia," p. 21. The comments of the Jewish journalist Chatskin (*Russkii vestnik*, Sept. 1858, p. 136), indicate how Odessa was seen by russified Jewish intellectuals in this period. Chatskin defended the honor of his coreligionists during the controversy over a series of anti-Jewish articles in *Illiustratsiia* in 1858 by acknowledging the low cultural level of Jews in "West Russia" but asserting that enlightened Odessa Jewry should be taken into account in order to balance the picture. See Klier's summary in "The *Illiustratsiia* Affair of 1858," p. 125.

3. *Odessa, 1794–1894*, p. 190.

4. Lestchinsky, "Odessa," pp. 814–15; Subbotin, 2: 219; Ianson, p. 401. On Jewish bankers in Odessa in this period see Margolis, p. 59. Herlihy notes that a few of Odessa's Greek magnates did benefit from the Crimean War. See "Greek Merchants," pp. 416–17.

5. *Odesskii vestnik*, Feb. 14, 1851. The city's wealthiest merchant, Fedor Rodocannachi, declared a turnover of nearly 2 million rubles, as compared with the richest Jews, Abram Rafalovich (568,834 rubles) and Joachim Efrusi (366,126 rubles).

6. Bliumenfeld, May 1884, p. 2.

7. La Fite de Pellepore, 1: 300–302.

8. Schmidt, p. 511.

9. Tarnopol, *Notices*, p. 178.

10. *Ibid.*, pp. 143, 144.

11. See Hertzberg, pp. 179–93 for a discussion of Isaac Benarroch Pinto's *Apologie pour la nation Juive* (Amsterdam, 1762). A Hebrew translation of Simone Ben Isaac Simhah Luzzatto's *Discorso circa il stato de gl'Hebrei et in particolar dimoranti nell'-inclite città di Venetia* (1638) is *Ma'amar al yehudei venetsiah* (Jerusalem, 1950), by Dan Lates, with its fine introduction by Ricardo Bachi. Altmann (pp. 449–61) evaluates Christian Wilhelm Von Dohm's *Ueber die buergerliche Verbesserung der Juden* (1781, 1783). On the Russian Haskalah's use of economic arguments see M. Levin, pp. 160–86.

12. On the local Jewish school see Gottlober, 2: 98–99; for information on the Jewish hospital see *Odessa, 1794–1894*, p. 502, and Tarnopol, *Notices*, pp. 111–13. Religious education in the city is described in Slouschz, p. 29.

13. *Ha-Magid*, Oct. 6, 1859, p. 155.

14. *Sion'*, July 28, 1861, p. 64; Oct. 13, 1861, p. 239. See also *Odessa, 1794–1894*, p. 502; Beilinson, pp. 72–76. *Odesskii vestnik*, June 29, 1863; *Vestnik Russkikh Evreev*, Oct. 7, 1872, pp. 426–29.

15. *Den'*, Jan. 30, 1870, p. 66.

16. Tsinberg, *Istoriia*, pp. 29–34; Klier, "The Jewish Question." With the confidence typical of this period, a Jewish student from Zhitomir stated that the November 27, 1861, decree allowing Jews with certain academic degrees to enter government service was virtually a declaration of civic emancipation. See *Ha-Melits*, 2 (Feb. 8, 1862): 301. Dubnow observed that "because the old conditions were so inexpressibly ugly and unbearable, the mere loosening of the chains of servitude [during the reign of Alexander II] was hailed as a pledge of complete liberation," *History of the Jews*, 2: 155.

17. See Skinner, pp. 210–26; Shohat, "Ha-hanhagah," p. 203; Subbotin, 2: 195–96; *Jewish Chronicle*, Nov. 12, 1858, p. 6. See *Odesskii vestnik*, Feb. 5, 1851, pp. 1–2, for a list of the candidates elected to municipal office that year. Of the 50 members of the committee established in 1863 to reformulate the guidelines of the municipal government, at least 14 were Jewish; see *Odesskii vestnik*, Dec. 10, 1863, p. 596. In 1876 when the municipal duma set up a commission to examine the state of local trade, two of its four members were Jewish; see *Odessa, 1794–1894*, p. 235. On the status of Jews in municipal affairs elsewhere in the Pale before 1861, see Margolis, pp. 51–52. In the 1880's several prominent Odessa Jews became consuls for foreign states and countries: Simon Gurevich (Denmark), Ignace Efrati (Sweden and Norway), F. Rafalovich (Belgium), David Rafalovich (Hesse-Kassel), and Auguste Wolff (Mecklenburg).

18. On the revision of the concept of philanthropy in the nineteenth century, see Briggs, pp. 64–67. Traditional Eastern European Jewish attitudes toward charity are explored in Levitats, pp. 105–22, and Glicksman.

19. Balmuth, p. 2.

20. Klier, "The Jewish Question," p. 302; Berezina, p. 31.

21. Balmuth, p. 3.

22. Slutsky, p. 42; "Razsvet," *Evreiskaia entsiklopediia*; Bernstein, p. 83; Beilinson, p. 47.

23. *Razsvet*, May 19, 1861, pp. 830–31. On Pirogov see Shtraikh and Mogilevskii.

24. "Pirogov, Nikolai Ivanovich," *Evreiskaia entsiklopediia*; Morgulis, "Nikolai Ivanovich Pirogov," pp. 1–13.

25. Klier, "*Odesskii vestnik's* Annus Mirabilis of 1858," p. 42; Skabichevskii, pp. 411–16; Berman, *Do stolitnikh*, pp. 7–8.

26. See *Odesskii vestnik*, 1858, nos. 6, 7, and 14. See also Skabichevskii, p. 411.

27. On Troinitskii see "Iz bumag," p. 557, and Nikitenko, p. 242.

28. Slutsky, p. 41. Among the articles on Jewish themes published in the *Odesskii vestnik* after 1858 are those concerning the conflict over Rabbi Schwabacher, as cited later in this chapter.

29. Klier, "*Odesskii vestnik's* Annus Mirabilis of 1858," p. 43.

30. For example, see *Odesskii vestnik*, no. 65 (1849); no. 95 (1850); nos. 28, 78 (1851); nos. 29, 54, 105 (1854).

31. Sosis, "Obshchestvennyia," p. 26.

32. The article was reprinted in N. I. Pirogov, *Sochineniia*, 1: 54–65. In 1858, Alexander Tsederbaum translated it into Hebrew and published it in lithograph form in Odessa as *Talmud Torah be-Odessa*, adding an eighteen-page introduction to the six pages of Hebrew text. Herman Horowitz (whom Tarnopol lists as a Jewish writer in Odessa; *Notices*, p. 183) translated the article into English from the Russian and wrote a short introductory note. His translation was published in the *Jewish Chronicle*, May 14, 1858, p. 170.

33. Pirogov, *Sochineniia*, 1: 54–55, 57. Pirogov's position that Jews should not have to demonstrate assimilation in order to be granted emancipation was unusual for a Russian liberal of this period. More in keeping with the sentiments of his contemporaries were Pirogov's comments, later in the same essay, that the Jewish religion had been abused and distorted, but nonetheless retained at its core "nothing less than a mutilated good." The thrust of the essay suggests, however, an unconditional acceptance of Jewish emancipation.

34. Pirogov, *Sochineniia*, 1: 65.

35. Especially important was the response of the *Sankt Peterburgskiia vedomosti*, no. 81 (1858), summarized by Klier in "The Jewish Question," pp. 315–16. Also see the same newspaper, no. 101 (1858), and *Sovremennik*, no. 69 (1858).

36. Sosis, "Obshchestvennyia," p. 28.

37. On the reasons for the closing of *Razsvet* and *Sion'*, see Orbach, pp. 38–42, 51. Students of Yiddish literature have only recently become interested in Tsederbaum's role in establishing the Eastern European Jewish press. As Brainin observed in his short biographical sketch of Tsederbaum (*Zikhronot*, p. 3), "Five years have now passed since his death and there has been no writer, from all his many acquaintances and coworkers, who has cared to mention his name, either in praise or scorn." Brainin exaggerates in claiming that Tsederbaum's contribution has been entirely overlooked—see, for instance, *He-Asif*, Aug. 1893, pp. 169–71; and *Ha-Magid*, June 7, 1893, pp. 4–6. But the thrust of his statement is nonetheless accurate. For two recent appraisals of Tsederbaum see Shmeruk, chap. 8, and Orbach, pp. 54–71 and *passim*.

38. Brainin, *Zikhronot*, pp. 4–6, 9–10; Ha-Cohen, 1: 94; see the highly unfavorable portrait of Tsederbaum in Kabak, pp. 114–21. According to Orbach (p. 131), the controversy generated by Kovner's articles gave *Ha-Melits* "a freshness and an intimacy it had previously lacked."

39. See Etkes, "Teudah be-yisrael," pp. 7–8.

40. Miron, *Traveler*, p. 43. According to Tsitron (p. 12), the Yiddish spoken in Odessa was particularly impure, a "mishmash of Volhynian Yiddish with a Galician dialect."

41. Miron, *Traveler*, pp. 35, 47.

42. Tsitron, pp. 48–49. Bernstein, p. 88. Miron observes in *The Traveler Disguised*, p. 3, that while Avraham Mapu's Hebrew novel *Ahavat Zion* (1853) was considered an unqualified success for having sold 1,200 copies in the first two years after it was published, the Yiddish writer Isaac Meir Dick could boast in the 1860's that his novelettes had sold 100,000 copies.

43. Lilienblum, *Ketavim autobiografi'im*, 2: 15–18.

44. Deinard, *Zikhronot bat ami*, 1: 141.

45. Brainin, *Zikhronot*, p. 3.

46. Dubnow, *History of the Jews*, 2: 42–43; Bernshtayn, p. 17. On the origins of censorship regulations concerning Hebrew books, see B. Katz, 2: 176.

47. Abramovitsch, *Fishke*, pp. 133–35. The bibliographic information comes from Moses Marx's untitled and undated manuscript, listed as

"Jewish Books Published in Odessa in the Nineteenth Century," Hebrew Union College, Jewish Institute of Religion, Klau Library, Cincinnati, Ohio.

48. Tcherikover, pp. 239–40. A particularly rich source on the Odessa ORPME is Rosenthal, 2: 129–55.

49. Tcherikover, p. 241.

50. Mandelstamm, pt. 1, p. 98.

51. *Ibid.*

52. Quoted in Trivush, p. 61.

53. Jabotinsky, *Piatero*, p. 91.

54. Braudes, p. 7.

55. Brooks, pp. 25–26.

56. See, for instance, *Odesskii vestnik*, Nov. 14, 1861, p. 559. Compare this mild criticism of unwise allocations by the local Jewish community with the changes made in the late 1860's. See chap. 6, pp. 117–18.

57. Shohat, *Mosad*, pp. 43–46.

58. *Ibid.*, p. 9.

59. *Ibid.*, pp. 13–16; "Odessa," *Ha-Eshkol (Allgemeine entsiklopedie)* (Warsaw, 1888).

60. S. Levin, p. 99.

61. Shohat, *Mosad*, p. 20.

62. *Razsvet*, Sept. 16, 1860, p. 267.

63. Reikhesburg, pp. 8–13; *Voskhod*, June 1890, pp. 50–52; "Schwabacher, S. L.," *Evreiskaia entsiklopediia*.

64. Reikhesburg, p. 12.

65. *Razsvet*, May 27, 1860, p. 1.

66. *Ibid.*, June 3, 1860, pp. 19–20.

67. *Ibid.*, June 24, 1860, pp. 85–86.

68. *Ibid.*, p. 86.

69. Reikhesburg, p. 14.

70. Tarnopol, *Notices*, p. 66.

71. "Poiasneniia," p. 2.

72. Reikhesburg, p. 14.

73. *Sion'*, Feb. 2, 1862, p. 498. See also Feb. 9, 1862, pp. 508–11.

74. "Poiasneniia," p. 1.

75. *Ibid.*, pp. 3–5.

76. The commission suggested, ostensibly for considerations of space, that the altar be moved from the center of the sanctuary to the front of the room—where it was located in contemporary German synagogues.

77. *Sion'*, Oct. 13, 1861, p. 240.

78. "Poiasneniia," p. 5.

79. *Odesskii vestnik*, Nov. 24, 1862.

80. *Ibid.*, Mar. 16, 1863, pp. 139–40.

81. *Ibid.*, p. 140. On Dovid Twersky's visit see Osip Rabinovich, "Tsadik v tsenakh Odessy." See also the discussion on this essay in chap. 4.

82. See Slutsky's comments on *Sion'* (pp. 46–52).

83. See *Sion'*, Sept. 1, 1861, p. 141.
84. *Ibid.*
85. *Ibid.*, p. 149.
86. *Ibid.*, pp. 142–43.
87. *Ibid.*, pp. 143–44.
88. *Ibid.*

Chapter Four

1. Russian-language supplement to *Ha-Karmel*, Dec. 8, 1861.
2. As it happens, all studies dealing with Odessa's Jewish intelligentsia of the 1860's have focused almost exclusively on the ways such intellectuals balanced their apparently contradictory commitments in order to criticize as well as defend Jewish communal interests. See, for instance, Tsinberg, *Di geshikhte*, vol. 9; Slutsky, pp. 37–85; Orbach, chap. 2 and *passim*. For a recent review of Osip Rabinovich's literary works, see Simon Markish, "Osip Rabinovič," pp. 5–30, 135–58.
3. Garmiza, p. 21.
4. Gessen, *Galleria*, pp. 7–8.
5. *Ibid.*, p. 14; Garmiza, p. 16.
6. See "Advokatura v Rossii," *Evreiskaia entsiklopediia*.
7. Gessen, *Galleria*, p. 14.
8. *Razsvet*, Sept. 23, 1860, pp. 283–84.
9. For a general discussion of this literature, see Mintz, pp. 71–110.
10. Gessen, *Galleria*, p. 15.
11. Garmiza, p. 18.
12. *Odesskii vestnik*, Nov. 18, 1850.
13. See Owen, pp. 1–28; Bill, pp. 245–58.
14. *Odesskii vestnik*, Nov. 15, 1850.
15. Tsinberg, *Di geshikhte*, 9: 64–65.
16. Gessen, *Galleria*, pp. 15–16; Garmiza, p. 18.
17. Gessen, *Galleria*, p. 18; the death of his father in 1852 may also have affected his productivity. On the general decline of cultural activity at the end of Nicholas's reign, see Lincoln, *Nicholas I*, pp. 316–24.
18. In the 1858 *Odesskii vestnik*, Rabinovich published "Istoriia odnoi palka" (June 7, pp. 291–92); a selection from "Kaleidoskop" (Jan. 7, pp. 7–8), and "O Moshkakh i Ios'kakh" (Jan. 23, p. 39).
19. "O sobstvennykh imenakh evreev," *Novorossiiskii literaturnyi sbornik* (1859).
20. See Tchernikhovsky's rather jaundiced appraisal of Jewish literature in Russian, "Russkoevreiskaia khudozhestvennaia literatura," *Evreiskaia entsiklopediia*.
21. "O Moshkakh i Ios'kakh," *Sochineniia*, 3: 51, 53, 56, 59, 62.
22. Dumashevskii, pp. 111–12. On Dumashevskii see Rashkovskii, pp.

29–36. That "Moshkakh" was the first article on a Jewish theme in the 1858 *Odesskii vestnik* might have contributed to the surprise of readers like Dumashevskii who had high expectations for the periodical.

23. Dumashevskii, pp. 111–12.

24. See the informative discussion in Slutsky, pp. 301–5; see also Klier, "The Jewish Question," pp. 301–19.

25. Gessen, *Galleria*, p. 40; Garmiza, p. 20. On the influence of *Shtrafnoi* on the work of Perets Smolenskin, see Klausner, *Historiah*, 5: 37.

26. Tsinberg, *Istoriia*, pp. 39–45; Slutsky, pp. 41–43.

27. Slutsky, p. 52.

28. Quoted in Orbach, pp. 35–36.

29. See Tsinberg's discussion of maskilic beliefs about the way in which Jewish–non-Jewish relations would improve in *Di geshikhte*, 9: 64–65.

30. "Iz bumag," p. 556.

31. *Den'*, June 27, 1869, pp. 101–2.

32. *Ibid.*, p. 101.

33. *Razsvet*, Oct. 14, 1860, pp. 331–32.

34. *Razsvet*, May 27, 1860, p. 1.

35. *Razsvet*, Dec. 2, 1860, p. 443.

36. Dovid Twersky, member of an eminent Hasidic family, lived in Talnoye, in Kiev province. See *Otsar ha-rabanim*, p. 111, citation no. 5178; "Chernobyl'skaia familiia tsadikov," *Evreiskaia entsiklopediia*.

37. *Razsvet*, Dec. 2, 1860, p. 443.

38. *Ibid.*, pp. 443–44.

39. *Ibid.*, p. 444.

40. Faddei Berezkin, "Istoriia khasidizma," *Odesskii vestnik*, Feb. 18, 1861, pp. 83–84.

41. Tarnopol, *Opyt'*, p. 19. Tarnopol observed in *Notices* that those Odessa Hasidim who engaged in commercial activity generally showed a commendable honesty; he also complimented Hasidim for their exemplary family life. See pp. 73, 138.

42. *Razsvet*, June 17, 1860, p. 52.

43. *Ibid.*

44. *Razsvet*, June 3, 1860, p. 19.

45. *Razsvet*, Nov. 18, 1860, p. 412.

46. In the absence of subscription lists, we can determine the approximate size of *Razsvet*'s Odessa readership by the lists of contributors to the philanthropic causes promoted by the newspaper, which generally specified the city of each giver. The most extensive campaign was a collection for Christians being massacred by Druze and Moslems in Syria. Of the 545 contributors to the fund—the newspaper having at no time, according to Rabinovich himself, more than 640 subscribers—240 were listed as

living in Odessa. Forty-eight lived in Kremenchug, 42 in Kishinev, 39 in Dvinsk, 37 in Ekaterinoslav, 28 in St. Petersburg, and 16 in Kherson. See *Razsvet*, nos. 11–24, 26, 27, 29.

47. See Gessen, "Pis'ma O. A. Rabinovicha," p. 80. Rabinovich is more equivocal on this point in his article in *Razsvet*, June 1, 1860; yet even here he expressed optimism as to the potential outcome of Jewry's russification.

48. *Razsvet*, June 10, 1860, pp. 35–36.

49. *Jewish Chronicle*, Jan. 20, 1860, p. 6.

50. Dumashevskii, p. 111.

51. *Yalkut Volin*, pp. 6–8.

52. Tchernowitz, *Pirkei hay'im*, pp. 181–82.

53. Lestchinsky suggests this reason for the difference in the cultural development of the Jewish commercial elites of Warsaw and Odessa. See *Ha-Tefutsah ha-yehudit*, p. 94. See also Kahan, "Notes," p. 112.

54. Marek, pp. 166–68; Pozner, pp. 54–61; "Prosveshchenie," *Evreskaia entsiklopediia*; Slutsky, p. 27; *Ha-Melits*, July 2, 1864, pp. 402-3. In the city of Grodno, for instance, 10 Jewish students attended the city's two gymnasiums in 1867, and by 1870 there were 40. (In 1887 the city's Jewish population was 27,373.) See Rabin, p. 95.

55. Smolenskin, *Ha-Toeh*, 4: 112.

56. See Tsederbaum's observations in *Ha-Melits*, 4 (1864): 403. In 1864 a commission evaluating the government-sponsored Jewish school system recommended that it be closed since local Jewish parents did not hesitate to send their children to Russian schools. See the report of A. Postel, as translated and summarized in *Ha-Melits*, 4 (1864): 405–6.

57. *Trudy Odesskago statisticheskago komiteta* (Odessa, 1867), pp. 179–93; Druianov, *Pinsker u-zemano*, p. 20.

58. Smolenskin, *Simhat hanef*, p. 25.

59. *Ibid.*, p. 23. Indeed, Smolenskin, who lived in Odessa between 1862 and 1867 and supported himself as a tutor, offered French lessons though he had only a rudimentary knowledge of the language. See Brainin, *Perets ben Moshe Smolenskin*, p. 31.

60. Smolenskin, *Simhat hanef*, pp. 60–61. See also Levanda, in *Den'*, Aug. 1, 1860, p. 510.

61. Quoted in the *Jewish Chronicle*, Nov. 26, 1858.

62. See, for instance, Y. Berman, p. 25.

63. Russian supplement to *Ha-Karmel*, May 17, 1860, p. 30. See chap. 7, p. 134.

64. Jabotinsky, *Autobiografiah*, pp. 19–21.

65. Quoted in Mintz, p. 90.

66. See pp. 141–50.

67. Tsinberg, *Istoriia*, pp. 43–44.
68. *Budushchnost'*, vol. 1, no. 2, (1900).
69. Tarnopol in *Ha-Magid*, Nov. 21, 1860, pp. 178–79.
70. Tsinberg, *Istoriia*, p. 44.
71. Tarnopol, *Opyt'*, p. 20. Tarnopol's political conservatism is particularly evident in his comments on the deleterious impact of the uprisings of 1848 on local commercial life (*Notices*, p. 141).
72. *Opyt'*, pp. 20–23, 183–84.
73. *Ibid.*, pp. 19–20.

Chapter Five

1. Gessen, *Istoriia*, 2: 206; *Jewish Chronicle*, May 19, 1871.
2. Orshanskii, p. 156.
3. Sosis, "Period 'obruseniia,'" p. 132; Kornilov, p. 381.
4. Gessen, *Istoriia*, 2: 200–201; John D. Klier, "Iakov Brafman's *Book of the Kahal* and Its Enemies," paper presented at the Midwest Slavic Conference, May 4, 1980; Hans Rogger, "Government, Jews, Peasants," p. 17.
5. Mishkinsky, pp. 49–52; Druianov, *Pinsker u-zemano*, pp. 102–4.
6. *Jewish Chronicle*, May 19, 1871; Skinner, pp. 229–31; Sosis, "Period 'obruseniia,'" p. 142. The sections of the 1870 municipal code directly relevant to Jews are reproduced in Levanda, no. 1041, pp. 1124–25.
7. Sosis, "Period 'obruseniia,'" pp. 129–30; Orshanskii, pp. 8–9. An article in *Ha-Melits*, May 11, 1868, p. 152, describes how Jewish emigrants from Lithuania to the Ukraine returned home considerably poorer than they had been.
8. See Isaak Babel, *Benya Krik*.
9. Natanson, "Zikhronot," p. 198; Lestchinsky, "Odessa," pp. 814–19.
10. Tchernikhovsky, "Lilienblum," p. 840.
11. Oislender, p. 150.
12. *Ibid.* I have been unable to locate Dantsig's novel, which is described on the same page. See Tarnopol's description of the city's slums in *Notices*, pp. 152–53. On Moldavanka, see also Smolenskin, *Ha-Toeh*, 1: 87–91; Borovoi, "Odessa," p. 44; Epstein, pp. 42–43. For a more sanguine description of the condition of Odessa's working class in the 1870's, see Lilienblum, *Kol kitvey*, 2: 137.
13. Borovoi, "A fargesener nihilist," pp. 474–84; Frankel, pp. 28–37.
14. "Greece," *Encyclopedia Judaica*; Shparo, p. 40.
15. Kogen, pp. 263–64. On Odessa's Greek community and their participation in anti-Ottoman agitation in the 1820's and earlier, see Karidis, "A Greek Mercantile paroikia," pp. 111–36.
16. Kogen, pp. 262–66.

17. Smol'ianinov, *Istoriia*, p. 182.

18. Lestchinsky, "Di sotsiale ontviklung," p. 203.

19. Sosis, "Obshchestvennyia," pp. 35–36.

20. *Ibid.*, p. 26; "Galats," *Evreiskaia entsiklopediia*.

21. Sosis, "Obshchestvennyia," pp. 36–37; "Goneniia na evreev v Odesse," *Odesskii vestnik*, June 27, 1859, pp. 300–301; *Ha-Magid*, Aug. 24, 1859.

22. Slutsky, pp. 41–42.

23. Sosis, "Obshchestvennyia," pp. 38–39.

24. *Ibid.*, pp. 40–41.

25. Morgulis, "Bezporiadki," pp. 44–45. This article contains a detailed description of the pogrom based on information collected immediately after the disturbance by A. Passover and I. A. Chatskin. The *Odesskii vestnik*'s reports on the pogrom were reprinted in *Illiustrirovannaia gazeta*, Apr. 22, 1871, pp. 225–27 (the *Odesskii vestnik* for the years after 1863 is unavailable outside the Soviet Union); the articles on the pogrom in the *Sankt Peterburgskiia vedomosti* were quoted at length in both *Vestnik Russkikh Evreev*, May 23, 1871, pp. 638–41, and *Den'*, May 22, 1871. Many Jewish newspapers abroad carried news about the pogrom, but the best coverage may be found in the 1871 *Allgemeine Zeitung des Judenthums*, Apr. 25, May 2, May 9, May 23, June 20, and July 11. I came upon a copy of the anonymous pamphlet *Opisanie Odesskikh ulichnykh bezporiadkov* after writing this chapter, but its report—perhaps written by Passover and Chatskin—does not contradict other sources.

26. *Den'*, May 29, 1871, p. 330; *Hebrew Leader*, May 12, 1871.

27. Morgulis, "Bezporiadki," pp. 49–50; *Illiustrirovannaia gazeta*, Apr. 22, 1871, pp. 225–26; *Jewish Chronicle*, May 19, 1871; *Allgemeine Zeitung des Judenthums*, May 2, 1871, pp. 358–59. For an account of the sacking of Rabinovich's home, see Y. Berman, p. 59. On the loss of Aksenfeld's works, see Reisen, 1: 161.

28. Morgulis, "Bezporiadki," pp. 50–55; Chudnovskii, pp. 42–45; *Illiustrirovannaia gazeta*, Apr. 22, 1871, pp. 226–27; *Hebrew Leader*, May 12, 1871. For a particularly vivid description of the pogrom, see the deposition of William Newmann, an Englishman living in Odessa, PRO, FO 258/7.

29. Morgulis, "Bezporiadki," pp. 55–61; *Evreiskaia starina*, Apr.–June 1913, pp. 201–2; *Illiustrirovannaia gazeta*, Apr. 22, 1871, p. 227. On June 23, 1871, the *Jewish Chronicle* quoted the correspondent of Vienna's *Neue Freie Presse* as saying, "Four thousand families are in utter destitution, . . . sixteen persons have been murdered; sixty seriously wounded; females have been brutally violated; a mother who was trying to prevent her daughter being outraged had her ears cut off, and died from loss of blood."

30. Orshanskii, pp. 161–68.

31. See, for instance, the *Jewish Chronicle*, July 28, 1871.

32. On the response of the Russian intelligentsia to the charges of *Illiustratsiia*, see Tsinberg, *Istoriia*, pp. 34–35.

33. Orshanskii, "K kharakteristike," p. 161; *Jewish Chronicle*, May 19, 1871.

34. See *Vestnik Russkikh Evreev*, May 23, 1871, pp. 638–41; *Den'*, May 22, 1871, pp. 313–16.

35. Morgulis, "Bezporiadki," pp. 42–44.

36. *Den'*, May 29, 1871.

37. Klier, "The Jewish *Den'*," pp. 25–26, 31. Klier observes that the *Den'* article dealing with the pogrom appeared without the familiar formula "Due to circumstances beyond our control . . . ," which would have alerted readers that censorship restrictions prohibited a fuller discussion of the topic.

38. Slutsky, pp. 68–69. See Shohetman's list of Jewish periodicals published in Odessa (pp. 98–105).

39. Tcherikover, pp. 249–52. See chap. 6, p. 140.

40. *Opisanie Odesskikh ulichnykh bezporiadkov*, pp. 11–12.

41. Kulisher, "K 25-letiiu so dnia smerti I. G. Orshanskago," p. 29.

42. "Orshanskii, Ilya Grigor'evich," *Evreiskaia entsiklopediia*; *The Christian*, Mar. 3, 1887.

Chapter Six

1. *Ha-Tsefirah*, Oct. 15, 1876, p. 315.

2. *Razsvet*, Aug. 2, 1880, pp. 1376–77.

3. "Prosveshchenie," *Evreiskaia entsiklopediia*; Tsinberg, *Istoriia*, p. 233; Slutsky, p. 27; *Razsvet*, Oct. 4, 1879, pp. 126–28; Sinel, p. 203.

4. *Ha-Magid*, Apr. 30, 1879, p. 133.

5. *Russkii evrei*, Oct. 1, 1879, p. 156; *Ha-Tsefirah*, Sept. 23, 1874, pp. 90–91; *Ha-Magid*, Feb. 7, 1872, p. 62.

6. *Razsvet*, Oct. 25, 1879, pp. 269–71; Sept. 18, 1880, pp. 1499–1501.

7. Rosenthal, *Toledot*, 2: 158.

8. See, for instance, *Razsvet*, Oct. 11, 1879, pp. 169–70, Nov. 15, 1879, pp. 376–77, April 17, 1880, pp. 611–15; *Ha-Magid*, Apr. 30, 1879, p. 133.

9. Lilienblum, *Igrot*, p. 80; Lilienblum, *Ketavim autobiografi'im*, 2: 16–17; Aaron Lita, "Ben kefar she-ba le-krakh; pirkei zikhronot al' Odessa," *He-Avar*, 14 (1967): 178; *Ha-Tsefirah*, Feb. 18, 1876, pp. 58–59.

10. File on Michael Zametkin, Bund Archives of the Jewish Labor Movement.

11. *Ha-Lebanon*, July 25, 1874, p. 29.

12. *Ha-Magid*, July 23, 1873, pp. 265–66.

13. *Razsvet*, May 8, 1880; PRO, FO 258/8.
14. *Ha-Tsefirah*, Aug. 26, 1874, pp. 58–59.
15. *Ha-Tsefirah*, Feb. 25, 1876, p. 68.
16. *Ha-Tsefirah*, Sept. 20, 1878, p. 301.
17. PRO, FO 181/591. See also Deich, pp. 37–42, and *passim*.
18. PRO, FO 181/547; *Odessa, 1794–1894*, pp. 98–101. The firm was late in providing the services to the city it had contracted for.
19. *Jewish Chronicle*, May 25, 1877, p. 6.
20. *Ha-Tsefirah*, Dec. 19, 1877, pp. 379–80.
21. *Ha-Tsefirah*, Sept. 23, 1874, pp. 90–91; see also *Ha-Tsefirah*, June 30, 1876, pp. 204–5. The writer was Elimelekh Veksler, an Odessa correspondent for Warsaw's *Ha-Tsefirah*, whose many reports offer a reliable and detailed source of local news. See his autobiographical sketch in Sokolow, pp. 140–46.
22. *Ha-Tsefirah*, Mar. 15, 1877, pp. 92–93.
23. *Razsvet*, June 26, 1880, pp. 1016–17; Dec. 22, 1879, pp. 578–79.
24. Lilienblum, *Ketavim autobiografi'im*, 2: 145–46. On the yeshiva itself see *Razsvet*, Oct. 18, 1879, p. 213.
25. On Beseda see *Russkii evrei*, Dec. 5, 1879, pp. 515–16, and *Ha-Tsefirah*, Feb. 10, 1875, p. 42. An optimistic appraisal of Jewish-gentile relations in nearby Anan'ev may be found in *Razsvet*, Jan. 31, 1880, pp. 171–72. The article mentions several local philanthropic efforts involving Jews and gentiles but offers no evidence of increased social interaction.
26. *Razsvet*, Aug. 28, 1880, pp. 1376–77. For a discussion of the impact of the Russo-Turkish war on relations between Russians and Jews, see Tsinberg, *Istoriia*, pp. 234–35.
27. *Russkii evrei*, Sept. 9, 1879, p. 37.
28. PRO, FO 257/7.
29. PRO, FO 257/15.
30. Chudnovskii, p. 30.
31. Harkavi and Goldberg, pp. 21–26; *Ha-Karmel*, Oct. 6, 1866, p. 163; Afans'ev-Chuzbinskii, pp. 57–60.
32. Zolotov, *Khlebnyi eksport Rossii*, pp. 38, 98, 113; "Nikolaev," *Entsiklopedicheskii slovar'*; PRO, FO 257/15. For a discussion of the deterioration of Odessa's port facilities in the 1860's, see PRO, FO 258/6.
33. *Russkii evrei*, Sept. 9, 1879, pp. 40–41, and Oct. 1, 1879, pp. 156–57.
34. PRO, FO 257/7.
35. *Russkii evrei*, Oct. 1, 1879, pp. 156–57.
36. *Ibid.*
37. *Razsvet*, July 31, 1880, pp. 1218–21.
38. *Ha-Magid*, Jan. 29, 1873, p. 40.
39. Gruzenberg, p. 5.

40. See, for instance, PRO, FO 257/7 on relations between Jews and authorities in the city of Kherson.

41. Zolotov, *Khlebnyi eksport Rossii*, pp. 112–14; Siegelbaum, pp. 121–23.

42. PRO, FO 181/547.

43. Siegelbaum, pp. 127–28; Zolotov, *Khlebnyi eksport Rossii*, pp. 114–15.

44. PRO, FO 181/547.

45. *Ibid.*

46. Zolotov, *Khlebnyi eksport Rossii*, p. 44. For a report on the railway system in South Russia, see PRO, FO 257/15.

47. Siegelbaum, pp. 128–31.

48. *Ha-Magid*, Nov. 25, 1874, p. 410, Dec. 2, 1874, pp. 417–18; *Ha-Tsefirah*, May 12, 1875, pp. 138–39.

49. *Ha-Tsefirah*, Aug. 26, 1874, p. 58, June 20, 1875, p. 219, Nov. 24, 1875, pp. 207–8; *Russkii evrei*, Feb. 4, 1881.

50. *Ha-Tsefirah*, Oct. 15, 1875, pp. 324–25; Mar. 25, 1879, p. 99.

51. Halkin discusses the equation of Haskalah with education, pp. 37–38.

52. See, for instance, Sosis, *Di geshikhte*, p. 127; Tsinberg, *Istoriia*, pp. 234–35.

53. Rosenthal, 2: 155–60; Tcherikover, pp. 291–94.

54. See B. Netanyahu's translation of Pinsker's work in *Road to Freedom*.

55. E. R. Malachi, "Le-Korot toledot Pinsker," a newspaper clipping from *Ha-Arets* (n.d.) in CZA A9/175, AM 646-1.

56. Though based on secondhand reports, the standard account of his conversion is in Lilienblum, *Kol kitvey*, 4: 182. An annotated bibliography of secondary material on Pinsker may be found in CZA A9/175 AM/646/1. An indication of how little is known about Pinsker in the 1870's is the cursory review Druianov gives of this period in his otherwise detailed *Pinsker u-zemano*, pp. 96–128. A brief but perceptive biographical sketch is included in Vital, pp. 122–32.

57. Lilienblum's autobiographies, *Hat'ot Neurim* (1876) and *Derekh Teshuva* (1899), have been meticulously annotated by Shlomo Breiman in Lilienblum, *Ketavim autobiografi'im*. Breiman includes a biography in 1: 7–70. Also useful is his introduction to the correspondence between Lilienblum and the poet Y. L. Gordon; see Lilienblum, *Igrot*, pp. 9–61. (Lilienblum integrated several of his letters to Gordon into his first autobiography.) An appendix to Breiman's introduction to *Ketavim autobiografi'im*, 1: 71–74, contains a bibliography of secondary works, mostly relevant to Lilienblum's career after 1881. Y. Klausner's bibliography on Lilienblum is helpful; see his *Historiah*, 4: 190–92.

58. The first volume of *Hat'ot Neurim* reviews Lilienblum's life until his arrival in Odessa. Sec *Ketavim autobiografi'im*, vol. 1.

59. Lilienblum, *Ketavim autobiografi'im*, 2: 23, 103.

60. See Breiman's introduction to *Ketavim autobiografi'im*, 1:20-23.

61. Lilienblum, *Kol kitvey*, 2: 5–6.

62. Lilienblum, *Ketavim autobiografi'im*, 2: 23, 50–51, 115, 132. For a discussion of the Yiddish articles that Lilienblum published in 1870, when he was an editor of *Kol Mevasser*, see Reisen, 2: 158–59.

63. Pomper, p. 72. See also Venturi, pp. 316–30. For a perceptive overview of Pisarev, see Lampert, pp. 295–338.

64. Brower, pp. 69–107.

65. On Lilienblum's belief in his own specialness, see *Ketavim autobiografi'im*, 2: 76. Deich suggests, in his study of Jews in the Russian revolutionary movement, that nihilism's stress on elitism was an important reason for its appeal among young Jews.

66. See, for instance, Lilienblum, *Ketavim autobiografi'im*, 2: 15–18.

67. Lilienblum, *Kol kitvey*, 2: 49–51, 96.

68. Lilienblum, *Ketavim autobiografi'im*, 2: 114.

69. *Ibid.*, p. 93.

70. Lilienblum, *Kol kitvey*, 2: 116.

71. On Mapu's novel, see Patterson, *Abraham Mapu*, pp. 26–38 and *passim*.

72. Lilienblum, *Kol kitvey*, 2: 53–54.

73. *Ibid.*, 2: 52, 55.

74. *Ibid.*, 2: 57–58.

75. *Ibid.*, 2: 59, 62–63.

76. *Ibid.*, 2: 96, 103–4. See also Lilienblum, *Ketavim autobiografi'im*, 2: 79. This contrast between small-town and big-city Jewish youths is a persistent motif in Kovner's nihilist writings. See Sosis, *Di geshikhte*, pp. 118–21.

77. For example, on the Jewish nihilists Abraham Uri Kovner and Joseph Yehudah Lerner, see Weinreich; Borovoi, "A fargesener nihilist," pp. 473–84; and Sokolow, p. 66.

78. Lilienblum, *Ketavim autobiografi'im*, 2: 94.

79. Lilienblum, *Kol kitvey*, 2: 15, and *Ketavim autobiografi'im*, 2: 74, 123–25. See also Breiman's introduction to *Ketavim autobiografi'im*, p. 51.

80. Kramer, pp. 24–25; Ginzburg, *Meshumodim*, pp. 171–93.

81. Lilienblum's most politically radical statement is "Mishnat Elisha ben Avuyah," an 1878 Hebrew essay espousing productivization and social justice rather than socialism per se. Reprinted in *Kol kitvey*, 2: 180–200.

82. Lilienblum, *Ketavim autobiografi'im*, 2: 51, 81.

83. *Ibid.*, p. 51.

84. *Ibid.*, p. 97.
85. *Ibid.*, pp. 96–99, 133–35.
86. Quoted in Druianov, "Mi-'Sefer zikhronot,'" p. 402.
87. Lilienblum, *Ketavim autobiografi'im*, 2: 53–62, 74, 116–18.
88. *Ibid.*, 2: 126–28.
89. *Ibid.*, 2: 12. For a brief sketch of Shereshevsky (who, after he left Odessa for Rostov-on-Don, supported himself as a Jewish bookseller and as a secretary of the local Jewish burial society), see Kressel, *Leksikon*, p. 981.
90. Tchernowitz, *Masekhet zikhronot*, p. 42. Also see Lilienblum, *Ketavim autobiografi'im*, 2: 124; Lilienblum, *Kol kitvey*, 2: 52.
91. See in particular the bitter letter to his wife published in *Hat'ot Neurim*, as reprinted in *Ketavim autobiografi'im*, 2: 39–43.
92. Lilienblum, *Ketavim autobiografi'im*, 2: 10.
93. See Lilienblum, *Kol kitvey*, 1: 168–78, and 2: 122–54.
94. Lilienblum, *Ketavim autobiografi'im*, 2: 168.
95. See Frankel, p. 86.
96. *Ibid.*, p. 87.

Conclusion

1. See Levinsky, 2: 494–502.
2. Braudes, p. 47.

Bibliography

Because archival material pertaining to Jews in Tsarist Russia is inaccessible (except for certain specialized collections concerning Lithuanian Jewry, Jewish socialism, and Zionism), the Jewish and non-Jewish press must be a primary resource. The *Odesskii vestnik*—which appeared twice weekly from 1828 to 1853 and thrice weekly until 1864, when it became a daily—was chiefly a commercial organ, but it devoted considerable space to Jewish affairs. Of course, reports in the *Vestnik* that do not deal specifically with Jews can also illuminate local Jewish history. The Jewish weekly newspapers published in Odessa from 1860 to 1871—*Razsvet*, *Sion'*, *Den'*, *Ha-Melits*, and (to a lesser extent) *Kol Mevasser*—naturally contain much highly useful information. Other Jewish newspapers, which catered to a Russian Jewish or Polish Jewish readership and were published outside of Odessa, also carried news about Odessa, especially *Ha-Magid*, *Ha-Karmel*, and *Ha-Tsefirah*. The coverage of Odessa by the correspondent of Warsaw's *Ha-Tsefirah* was particularly detailed and reliable. (To be sure, as such newspapers were produced for didactic purposes by proponents of Jewish enlightenment, one must use them prudently and extract carefully the wealth of available data from often highly tendentious articles.) Periodicals such as *Ha-Boker or*, *Ha-Shahar*, *Knesset Israel*, and *Voskhod* focused much attention on Odessa, as did later journals such as *Evreiskaia starina*, *Perezhitoe*, and *Reshumot*. Two Russian newspapers with especially good coverage of Odessa Jewish affairs are the *Sankt Peterburgskiia vedomosti* and *Illiustrirovannaia gazeta*. Jewish newspapers abroad paid considerable attention to Odessa, especially the *Allgemeine Zeitung des Judenthums*, *Der Orient*, the *Jewish Chronicle*, and the *Hebrew Leader*.

Some archival material directly relevant to this study can be found in the YIVO Institute for Jewish Research, in New York. The Bund Archives of the Jewish Labor Movement, also in New York, are a useful source of information on Jewish labor leaders born in the New Russia region. The Mosessohn Collection, Klau Library, Hebrew Union College–Jewish Institute of Religion, Cincinnati, Ohio, is a unique and still uncatalogued cache of primary material that belonged to Moshe Ha-Dayyan, an important Odessa rabbi. The Klau Library also has a manuscript by Moses Marx that lists Hebrew and Yiddish books published in Odessa in the nineteenth century. The files on Lilienblum and Pinsker in the Druianov collection of the Central Zionist Archives (Jerusalem) contain material on these men's activities in the 1870's. Birthday greetings to Moses Montefiore in the Mocatta Library, London, provide information about Odessa's Jewish leadership in the second half of the nineteenth century. One can find data on the Jewish community, particularly in the last quarter of the nineteenth century, in British Consular Reports from Odessa in the Public Record Office, Kew.

Abramovitsch, Sh. Y. *Fishke der krumer*. Odessa, 1888.

———. *Kol kitvey Mendele Mocher Seforim*. Tel Aviv, 1947.

Adamson, Sidney. "Odessa—The Portal of an Empire." *Harper's Monthly Magazine*, vol. 25, 1912.

Afans'ev-Chuzbinskii, A. *Poezdka v iuzhnuiu Rossiiu*. St. Petersburg, 1861–63.

Alfasi, Yitshak. *Ha-Hasidut*. Tel Aviv, 1974.

Allen, W. E. D. *The Ukraine*. Cambridge, Eng., 1940.

Alston, Patrick. *Education and the State in Tsarist Russia*. Stanford, 1969.

Altmann, Alexander. *Moses Mendelssohn: A Biographical Study*. Philadelphia, 1973.

Anderson, Barbara A. *Internal Migration During Modernization in Late Nineteenth-Century Russia*. Princeton, 1980.

Aronson, I. Michael. "Geographical and Socioeconomic Factors in the 1881 Anti-Jewish Pogroms in Russia." *Russian Review*, vol. 39, Jan. 1980.

Arsh, G. L. *Eteristskoe dvizhenie v Rossii*. Moscow, 1970.

Avtsinski, Levi. *Nahalat avot*. Vilna, 1912.

Babel, Isaak. *Benya Krik, The Gangster and Other Stories*. Edited and translated by Avram Yarmolinsky. New York, 1948.

———. *Izbrannoe*. Moscow, 1966.

Balmuth, David. *Censorship in Russia, 1865–1905*. Washington, D.C., 1979.

Baron, Salo Wittmayer. *The Russian Jew Under Tsars and Soviets*, 2d ed. New York, 1976.

———. *A Social and Religious History of the Jews.* 3 vols. New York, 1937.

Bartlett, Roger P. *Human Capital: The Settlement of Foreigners in Russia, 1762–1804.* Cambridge, Eng., 1979.

Batiushkov, K. N. *Sochineniia*, 4th ed. 3 vols. St. Petersburg, 1885–87.

Beable, William Henry. *Commercial Russia.* New York, 1919.

Beilinson, Moshe. *Alei hadas.* Odessa, 1865–66.

Beletskii, A. *Vopros ob obrazovannii russkikh evreev v tsarstvovanie Imperatora Nikolaia I.* St. Petersburg, 1894.

Ben-Ami, Mordecai [Rabinowicz]. "Zikhronot al Odessa bi-tekufat ha-haskalah." *Bitzaron*, vols. 42 (1960) and 43 (1961). See the Russian version in *Evreiskaia starina*, vol. 7, 1914.

Bendix, Richard. "Tradition and Modernity Reconsidered." *Comparative Studies in Society and History*, vol. 9, 1967.

Berezina, V. G. et al. *Ocherki po istorii russkoi zhurnalistiki i kritiki.* Leningrad, 1965.

Berlin, M. *Ocherk etnografii evreiskago narodnonaseleniia v Rossii.* St. Petersburg, 1861.

Berlin, P. A. *Russkaia burzhuaziia v staroe i novoe vremia.* Moscow, 1922.

Berman, Ia. Z. *Do stolitnikh reokovyn zasnuvannia hazety "Odesskii Vestnik" (1827–1927).* Kiev, 1928.

Berman, Yekutiel. *Ha-Shododim ba-tsohora'im.* Vienna, 1877.

Bernshtayn, Mordkhe V. "Di yidishe drukerayen in ukraine." *Yivo Bleter*, vol. 45, 1975.

Bernshtein, S. *Istoricheskii i torgovo-ekonomicheskii ocherk Odessy.* Odessa, 1881.

Bernstein, Simon. *Ba-Hazon ha-dorot.* New York, 1928.

Bill, Valentine Tscherbotiarioff. "The Dead Souls of Russia's Merchant World." *Russian Review*, vol. 15, Oct. 1956.

Biuletin fun der katedre far yidisher kultur ba der alukrainisher visenshaftlekher akademie, no. 1, Kiev, Dec. 1, 1928.

Black, C. E. *The Dynamics of Modernization: A Study in Comparative History.* New York, 1966.

Blackwell, William L. *The Beginnings of Russian Industrialization, 1800–1860.* Princeton, 1968.

Bliumenfeld, G. "Torgovo-promyshlennaia deiatelnost' evreev v Odesse." *Voskhod*, vol. 4, Apr.–May 1884.

Borovoi, S. Ia. *Evreiskaia zemledelcheskaia kolonizatsiia v staroi Rossii.* Moscow, 1928.

———. "Evrei v Zaporozhskoi Sechi." *Istoricheskii sbornik*, vol. 1, 1934.

———. "A fargesener nihilist (Yehudah Leib Lerner)." *Filologishe shriftn*, vol. 3, 1929.

———. *Kredit i banki Rossii.* Moscow, 1958.

———. "Odessa (k 150-letiiu so dniia osnovannia)." *Istoricheskii zhurnal*, no. 5–6, 1944.

———. "Tsu der geshikhte fun der ershter rusish-yidisher tsaytshrift." *Historishe shriftn*, vol. 1, 1929.

———. "Yisroel Aksenfeld," in *Mendele un zain tsayt*. Moscow, 1940.

Brainin, Reuven. *Perets ben Moshe Smolenskin*. Warsaw, 1897.

———. *Zikhronot: sirtutim me-hayei A. Tsederboim u-tehunato*. Cracow, 1899.

Bramson, L. M. *K istorii nachal'nago obrazovaniia evreev v Rossii*. St. Petersburg, 1896.

Braudes, Reuven. *Shete ha-ketsavot*. Warsaw, 1888.

Brawer, A. Y. *Galitsiah vi-yehudeha*. Jerusalem, 1956.

Breiman, S. [Shlomo Breiman]. "Pulmus ha-tikunim ba-da'at ba-sifrut ha-ivrit be-emtsah ha-me'ah hatesha-esreh." *He-Avar*, vol. 1, Dec. 1952.

Bremner, Robert. *Excursions in the Interior of Russia*. London, 1840.

Briggs, Asa. *Victorian Cities*. Harmondsworth, Eng., 1977.

Brooks, Shirley. *The Russians of the South*. London, 1854.

Brower, Daniel. *Training the Nihilists: Education and Radicalism in Tsarist Russia*. Ithaca, N.Y., 1975.

Brutskus, Boris D. *Statistika evreiskago naseleniia*. St. Petersburg, 1909.

Chadwick, Owen. *The Secularization of the European Mind in the Nineteenth Century*. Cambridge, Eng., 1975.

Chudnovskii, S. L. *Iz davnikh let: vospominaniia*. Moscow, 1934.

Cohen, Israel. *Vilna*. Philadelphia, 1943.

Curtis, William E. *Around the Black Sea*. New York, 1911.

Dawidowicz, Lucy. "Yiddish: Past, Present, and Perfected," in *The Jewish Presence*. New York, 1978.

Deich, Lev G. *Rol' evreev v russkom revoliutsionnom dvizhenii*. Berlin, 1923.

Deinard, Ephraim. *Toledot even reshef*. Warsaw, 1875.

———. *Zikhronot bat ami*. 2 vols. Arlington, N.J., 1920.

DeRibas, A. *Staraia Odessa, istoricheskie ocherki i vospominaniia*. Odessa, 1913.

Dinur, Benzion. *Be-Mifneh ha-dorot*. Jerusalem, 1955.

———. "Demutah ha-historit shel ha-yahadut ha-rusit u-ve'ayot ha-heker bah." *Zion*, vol. 22, 1957.

Ditiatin, I. *Ustroistvo i upravlenie gorodov Rossii*. 2 vols. St. Petersburg, 1875–77.

Dobroliubskii, K. P., ed. *Odesskii universitet za 75 let (1865–1940)*. Odessa, 1940.

Druianov, A. "Mi-'Sefer zikhronot' shel Lilienblum." *Reshumot*, vol. 2, 1927.

———. *Pinsker u-zemano*. Jerusalem, 1953.

Druzhinina, E. I. *Iuzhnaia Ukraina 1800–1825 g.g.* Moscow, 1970.

———. *Severnoe prichernomorie v 1775–1800 g.g.* Moscow, 1959.

Dubnow, Simon M. *History of the Jews in Russia and Poland.* Translated by I. Friedlaender. 3 vols. Philadelphia, 1916–20.

———. *Kniga zhizni.* Vols. 1 and 2, Riga, 1934–35; vol. 3, New York, 1957.

———. *Ob izuchenii istorii russkikh evreev.* St. Petersburg, 1891.

Duker, A. G. "*Evreiskaia starina.* Bibliography of the Russian-Jewish Periodical." *Hebrew Union College Annual*, vols. 8 (1931) and 9 (1932).

Dumashevskii, A. "Po povodu stat'i 'O Moshkakh i Ios'kakh.'" *Odesskii vestnik*, Mar. 4, 1858.

Dyos, H. J., ed. *The Study of Urban History.* New York, 1968.

Eisenstadt, B. M. *Rabbane minsk va-hahamehah.* Vilna, 1898.

Eliav, Mordecai. *Ha-Hinukh ha-yehudi be-germaniah bi-yeme ha-haskalah ve-ha-emantsipatsiah.* Jerusalem, 1961.

Encyclopedia Judaica. 16 vols. Jerusalem, 1972.

Endelman, Todd. *The Jews of Georgian England, 1714–1830: Tradition and Change in a Liberal Society.* Philadelphia, 1979.

Entsiklopedicheskii slovar. 82 vols. and 4 supplementary vols. St. Petersburg, 1890–1907.

Epstein, Melech. *Pages From a Colorful Life.* Miami Beach, Fla., 1971.

Erik, Max. *Etyudn tsu der geshikhte fun der haskole.* Minsk, 1934.

Etkes, Emmanuel. "Ha-Gr'a ve-ha-haskalah: tadmit u-metsiut," in *Perakim le-toledot ha-hevrah ha-yehudit bi-yeme ha-benayim uba-'et ha-hadashah mukdashim le-prof. Ya'akov Katz.* Jerusalem, 1980.

———. "Parashat ha-haskalah mi-ta'am veha-temurah be-ma'amad tenuat ha-haskalah be-rusiah." *Zion*, vol. 43, 1978.

———. *Rav Yisrael Salanter ve-reshitah shel tenu'at ha musar.* Jerusalem, 1982.

———. "*Teudah be-yisrael*: bein temurah le-masoret," Introduction to facsimile edition of *Teudah be-yisrael* (1827). Jerusalem, 1977.

Eton, William. *A Concise Account of the Commerce and Navigation of the Black Sea from Recent and Authentic Information.* London, 1805.

Ettinger, Shmuel. "Ha-Yesodot ve-ha-megamot be-itsuv mediniut ha-shilton ha-rusi kelapei ha-yehudim im halukat polin." *He-Avar*, vol. 19, Sept. 1972.

Evreiskaia entsiklopediia. 16 vols. St. Petersburg, 1908–13.

Falk, M. E. *The Industrialization of Russia, 1700–1914.* London, 1972.

Fedor, Thomas S. *Patterns of Urban Growth in the Russian Empire During the Nineteenth Century.* Chicago, 1975.

Feinstein, A. L. *Ir tehillah . . . brisk.* Warsaw, 1886.

Fin, S. J. *Kiriah ne'emanah.* Vilna, 1860.

Finkel, J. L. "Odesskie evrei." *Zhurnal ministerstva narodnago prosveshcheniia*, vol. 10, 1843.

———. "Zur Geschichte der Juden in Odessa." *Der Orient*, July 16, July 30, Aug. 6, Aug. 13, 1844.

Fischer, George. *Russian Liberalism: From Gentry to Intelligentsia*. Cambridge, Mass., 1958.

Flynn, James T. "S. S. Uvarov's 'Liberal' Years." *Jahrbücher für Geschichte Osteuropas*, vol. 20, Dec. 1972.

Frankel, Jonathan. *Prophecy and Politics: Socialism, Nationalism, and the Russian Jews, 1862–1917*. Cambridge, Eng., 1981.

Frenk, Asriel Nathan. *Yehude polin bi-yme milhamot Napoleon*. Warsaw, 1912.

Garmiza, Ya'akov. "Toledot Yosef ben Aharon Rabinovich." *Ha-Shahar*, vol. 6, 1875.

Gessen, Iulii I. [Hessen, J.]. *Evrei v Rossii*. St. Petersburg, 1906.

———. *Galleria evreiskikh deiatelei*. St. Petersburg, 1898.

———. *Istoriia evreiskogo naroda v Rossii*, 2d ed. 2 vols. Leningrad, 1925–27.

———. "K istorii evreiskikh tipografii." *Evreiskaia starina*, vol. 1, 1909.

———. "K istorii korobochnago sbora v Rossii." *Evreiskaia starina*, vol. 3, 1911.

———. "Pis'ma O. A. Rabinovicha." *Evreiskaia starina*, vol. 3, 1911.

———. "Smena obshchestvennykh techenii: I. B. Levinsohn i d-r M. Liliental." *Perezhitoe*, vol. 3, 1911.

———. *Zakon i zhizn'*. St. Petersburg, 1911.

Getzler, Israel. *Martov: A Political Biography of a Russian Social Democrat*. Cambridge, Eng., 1967.

Ginzburg, Shaul [S. M.]. *Historishe verk*. 3 vols. New York, 1937.

———. *Meshumodim in tsarishn rusland*. New York, 1946.

———. *Otechestvennaia voina 1812 goda i russkie evrei*. St. Petersburg, 1912.

Glicksman, William M. *Jewish Social Welfare Institutions in Poland*. Philadelphia, 1976.

Goldberg, Reuven. "Sofrei ha-haskalah ha-ivri'im ha-rishonim bi-d'rom rusiah." Master's thesis, Hebrew University, 1947.

Gottlober, Abraham Baer. *Zikhronot u-masa'ot*. Edited by Reuven Goldberg. 2 vols. Jerusalem, 1976.

Green, Arthur. *Tormented Master: A Life of Rabbi Nahman of Bratslav*. University, Ala., 1979.

Greenbaum, Alfred Abraham. "Jewish Scholarship in the Soviet Union, 1918–1941." Typescript (1959).

Greenberg, L. S. *A Critical Investigation of the Works of Rabbi Isaac Baer Levinsohn*. New York, 1930.

Greenberg, Louis. *The Jews in Russia.* 2 vols. in one. New York, 1976.

Grossman, Leonid. *Ispoved odnogo evreia.* Moscow, 1924.

Gruzenberg, O. O. *Vchera: vospominaniia.* Paris, 1938.

Guensburg, M. A. *Magid emet.* Leipzig, 1842.

Guernsey, A. H. "The Steppes, Odessa and the Crimea." *Harper's New Monthly Magazine,* vol. 9, June 1854.

Gurland, Ya'akov. *Kevod ha-bayit.* Vilna, 1858.

Ha-Cohen, Mordecai Ben-Hillel. *Olami.* 5 vols. Jerusalem, 1927–29.

Hagemeister, Julius de. *Report on the Commerce of the Ports of New Russia, Moldavia and Wallachia Made to the Russian Government in 1835.* London, 1836.

Halevy, Zvi. *Jewish Schools Under Czarism and Communism: A Struggle for Cultural Identity.* New York, 1976.

Halkin, Simon. *Modern Hebrew Literature.* New York, 1972.

Hamm, Michael F., ed. *The City in Russian History.* Lexington, Ky., 1976.

Hans, Nicholas A. *History of Russian Educational Policy (1701–1917).* London, 1931.

Harkavi, Tsvi, and Ya'akov Goldberg, eds. *Sefer Yekaterinoslav-Dnepropetrovsk.* Jerusalem, 1972.

Harvey, M. L. "The Development of Russian Commerce on the Black Sea and Its Significance." Ph.D. diss., University of California, Berkeley, 1938.

Haxthausen, August von. *The Russian Empire, Its People, Institutions and Resources.* Translated by Robert Farie. 2 vols. London, 1856.

Heilman, Samuel C. "The Many Faces of Orthodoxy." *Judaism,* vol. 2, Feb.–May 1982.

Herlihy, Patricia. "Death in Odessa: A Study of Population Movement in a Nineteenth-Century City." *Journal of Urban History,* vol. 4, Aug. 1978.

———. "The Ethnic Composition of the City of Odessa in the Nineteenth Century." *Harvard Ukrainian Studies,* vol. 1, Mar. 1977.

———. "Greek Merchants in Odessa in the Nineteenth Century." *Harvard Ukrainian Studies,* vol. 3–4, 1979–80.

———. "Odessa Staple Trade and Urbanization in New Russia." *Jahrbücher für Geschichte Osteuropas,* vol. 21, 1973.

———. "Russian Grain Trade and Mediterranean Markets, 1774–1861." Ph.D. diss., University of Pennsylvania, 1963.

———. "Ukrainian Cities in the Nineteenth Century," in *Rethinking Ukrainian History,* edited by Ivan L. Rudnytsky. Edmonton, Alberta, 1981.

Hertzberg, Arthur. *The French Enlightenment and the Jews.* New York, 1968.

Holde, Arthur. *Jews in Music: From the Age of Enlightenment to the Present.* New York, 1959.

Holderness, Mary. *Journey from Riga to the Crimea*, 2d ed. London, 1827.

Hommaire de Hell, Xavier. *Travels in the Steppes of the Caspian Sea, the Crimea, the Caucasus. . . .* London, 1847.

Hyman, Paula. "The History of European Jewry: Recent Trends in the Literature." *Journal of Modern History*, vol. 54, June 1982.

Iakovkina, N. I. "Uchastie dvorian v iuzhno-russkoi torgovle (pervaia polovina 19v)," in *Problemy obshchestvennoi mysli i ekonomicheskaia politika Rossii 19–20 vekov*, edited by N. G. Sladkevich. Moscow, 1972.

Ianson, Iu. *Statisticheskoe issledovanie o khlebnoi torgovle v Odesskom raione.* St. Petersburg, 1870.

Iuzhakov, S. "Iubilei Odessy." *Russkoe bogatstvo*, no. 9, 1894.

Ivask, U. G. *Evreiskaia periodicheskaia pechat' v Rossii.* Tallinn, 1935.

"Iz bumag Aleksandra Grigorievicha Troinitskago." *Russkii arkhiv*, bk. 1, 1894.

Jabotinsky, Vladimir [Ze'ev Jabotinsky]. *Autobiografiah.* Jerusalem, 1947.

———. *Piatero.* Paris, 1936.

Jewish Encyclopedia. 12 vols. New York, 1901–6.

Jick, Leon A. *The Americanization of the Synagogue, 1820–1870.* Hanover, N.H., 1976.

Joffe, Judah A., and Yudel Mark, eds. *Groiser verterbukh fur der yidisher shprakh.* New York, 1961.

Kabak, A. A. *Sipur beli giborim.* Tel Aviv, 1945.

Kabuzan, V. M. *Zaselenie Novorossii (Yekaterinoslavskoi i Khersonskoi gubernii) v 18–pervoi polovine 19 v.* Moscow, 1976.

Kahan, Arcadius. "Economic Opportunities and Some Pilgrims' Progress: Jewish Immigrants from Eastern Europe to the U.S., 1890–1914." *Journal of Economic History*, vol. 38, no. 1, Mar. 1978.

———. "Notes on Jewish Entrepreneurship in Tsarist Russia," in *Entrepreneurship in Imperial Russia and the Soviet Union*, edited by Gregory Guroff and Fred V. Carstensen. Princeton, 1983.

Kahane, David. "Lilienthal ve-haskalat ha-yehudim be-rusiah." *Ha-Shiloah*, vol. 27, 1912.

———. "Zikaron be-sefer mishpaha." *Knesset Israel* (Warsaw), vol. 1, 1886.

Karidis, Viron [B. A. Karidis]. "The Greek Communities in South Russia: Aspects of Their Formation and Commercial Enterprise, 1774–1829." Master's thesis, University of Birmingham, 1976.

———. "A Greek Mercantile *paroikia*: Odessa 1774–1829," in *Balkan Society in the Age of Greek Independence*, edited by Richard Clogg. London, 1981.

Katsnelson, G. *Ha-Milhama ha-sifrutit bein ha-haredim ve-ha-maskilim.* Tel Aviv, 1954.

Katz, Benzion. *Rabanut, hasidut, haskalah.* 2 vols. Tel Aviv, 1956–58.

Katz, Jacob. *Out of the Ghetto: The Social Background of Jewish Emancipation, 1770–1870*. New York, 1978.

———. *Tradition and Crisis: Jewish Society at the End of the Middle Ages*. New York, 1971.

Kaufman, A. E. "Za mnogo let." *Evreiskaia starina*, vol. 6, 1913.

Kirpichnikov, A. "Stoletie Odessy." *Istoricheskii vestnik*, vol. 57, Sept. 1894.

Kirzshnits, A. *Di yidishe prese in der gevezener rusisher imperie, 1823–1916*. Moscow, 1930.

Kizevetter, A. A. *Mestnoe samoupravlenie v Rossii*. Moscow, 1910.

Klausner, Yisrael. *Toledot ha-kehillah ha-ivrit be-vilna*. Vilna, 1938.

Klausner, Yosef. *Historiah shel ha-sifrut ha-ivrit ha-hadashah*. 6 vols. Jerusalem, 1953–58.

———. *Yotsrim u-vonim*, vol. 1. Tel Aviv, 1925.

Kleinman, Moshe. *Demu'yot ve-komot*. Paris, 1928.

Klier, John D. "The Ambiguous Legal Status of Russian Jewry in the Reign of Catherine II." *Slavic Review*, vol. 35, Sept. 1976.

———. "The *Illiustratsiia* Affair of 1858: Polemics on the Jewish Question in the Russian Press." *Nationalities Papers*, vol. 5, Fall 1977.

———. "The Jewish *Den'*, the Censorship, and the Literary Mice, 1869–1871." Typescript (undated).

———. "The Jewish Question in the Reform Era Russian Press." *Russian Review*, vol. 39, July 1980.

———. "Kievlianin and the Jews: A Decade of Disillusionment, 1864–1873." *Harvard Ukrainian Studies*, vol. 5, no. 1, 1981.

———. "*Odesskii Vestnik*'s Annus Mirabilis of 1858." *Canadian Slavonic Papers*, vol. 23, no. 1, 1981.

Koch, Charles. *The Crimea and Odessa*. Translated by Joanna B. Horner. London, 1855.

Kogen, David [Kahane]. "Pervyia desiatiletiia evreiskoi obshchiny v Odesse i pogrom 1821 g." *Evreiskaia starina*, vol. 3, 1911.

Kohl, Johann Georg. *Russia. St. Petersburg, Moscow, Kharkoff, Riga, Odessa, the German provinces on the Baltic, the Steppes, the Crimea, and the Interior of the Empire*. London, 1848.

Kornilov, Alexander. *Modern Russian History*. Translated by Alexander S. Kaun; edited and abridged by Robert Bass. New York, 1966.

Kotik, A. *Dos lebn fun a yidishn inteligent*. New York, 1925.

Kovbasiuk, S. M., ed. *Odessa. Ocherki istorii goroda-geroia*. Odessa, 1957.

Kovner, Abraham Uri. *Kol kitvey Avraham Uri Kovner*. Edited by Israel Zamorah. Tel Aviv, 1947–48.

Kramer, Sh. *Ha-Mevaker ha-niddah: hayei A. U. Kovner*. Merhavia, 1946.

Krawchenko, Bohdan. "The Social Structure of the Ukraine at the Turn of the Twentieth Century." *East European Quarterly*, vol. 16, Summer 1982.

Kressel, Getsel. *Leksikon ha-sifrut ha-ivrit ba-dorot ha-aharonim.* 2 vols. Tel Aviv, 1965–67.

Kulisher, M. "Evrei v kieve: istoricheskii ocherk." *Evreiskaia starina*, vol. 6, 1913.

———. "K 25-letiiu so dnia smerti I. G. Orshanskago." *Voskhod*, Nov. 23, 1900.

Kunitz, Joshua. *Russian Literature and the Jew: A Sociological Inquiry into the Nature and Origin of Literary Patterns.* New York, 1929.

Kupernik, A. *Le-Korot benei yisrael be-kiev.* Berdichev, 1891.

Kuznets, Simon. "Immigration of Russian Jews to the United States: Background and Structure." *Perspectives in American History*, vol. 9, 1975.

Lachower, F. [Yeruham Fishel]. *Toledot ha-sifrut ha-hadashah.* 3 vols. Tel Aviv, 1928–31.

La Fite de Pellepore, Vladimir de. *La Russie historique, monumentale et pittoresque.* 2 vols. Paris, 1862–65.

Lampert, E. *Sons Against Fathers.* Oxford, 1965.

Lefkowitz, David. *The Unpublished Masterpieces of David Nowakowsky.* New York, 1979.

Leikina-Svirskaia, V. R. *Intelligentsiia v Rossii vo vtoroi polovine 19 veka.* Moscow, 1971.

Lerner, Osip [Judah]. *Evrei v Novorossiiskom krae.* Odessa, 1901.

Lestchinsky, Jacob [Yakov Leshchinsky]. "Berditchever yidishe kehile fun 1789 biz 1917." *Bleter far yidishe demografye, statistik un ekonomik* (Berlin), Apr. 15, 1923.

———. *Ha-Tefutsah ha-yehudit.* Jerusalem, 1960.

———. *Matsavam ha-kalkali shel ha-yehudim be-eropa ha-mizrahit ve-ha-merkazit.* Tel Aviv, 1934–35.

———. "Odessa." *Eshkol entsiklopedia yisre'elit*, vol. 1. Berlin and Jerusalem, 1929.

———. "Di sotsiale ontviklung fun ukrainer yidntum," in *Yidn in ukraine.* New York, 1961.

———. *Dos yidishe folk in tsifern.* Berlin, 1922.

———. *Der yidisher arbayter in rusland.* Vilna, 1906.

Levanda, V. O. *Polnyi khronologicheskii sbornik zakonov i polozhenii kasaiushchikhsia evreev . . . 1649–1873.* St. Petersburg, 1874.

Levin, Mordecai. *Erkei hevrah ve-kalkalah ba-ideologiah shel ha-haskalah.* Jerusalem, 1975.

Levin, Shmarya. *The Arena.* Translated by Maurice Samuel. New York, 1932.

Levinsky, E. L. *Kitvey E. L. Levinsky.* 2 vols. Tel Aviv, 1935.

Levinsohn, I. B. *Beit yehuda.* Vilna, 1839.

———. *Teudah be-yisrael.* Vilna, 1828.

Levitats, Isaac. *The Jewish Community in Russia, 1772–1844*. New York, 1943.

Lichtenshtadt, Moses Avigdor. *Mi-maharat ha-shabbat*. Odessa, 1860.

Lifshiz, Yaakov Halevi. *Zikhron Ya'akov*, 2d ed. 3 vols. Bnai Brak, 1967–68.

Lilienblum, Moshe Leib. *Igrot M. L. Lilienblum le-Y. L. Gordon*. Edited by Shlomo Breiman. Jerusalem, 1968.

———. *Ketavim autobiografi'im*. Introduced and annotated by Shlomo Breiman. 3 vols. Jerusalem, 1970.

———. *Kol kitvey Lilienblum*. 4 vols. Cracow, 1910–13.

Lilienthal, Sophie. *The Lilienthal Family Record*. San Francisco, 1930.

Lincoln, W. Bruce. "The Daily Life of St. Petersburg Officials in the Mid-Nineteenth Century." *Oxford Slavonic Papers*, n.s., vol. 8, 1975.

———. *Nicholas I: Emperor and Autocrat of All the Russias*. Bloomington, Ind., 1978.

Lowenstein, Steven M. "The Pace of Modernization of German Jewry in the Nineteenth Century," in *Leo Baeck Institute Yearbook*, vol. 21, London, 1976.

———. "The Rural Community and the Urbanization of German Jewry." *Central European History*, vol. 13, Sept. 1980.

Lozinskii, S. G., ed. *Kazennye evreiskie uchilishcha*, vol. 1. Petrograd, 1920.

Lyall, Robert. *Travels in Russia, the Krimea, the Caucasus, and Georgia*. 2 vols. London, 1825.

Maggid, David [H. L. Schteinschneider]. *Ir vilna*. Vilna, 1900.

———. *Sefer toledot mishpahot Ginzburg*. St. Petersburg, 1869.

Mahler, Raphael. *Divrei yemei yisrael, dorot aharonim*. 4 vols. Merhavia, 1962.

———. *Der kampf tsvishn haskole un khsides in Galitsie*. New York, 1942. Translated as *Ha-hasidut ve-ha-haskalah* (Merhavia, 1961).

Mandelstamm, Binyamin. *Hazon la-mo'ed*. 3 parts. Vienna, 1877.

Maor, Yitshak. "Eliyah Orshanski u-mekomo be-historiografiah shel yehude rusiah." *He-Avar*, vol. 20, Sept. 1973.

———. "Tekhum ha-moshav ha-yehudi." *He-Avar*, vol. 19, Sept. 1972.

Marek, P. *Ocherki po istorii prosveshcheniia evreev v Rossii*. Moscow, 1909.

Margolis, O. *Geshikhte fun yidn in rusland, 1772–1861*. Moscow, 1930.

Markgraf, R. *Zur Geschichte der Juden auf den Messen in Leipzig, von 1664–1839*. Birchofswerden, 1894.

Markish, Simon. "Osip Rabinovič." *Cahiers du monde russe et soviétique*, vol. 21, Jan.–Mar. and Apr.–June 1980.

Marrus, Michael R. *The Politics of Assimilation*. Oxford, 1971.

Mathes, William L. "N. I. Pirogov and the Reform of University Government, 1856–1866." *Slavic Review*, vol. 31, Mar. 1972.

Mayer, Bonaventura. *Die Juden unserer Zeit*. Regensburg, 1842.

McConnell, Alan. *Tsar Alexander I.* New York, 1970.
McLeod, Hugh. *Religion and the People of Western Europe.* Oxford, 1981.
Meisl, Joseph. *Haskalah, Geschichte der Aufklaerungsbewegung unter den Juden in Russland.* Berlin, 1919.
Mendelsohn, Ezra. *Class Struggle in the Pale.* Cambridge, Eng., 1970.
Mevorakh, Baruch. *Napoleon u-tekufato.* Jerusalem, 1968.
Meyer, Michael A., ed. *Ideas of Jewish History.* New York, 1974.
———. *The Origins of the Modern Jew: Jewish Identity and European Culture in Germany, 1749–1824.* Detroit, 1967.
———. "Where Does the Modern Period of Jewish History Begin?" *Judaism*, vol. 24, Summer 1975.
Mikhnevich, I. *Istoricheskii obzor sorokaletiia Rishelevskogo litseia s 1817 po 1857 g.* Odessa, 1857.
Minkowski, Pincus. "Mi-Sefer hay'ai." *Reshumot*, vols. 1–6, 1918–30.
Mintz, Alan. "Guenzberg, Lilienblum and the Shape of Haskalah Autobiography." *Association of Jewish Studies Review*, vol. 4, 1979.
Miron, Dan. *Bein hazon le-emet.* Jerusalem, 1979.
———. *A Traveler Disguised.* New York, 1973.
Mirov, N. T. *Geography of Russia.* New York, 1951.
Mishkinsky, Moshe. "Al emdatah shel ha-tenuah ha-mahaphanit ha-rusit le-gabe ha-yehudim bi-shenot ha-70 shel ha-me'ah ha-19 esreh." *He-Avar*, vol. 9, Sept. 1962.
Mogilevskii, B. *Zhizn' Pirogova.* Moscow, 1952.
Morgulis, M. G. "Bezporiadki 1871 goda v Odesse." *Evreiskii mir*, vol. 2, Dec. 1910.
———. *Dor ha-haskalah be-rusiah.* Vilna, 1910.
———. "Iz moikh vospominanii." *Voskhod*, vol. 15, nos. 2, 4, 7, 9, 11–12, (1895); vol. 17, nos. 4, 6 (1897).
———. "Nikolai Ivanovich Pirogov i ego otnoshenie k evreiskomu voprosu." *Voskhod*, May 1881.
Morozov, P. "Odessa v 1830 g.," in *Odesskii almanakh na 1831 g.* Odessa, 1831.
Morton, Edward. *Travels in Russia and a Residence at St. Petersburg and Odessa in the Years 1827–9.* London, 1830.
Mumford, Lewis. *The City in History.* New York, 1961.
Nadav, Mordecai. *Toledot kehillat pinsk, 1506–1880*, vol. 1. Tel Aviv, 1973.
Nadler, V. K. *Odessa v pervyia epokhi eia sushchestvovaniia.* Odessa, 1893.
Natanson, Bernard. *Sefer ha-zikhronot, divrei yemei hayei Ribal.* Warsaw, 1889.
———. "Zikhronot le-korot ha-ir Odessa." *Ha-Melits*, vol. 10, nos. 25–29, 31–32 (1870).
Netanyahu, B., ed. *Road to Freedom.* New York, 1944.
Nikitenko, Alexander. *Diary of a Russian Censor.* Edited and translated by Helen Saltz Jacobson. Amherst, Mass., 1975.

Odessa, 1794–1894. Izdanie gorodskogo obshchestvennogo upravleniia k stoletiiu goroda. Odessa, 1895.

Odesser adres kalendar. Odessa, 1897.

Oislender, N. "Mendeles mitgayer in di 60er, 70er yorn," in *Mendele un zain tsayt.* Moscow, 1940.

Olenin, K. L. *Vek, Odesskii istoricheskii al'bom, 1794–1894.* Odessa, 1894.

Opisanie Odesskikh ulichnykh bezporiadkov v dni sv. paskhi 1871 goda. Odessa, 1871.

Orbach, Alexander. *New Voices of Russian Jewry: A Study of the Russian-Jewish Press of Odessa in the Era of the Great Reforms, 1860–1871.* Leiden, 1980.

Orlov, A. *Istoricheskii ocherk Odessy s 1794 po 1803 g.* Odessa, 1885.

Orshanskii, Ilya. "K kharakteristike Odesskago pogroma." *Evrei v Rossii.* St. Petersburg, 1877.

Otsar ha-rabanim. Tel Aviv, 1975.

Otsar Yisrael. 10 vols. New York, 1924.

Owen, Thomas C. *Capitalism and Politics in Russia.* Cambridge, Eng., 1981.

Pancr, Sara Feigeh. *Mi-zikhronot yemei yalduti.* Warsaw, 1903.

Paperna, A. I. "Iz Nikolaevskoi epokhi." *Perezhitoe*, vol. 2, 1910.

———. "Vospominaniia." *Perezhitoe*, vol. 3, 1911.

———. "Zikhronot u-shemu'ot." *Reshumot*, vol. 1, 1918.

Patterson, David. *Abraham Mapu.* London, 1964.

———. *The Hebrew Novel in Czarist Russia.* Edinburgh, 1964.

Pearlmann, Moshe. "*Razsvet* 1860–61: The Origins of the Russian Jewish Press." *Jewish Social Studies*, vol. 24, July 1962.

Pen, S. *Evreiskaia starina v Odesse: K istorii evreev v pervoe 25-letie eo osnovaniia.* Odessa, 1903.

Philipson, David. *The Reform Movement in Judaism*, 2d ed. New York, 1931.

"Pinkas ha-hevrah halva'it be-Odessa" (1837). *Yedah am*, vol. 13, nos. 33–34, 1968.

Pinkerton, Robert. *Russia: or, Miscellaneous Observations on the Past and Present State of That Country and Its Inhabitants.* London, 1833.

Pinner, Ephraim Moses ben Alexander Susskind. *Prospectus der Odessaer Gesellschaft für Geschichte und Alterthümer Gehörenden Aeltesten Hebräischen und Rabbinischen Manuscripte.* Odessa, 1845.

Pinsker, Simha. *Likute kadmoniot.* Vienna, 1860.

Pipes, Richard. "Catherine II and the Jews: The Origins of the Pale of Settlement." *Soviet Jewish Affairs*, vol. 5, no. 2, 1975.

Pirogov, N. I. *Sochineniia.* 2 vols. St. Petersburg, 1887.

"Poiasneniia po delu Odesskoi glavnoi sinagogi." *Sion'*, Feb. 23, 1862.

Polons'ka-Vasylenko, M. D. "The Settlement of the Southern Ukraine." *Annals of the Ukrainian Academy of Arts and Sciences in the United States*, vol. 4–5, Summer–Fall 1955.

Pomper, Philip. *The Russian Revolutionary Intelligentsia.* New York, 1970.

Posner, Harry. "My Three Years in Odessa." *Reconstructionist,* vol. 34, June 28, 1968.

Pozner, S. V. *Evrei v obshchei shkole.* St. Petersburg, 1914.

Pravila Odesskoi glavnoi sinagogi po Rishel'evskoi ul. Odessa, 1896.

Priluker, Yakov M. *The New Israelite; or, Rabbi Shalom on the Shores of the Black Sea.* London, 1903.

———. *Under the Russian and British Flags.* London, 1912.

Puryear, V. J. "Odessa: Its Rise and International Importance (1815–1850)." *Pacific Historical Review,* vol. 3, June 1934.

Rabin, Dov, ed. *Grodno: Entsiklopedia shel galuyot.* Jerusalem, 1973.

Rabinovich, Osip. "O Moshkakh i Ios'kakh." *Odesskii vestnik,* Jan. 23, 1858.

———. *Sochineniia.* 3 vols. St. Petersburg, 1880–88.

———. "Tsadik v tsenakh Odessy." *Razsvet,* Nov. 25, 1860.

Rabinovitz, A. S. *Haftorah.* Tel Aviv, 1925–26.

Raisin, Jacob F. *The Haskalah Movement in Russia.* Philadelphia, 1913.

Rashin, A. G. *Naselenie Rossii za 100 let.* Moscow, 1956.

Rashkovskii, N. S. *Sovremennye russko-evreiskie deiateli.* Odessa, 1899.

Reikhel't, Nikolai N. [N. Lerner]. *Chernoe more i kavkaz.* St. Petersburg, 1900.

Reikhesburg, M. *Penei aryeh.* Odessa, 1889.

Reisen, Zalman. *Leksikon fun der yidisher literatur, prese, un filologie.* 4 vols. Vilna, 1928–29.

Rieber, Alfred J. *Merchants and Entrepreneurs in Imperial Russia.* Chapel Hill, N.C., 1982.

Rogger, Hans. "Government, Jews, Peasants, and Land in Post-Emancipation Russia." *Cahiers du monde russe et soviétique,* vol. 27, Jan.–Mar. and Apr.–Sept. 1976.

———. "Russian Ministers and the Jewish Question." *California Slavic Studies,* vol. 8, 1975.

Roi, J. F. A. de le. *Judentaufen im 19 Jahrhundert.* Leipzig, 1899.

Rosenthal, Leon [Judah Leib]. *Toledot hevrat marbei haskalah be-yisrael be-erets rusiah.* 2 vols. St. Petersburg, 1885–90.

Rubinow, Isaac. *Economic Condition of the Jews in Russia.* U.S. Bureau of Labor. Washington, D.C., 1907.

Ruppin, Arthur. *The Jews of the Modern World.* London, 1934.

Russkii biograficheskii slovar. 25 vols. St. Petersburg, 1896–1913.

"Russland." *Jüdische Statistik.* Berlin, 1903.

Ryndziunskii, P. G. *Gorodskoe grazhdanstvo doreformennoi Rossii.* Moscow, 1958.

Sadan, Dov. *Avnei bohan.* Tel Aviv, 1950–51.

———. *Avnei zikaron.* Tel Aviv, 1953–54.

Samter, N. *Judentaufen im 19ten Jahrhundert.* Berlin, 1906.

Saul, Norman E. *Russia and the Mediterranean, 1797–1807.* Chicago, 1970.

Scharfstein, Tsvi. *Toledot ha-hinukh be-yisrael ba-dorot ha-aharonim.* 5 vols. New York, 1960–66.

Schechtman, Joseph. *Rebel and Statesman: The Vladimir Jabotinsky Story.* 2 vols. New York, 1956–61.

Schmidt, A. *Materialy dlia geografii i statistiki Rossii, Khersonskaia guberniia.* St. Petersburg, 1863.

Scott, Charles Henry. *The Baltic, the Black Sea, and the Crimea.* London, 1854.

Seltzer, Robert M. "Simon Dubnow: A Critical Biography of His Early Years." Ph.D. diss., Columbia University, 1970.

Seton-Watson, H. "Two Contrasting Policies Towards Jews: Russia and Hungary," in *Jews and Non-Jews in Eastern Europe*, edited by Bela Vago and G. L. Mosse. Jerusalem, 1974.

Shatski, Yakov. *Geshikhte fun yidn in varshe.* 3 vols. New York, 1947–53.

———. "Haskole in zamosc." *Yivo Bleter*, vol. 36, 1952.

———. *Kultur-geshikhte fun der haskole in lite.* Buenos Aires, 1950.

———. Problemen fun yidisher historiografie." *Tsukunft*, vol. 40, Mar. 1955.

Shils, Edward. *Tradition.* London, 1981.

Shmeruk, Chone. *Sifrut yidish: perakim le-toledoteiah.* Tel Aviv, 1978.

Shohat, Azriel. "Ha-hanhagah be-kehillot rusiah im bitul ha-kahal." *Zion*, vol. 42, 1977.

———. *Im hilufei tekufot.* Jerusalem, 1960.

———. *Mosad "ha-rabanut mi-ta'am" be-rusiah.* Haifa, 1975.

Shohetman, Baruch. "Odessa," in *Arim ve-imahot be-yisrael*, edited by H. L. Ha-Cohen Fishman, vol. 2. Jerusalem, 1948.

Shparo, O. B. *Osvobozhdenie Gretsii i Rossiia (1821–1829).* Moscow, 1965.

Shtraikh, S. Ia. *N. I. Pirogov.* Berlin, 1923.

Shubert, A. I. *Moia zhizn'.* Leningrad, 1929.

Sicard, Charles. *Lettres sur Odessa.* St. Petersburg, 1812.

Siegel, Seymour. "The War of the *Kitniyot* (Legumes)," in *Perspectives on Jews and Judaism: Essays in Honor of Wolf Kelman*, edited by Arthur A. Chiel. New York, 1978.

Siegelbaum, Lewis. "The Odessa Grain Trade: A Case Study in Urban Growth and Development in Tsarist Russia." *Journal of European Economic History*, vol. 9, Spring 1980.

Simon, Leon. *Ahad Ha-am.* Philadelphia, 1960.

Sinel, Allen. *The Classroom and the Chancellery: State Educational Reform in Russia under Count Dmitry Tolstoi.* Cambridge, Mass., 1973.

Sistematicheskii katalog biblioteki obshchestva vzaimnago vspomoshchestvovaniia prikazchikov-evreev g. Odessy. Odessa, 1910.

Sistematicheskii ukazatel' literatury o evreiakh na russkom iazyke so vremeni vvedeniia grazhdanskago shrifta (1708 g.) do dekabria 1889. St. Petersburg, 1892.

Skabichevskii, A. M. *Ocherki istorii russkoi tsenzury*. St. Petersburg, 1892.

Skal'kovskii, A. A. "Iz portfelia pervago istorika v Odesse," in *Iz proshlago Odessy*, edited by I. Mikhailovich DeRibas. Odessa, 1894.

———. *Khronologicheskoe obozrenie istorii Novorossiskago kraia, 1731–1823*. 2 vols. Odessa, 1836–38.

———. "Odessa za 40 let nazad," in *Trudy Odesskago statisticheskago komiteta*, vol. 4. Odessa, 1870.

———. "O periodicheskikh izdaniiakh v Odesse." *Odesskii vestnik*, no. 1, 1858.

———. *Opyt' statisticheskago opisaniia Novorossiiskago kraia*. 2 vols. Odessa, 1850–53.

———. *Pervoe tridtsatiletie istorii goroda Odessy, 1793–1823*. Odessa, 1837.

Skinner, Frederick William. "City Planning in Russia: The Development of Odessa, 1789–1892." Ph.D. diss., Princeton University, 1973.

Slouschz, Shlomo. "Toledot hay'ai." *He-Avar*, vol. 5, Aug. 1957.

Slutsky, Yehuda. *Ha-'itonut ha-yehudit-rusit be-me'ah ha-teshah-esreh*. Jerusalem, 1970.

Smolenskin, Perets. *Ha-Toeh be-darkei ha-hayim*. 4 vols. Vienna, 1876.

———. *Simhat hanef*. Warsaw, 1905.

Smol'ianinov, K. *Istoriia Odessy*. Odessa, 1853.

———. "Pervye gorodskie vybory v Odesse." *Odesskii vestnik*, Feb. 7, 1851.

Sokolow, N. *Sefer zikaron*. Warsaw, 1889.

Sosis, I. *Di geshikhte fun di yidishe gezelshaftlekhe shtremungen in rusland in 19tn y.h.* Minsk, 1929.

———. "Obshchestvennyia nastroeniia 'epokhi velikikh reform.'" *Evreiskaia starina*, vol. 7, 1914.

———. "Period 'obruseniia.'" *Evreiskaia starina*, vol. 8, 1915.

———. *Di sotsial-ekonomishe lage fun di ruslendishe yuden*. Petrograd, 1919.

———. *Tsu der ontviklung fun der yidisher historiografie*. Minsk, 1929.

Stampfer, Shaul. "Shalosh yeshivot lita'ot ba-me'ah ha'tsha-esreh." Ph.D. diss., Hebrew University, 1981.

Stanislavskii, S. "Iz istorii i zhizni odnoi evreiskoi shkoly." *Voskhod*, vol. 4, 1884.

Stanislawski, Michael. *Tsar Nicholas I and the Jews: The Transformation of Jewish Society in Russia, 1825–1855*. Philadelphia, 1983.

Starr, S. Frederick. *Decentralization and Self-Government in Russia, 1830–1870*. Princeton, 1972.

Stoletie Odessy. Odessa, 1894.

Subbotin, A. P. *V cherte evreiskoi osedlosti*. 2 vols. St. Petersburg, 1890.

Talmud Torah be-Odessa, N. Pirogov. Translated into Hebrew and annotated by Alexander Tsederbaum. Odessa, 1858.

Tarnopol, Joachim. *Notices historiques et caractéristiques sur les israélites d'Odessa, précedées d'un aperçu général sur l'état du peuple israélite en Russie.* Odessa, 1855.

———. *Opyt' sovremennoi i osmotritel'noi reformy v oblasti iudaizma v Rossii.* Odessa, 1868.

Tcherikover, Elias. *Istoriia obshchestva dlia rasprostraneniia prosveshcheniia mezhdu evreiiami v Rossii.* St. Petersburg, 1913.

Tchernikhovsky, Shaul. "David Kahane." *Ha-Olam,* vol. 16, June 15, 1928.

———. "Moshe Leib Lilienblum." *Ha-Olam,* vol. 16, Nov. 2, 1928.

Tchernowitz, Chaim. *Masekhet zikhronot.* New York, 1945.

———. *Pirkei hay'im.* New York, 1954.

Thaden, Edward C., ed. *Russification in the Baltic Provinces and Finland, 1855–1914.* Princeton, 1981.

Trivush, Y. ' 'Partsufah shel Odessa ha-yehudit." *He-Avar.* vol. 1, 1952.

Trudy Odesskago statiticheskago komiteta. 5 vols. Odessa, 1865–70.

Trusov, Iurii S. *Khadzibei.* Kiev, 1974.

Tsederbaum, Alexander. *Keter kehunah.* Odessa, 1868.

———. *Zikhron mikrah kodesh.* Odessa, 1850.

Tsinberg, Yisrael [S. L. Tsinberg]. *Di geshikhte fun literatur bai yidn,* vols. 8 and 9. New York, 1943, 1966.

———. *Istoriia evreiskoi pechati v Rossii.* Petrograd, 1915.

Tsitron, Sh. L. *Di geshikhte fun der yidisher prese fun 1863 biz 1889.* Vilna, 1923.

Vakar, Nicholas. *Belorussia: The Making of a Nation.* Cambridge, Mass., 1956.

Venturi, Franco. *Roots of Revolution.* New York, 1960.

Vigel', F. F. *Vospominaniia.* 7 vols. Moscow, 1864–65.

Vital, David. *The Origins of Zionism.* Oxford, 1975.

Vol'skii, M. *Ocherk istorii khlebnoi torgovli Novorossiiskago kraia.* Odessa, 1854.

Vsevolozhskii, N. S. *Puteshestvie cherez iuzhnuiu Rossiiu, Krym i Odessu v 1836, 37 g.* 2 vols. Moscow, 1839.

Weinreich, M. *Fun beyde zaytn ployt.* Buenos Aires, 1955.

Weinryb, Bernard D. *The Jews of Poland: A Social and Economic History of the Jewish Community in Poland from 1100–1800.* Philadelphia, 1973.

———. *Neuste wirtschaftsgeschichte der Juden in Russland und Polen von der 1. polnischen Teilung bis zum Tode Alexanders II (1772–1881).* Breslau, 1934.

Weisbrem, Israel. *Bein ha-zemanim.* Warsaw, 1888.

Weiss, I. H. "Reshit tsemihat ha-haskalah be-rusiah." *Mi-Mizrah u-mima'arav*, vol. 1, 1894.

Weissenberg, S. "Der Gesundheitszustand der Juden in Odessa." *Zeitschrift für Demographie und Statistik der Juden*, vol. 5, 1909.

Wengeroff, Pauline. *Memoiren einer Grossmutter.* 2 vols. Berlin, 1908–10.

Westwood, J. N. *A History of the Russian Railways*. London, 1964.

Wilson, Bryan. *Religion in Sociological Perspective*. Oxford, 1982.

Wishnitzer, M. "Die Stellung der Brodyer Juden in internationalen Handel in der zweiten Hälfte des 18 Jhd," in *Festschrift zu Simon Dubnows siebzigstem Geburtstag*, edited by Ismar Elbogen et al., vol. 1. Berlin, 1930.

Wortman, Richard S. *The Development of a Russian Legal Consciousness*. Chicago, 1976.

Yakhinson, Y. *Sotsial-ekonomisher shteyger ba yidn in rusland in 19-tn y.h.* Kharkov, 1929.

Yalkut Volin, vol. 2, no. 12–13, Apr. 1951.

Yuditski, A. *Yidishe burzhuazye un yidisher proletariat in ershter helft 19-y.h.* Kiev, 1931.

Zagoruiko, V. *Po stranitsam istorii Odessy i Odesshchiny.* 2 vols. Odessa, 1957–60.

"Zastroenie goroda Gadzhibeia, teper' Odessy, v 1794 godu," in *Zapiski Odesskago obshchestva istorii i drevnostei*, vol. 3. Odessa, 1853.

Zeman, Z. A. B., and W. B. Scharlau. *The Merchant of Revolution: The Life of Alexander Israel Helphand (Parvus), 1867–1924*. London, 1965.

Zilbershtein, M. "Dva slova ob uchilishchakh." *Razsvet*, Oct. 7, 1860.

Ziunim mezuyanim be-batei ha-kevarot be-Odessa. Warsaw, 1888.

Zolotov, V. A. *Khlebnyi eksport Rossii cherez porty chernogo i azovskogo morei v 60–90 g. 19 v.* Rostov-on-Don, 1966.

———. *Vneshiaia torgovlia iuzhnoi Rossii v pervoi polovine 19 v.* Rostov-on-Don, 1963.

Index

Library of Congress Cataloging in Publication Data

Zipperstein, Steven J., 1950–
The Jews of Odessa.

Bibliography: p.
Includes index.
1. Jews—Ukraine—Odessa—Intellectual life.
2. Haskalah—Ukraine—Odessa—History. 3. Odessa (Ukraine)—Intellectual life. I. Title.
DS135.R930385 1985 947′.717 84-50152
ISBN 0-8047-1251-4 (alk. paper)